Ruby

'FORGET NOT'

The Whigham Coat of Arms

'FORGET NOT'

The autobiography of
Margaret, Duchess of Argyll

A STAR BOOK
published by
WYNDHAM PUBLICATIONS

A Star Book
Published in 1977
by Wyndham Publications Ltd.
A Howard and Wyndham Company
123, King Street, London W6 9JG

First published in Great Britain by
W. H. Allen & Co. Ltd. 1975

Printed in Great Britain by
Richard Clay (The Chaucer Press) Ltd, Bungay, Suffolk

ISBN 0 352 39686 5

Acknowledgments

In the autumn of 1974 several people offered to help me write this book, but, experienced as they were, I came to realise that only I could tell my story.

Therefore, directly after Christmas, my secretary, Miss Winifred Medus, who has been with me for ten years, and I began work on the manuscript, which was delivered to my publishers on April 13th, 1975. This delivery date could never have been achieved without Miss Medus's intelligence, expert shorthand and willingness to work over weekends, throughout the entire Easter holiday, and often for very long hours.

Once Mr Jeffrey Simmons, Managing Director of W. H. Allen, had read the book, he introduced me to Mr David Hately, one of W. H. Allen's senior editors.

As time was never on our side, David Hately worked tremendously hard in improving and trimming the book, despite wails of anguish from me over some of my favourite bits which he quietly but firmly eliminated. Throughout, he was the epitome of tact and patience, and, above all, was mindful of my interests.

I would like to offer my heartfelt thanks to Miss Medus and Mr Hately, without whose help this book would never have appeared.

Sources of Illustrations

All the photographs reproduced in this book have come from my private albums. While anxious to give credit where it is due, I am in the majority of cases unable to remember the original sources of photographs or photographers. However I would like to thank Dorothy Wilding, Lenare and Brodrick Haldane in particular. I am grateful for permission to use these photographs as illustrations in my book.

M.A.

To my father, of course,
and
to my grandchildren
David, Teresa and Edward

Chapter 1

Some moments of your life you never forget, no matter how long you live.

I remember the day of my presentation at court as a debutante, and the awe-inspiring sight of the throne room.

I remember choking back tears of emotion on my wedding day in 1933 as, to the thunder of the organ, I entered the Brompton Oratory on my father's arm to face three thousand people packing the church.

I remember the shadowy figure of a priest who was praying at the foot of my bed. Although I did not know it at the time, he had just administered the sacrament of Extreme Unction.

And I remember a summer afternoon in Paris. But this memory is of a different kind.

It was Wednesday, May 8th, 1963. There was not a cloud in the sky, and I was lunching with three friends on the lawns of the famous Pré-Catelan restaurant in the Bois de Boulogne. I was doing my best to appear relaxed, but my mind was six hundred miles away in an Edinburgh courtroom where judgement was being given in the Duke of Argyll's divorce action against me.

The case had dragged on for four bitter years, and I had contested it every inch of the way. This afternoon, the result of the exhausting struggle would at last be known. My character, my credibility, my reputation were all at stake—but I felt hopeful. Only an hour earlier, outside the Ritz Hotel, a reporter had told me he had heard from Edinburgh that I had won. I was not really surprised, because I had every expectation of winning. In fact, I had prepared for a celebration by putting on a pretty, new, red-feathered hat.

My three friends at the lunch party were very patient and understanding, for all of them knew the situation. A waiter approached our table and called me to the telephone. I walked across the lawn wondering how anyone could possibly have known where I was lunching. When I lifted the receiver I discovered that Sam White, Paris correspondent for the London *Evening Standard*, was on the line. He had tracked me down through Georges, the famous concierge at the Paris Ritz.

'Have you heard the result?' White asked.

I told him that I didn't expect the news until four o'clock.

'Well, I'm afraid you've lost, and the judge has clobbered you.'

I have no idea what I answered, except that I asked him several times if he was sure of his facts. He was.

In a daze I returned to the lunch table. My friends must have guessed from my face, even before I spoke, that something was wrong. 'I'm afraid I've lost,' I said, 'and badly. Please take no notice of me. Just go on talking and eating.'

They did their tactful best to pretend I wasn't there as I sat in my jaunty red-feather hat dripping silent tears on to my plate. Deliberately forcing me to regain my composure, they insisted that we should go shopping after lunch, and it was only when we got back to the Ritz that I realised just what the verdict would mean in terms of sensational publicity. The hotel lobby was packed, and we had to fight our way through a mob of reporters and photographers to get to the lift.

As soon as I reached my room I put through a call to my solicitor in Edinburgh. 'It couldn't be much worse,' he told me. 'I've never in my life heard such a cruel judgement.' He went on to repeat some of the things the judge, Lord Wheatley, had said about me. As he spoke, I knew I was listening to my world disintegrate. The words I was hearing constituted nothing less than a savage character assassination. I could scarcely believe that any man—let alone a judge—could be so merciless or capable of inflicting such unnecessary pain on another human being.

My first thought was to call Frances, my daughter, at Belvoir Castle to warn her of the judgement before she read about it in the newspapers. I also tried, unsuccessfully, to put through a call to New York to speak to my son, Brian Sweeny.

When I talked to Frances she was calm and extremely sensible. 'It's all right, Mummy,' she said quietly. 'It can't be helped.'

One of my friends at lunch was more than a friend. His name was Bill, and without his support I could scarcely have endured the nightmare through which I passed. He had already sustained and advised me for two years, understanding even better than my lawyers just what I was facing.

For forty-six years my life had been peaceful, uncontroversial, without a breath of scandal. I had wealth, I had good looks. As a young woman I had been constantly photographed, written about, flattered, admired, included in the Ten Best-Dressed Women in the World list, and mentioned by Cole Porter in the words of his hit song, 'You're the Top'. The top was what I was supposed to be. I had become a duchess and mistress of an historic castle. My daughter had also married a duke. Life was apparently roses all the way.

But slowly and insidiously the poison that eventually killed my marriage was beginning to work its destruction. The Duke of Argyll, who I still believe had loved me deeply as I had loved him, was a good-looking, charming man, but weak. He allowed himself to be surrounded by people who were intent on breaking up our lives. They succeeded.

After eight years of marriage my husband, in one of his unaccountable moods, obtained a court order barring me from his castle. For the first time in my life I was the subject of sensational publicity.

While he was still my husband, he had gone into the witness box to give evidence against me in a libel action! This was the case in which a well-known Queen's Counsel, Gilbert Beyfus, for dramatic effect described me as 'a poisonous liar'—in spite of the fact that I had not uttered one single word in evidence.

London society, meanwhile, was swept by wild rumours that

my private diaries were full of erotic material. The names of cabinet ministers, ambassadors and film stars were mercilessly bandied about as being mentioned in those diaries. My family and I became the victim of poison-pen writers.

Behind all these rumours, and unknown to the public, something even more sinister was going on. With the help of a Dr Petro—who later went to prison, and was struck off the medical register—my husband made a determined effort to have me certified insane. Unfortunately for Ian, Dr Petro asked a distinguished Harley Street specialist, Mr Ivor Griffiths, who had known me for twenty years, to supply the necessary signature of a second doctor on the committal papers. Ivor Griffiths laughed Petro out of his room and advised him not to approach any other Harley Street specialists on this subject.

When Ivor Griffiths told me of this episode, for the first time I was really frightened. If it had been the time of the Borgias it might have seemed feasible. But this was happening in the 'enlightened' 1960s, and to me it was—and still is—incredible.

I was also amazed that people who had known me all my adult life could be so ready to believe in the mud that was being thrown at me.

I was very much alone at the time.

My father, who was my staunchest ally, had died from throat cancer in 1960.

My daughter, Frances, the Duchess of Rutland, was preoccupied with her duties as a wife and mother at her home, Belvoir Castle.

My son, Brian Sweeny, was working in New York.

And then, in the words of the song, 'Along came Bill'.

Although Bill was as upset as I about the outcome of the divorce hearing, he was determined that we should have a happy evening. He booked a table at the Cri de Paris and said we would probably 'do the town' afterwards. And so it was I ended the worst day of my life dancing in a Paris nightclub with the man I loved— the one man, ironically, whom my husband might have named in the divorce, but never did.

Next morning's newspapers were filled with the sensational details of Wheatley's judgement. I refused to read any of them (and have never done so to this day). But Bill insisted on knowing what they were saying about me so that he could advise me what to do. As he sat there reading page after page, his face became very grim.

My one thought was to get back to London as quickly as possible in the hope of appealing against the judgement, and to 'face the music'. We booked our air tickets. I travelled under the family alias of 'Mrs Campbell' in an attempt to escape the press. Even though Georges managed to smuggle us out of the Ritz by a back exit, there were press cars following us all the way to the airport. In London, as the plane landed at Heathrow, I looked down from the window and saw the tarmac swarming with reporters, photographers and television cameramen. From where I sat they looked like an army of angry black ants.

I had put on what I thought was my prettiest outfit, and with the best smile I could manage I came down the steps to the whir of cine film and the clicking of cameras. The press were so persistent and overwhelming that it finally took police protection to enable me to leave the airport.

Bill's identity was unknown to the press. He was a high-ranking business executive and I was anxious to keep him out of the publicity, so we separated on board the plane, and I drove home alone.

Outside my London house in Upper Grosvenor Street, a crowd had gathered. My butler, Reay, warned of my arrival, was ready to open the front door and I hurried into the shelter of my home. I went straight upstairs to my bedroom, where my loyal and devoted maid, Isabel Bennett—then almost eighty— was waiting. She had looked after me for many years, and I saw at once from her face that she had read the judge's words.

'Oh, Your Grace . . .' she began falteringly, but got no further. I collapsed in her arms and burst into uncontrollable sobs.

Chapter 2

There had been a day twelve years earlier when I thought I had found lasting happiness.

It was March 24th, 1951, and Ian Argyll and I had just arrived at Inveraray, Argyll, in the western highlands. We had been married in London the day before. In my arms I carried the huge bouquet of Inveraray daffodils that the tenants of the Argyll estate had sent to London for my wedding. Those same tenants now lined the Castle drive to welcome me.

As we stepped out of the car, Duncan MacArthur, the family piper, began to play 'The Campbells are Coming' and we heard shouts of, 'Welcome home, Your Graces!' We walked slowly along behind the kilted piper, up the drive to the romantic grey castle with its four turrets, which I always called the 'pepper pots'. When we reached the front door Ian insisted—much to my embarrassment!—on carrying me over the threshold, complaining with a grin how heavy I was.

I had come home to Scotland, the land of my forefathers.

Through the years there has been a persistent misconception that I am an American. This is probably because I spent my childhood in New York. Actually both my parents were Scots, and I was born in Scotland. Whether the Campbell clansmen realised this is doubtful. They were also probably unaware that the Duke himself was only a quarter Scottish. His mother was an American, and his father was half English.

My Scottish ancestry goes back to the twelfth century—to Helias de Dundas, who was granted the lands of Dundas by King David I of Scotland.

For hundreds of years my ancestors lived on the same estate at Sanquhar in Dumfriesshire. Their lands lay close to the Kirk-yard, in which the family vault can still be seen. Nearby, carved on a stone, appears their coat of arms: an uprooted oak tree crested by a scimitar held in a clenched fist, together with the motto, *Certavi et Vici*—'I have striven and conquered'. The words seem strangely appropriate to my forebears, most of whom began life with few advantages and rose, in almost every case, to success and prominence.

The first of my ancestors to become notable in Scottish affairs was Sir James Dundas, the 1st of Arniston, who was Governor of Berwick in the sixteenth century.

His son, also Sir James, the 2nd of Arniston, was knighted by Charles I in 1641, and in 1662 was appointed a Judge of the Court of Session in Edinburgh. Sir James took his seat on the bench as Lord Arniston, but soon afterwards he lost that title for refusing to renounce the 'National and Solemn League of Covenant'.

The second Sir James's son also rose to the bench, while his grandson regained the title of Lord Arniston and fathered two remarkable sons of his own. The younger, Henry Dundas, became the first Viscount Melville and married, as his second wife, the Earl of Hopetoun's sister, Lady Jane Hope. The elder son, Robert Dundas, the 5th of Arniston, became successively Solicitor General for Scotland, Lord Advocate, the Member for Midlothian in the British Parliament and, finally, for twenty-seven years, Lord President of the Court of Session.

His son, yet another Robert Dundas, the 6th of Arniston, also became Lord Advocate, and was for eighteen years Lord Chief Baron of the Court of Exchequer in Scotland.

Whereas the Arniston line of the Dundas family produced mainly judges and lawyers, their cousins, who were called Dundas of Beechwood, were more often soldiers. Foremost among these was Sir David Dundas, who became Adjutant General in 1781, attended Frederick the Great's Review at Potsdam two years later, and whose *Regulations for Infantry and Cavalry* was for a long time the standard work on the subject.

In 1809 the General succeeded 'the grand old Duke of York' as Commander-in-Chief of the British Army when the Duke was forced to resign because of the scandalous traffic in military appointments carried on by his mistress, Mary Anne Clarke.

Dundas remained Commander-in-Chief until 1811, when it was deemed that the scandal had subsided sufficiently for the Duke to be reinstated. General The Right Honourable Sir David Dundas was then appointed Governor of the Royal Hospital at Chelsea, where he died in 1820 at the ripe old age of eighty-five.

The General's nephew, Sir Robert Dundas of Beechwood, had seven daughters. One of them, Jane, married Robert Whigham, Advocate and Sheriff of Perthshire, who was my great-grand-father. His eldest son, David Dundas Whigham, my grandfather, was born on August 22nd, 1832. He was educated at Winchester and Oriel College, Oxford, and was then called to the Scottish Bar.

The Whighams, who came originally from Crieff, were extremely wealthy. But as a young man my grandfather lost most of the fortune he inherited—more than a million pounds—in an Australian bank crash. This may be the reason why he never practised law, but chose instead to go into the wine trade, joining the old-established firm of Oliphant and Company of Ayr, which had been founded in 1766. On April 21st, 1864, he married Ellen Murray Campbell, whose father owned a magnificent Adam house called Craigie, which stood in beautiful grounds on the bank of the River Ayr a mile upstream from the town of Ayr itself. Ellen, my grandmother, was then twenty-three. She was to live to be almost ninety-one. She died in 1931, a year after my own coming out, and I can still remember her, but only slightly.

The Campbells were also rich, and they owned Ayr Race Course, but my grandmother never saw any of this wealth. Her sister inherited it all and later left it to a dogs' home because she thought no one had paid enough attention to her. Thus my grandparents could not afford, after their marriage, to live in the style they had both known as children, and for the rest of their lives their home was a small and rather modest villa called Dunearn, overlooking Prestwick Golf Course.

My Whigham grandfather was an excellent shot, a skilful rider to hounds, and a fine golfer. He won the Prestwick Golf

Club medal in 1865, the same year in which my grandmother gave birth to their first child, Robert.

They were to have ten children in all, six of them boys. Each son started life with neither wealth nor influence, and each was to make his fortune and become remarkable in his own right. So remarkable, in fact, that Gilbert Miller, the Broadway impresario, often talked of producing a play about them to be called *The Whigham Brothers*. They were such an example of that rare breed of Empire builders that Lord Beaverbrook was preparing a series of six profiles, one on each of the brothers, at the time of my father's death in 1960.

The eldest son, my Uncle Bob, was to become General Sir Robert Whigham, Deputy Chief of the Imperial General Staff at the War Office, Commander of the 62nd Division in the last victorious months of the 1914–18 war, Chief of Staff under Field Marshal Foch, and finally ADC General to King George V.

After him came two sisters, my aunts Maud and Ethel. Then, in 1869, was born the second son, Henry James Whigham, my Uncle Jim, who became an outstanding war correspondent. He was Foreign Editor of the London *Evening Standard*, drama critic of the *Chicago Tribune*, the author of three books, editor of New York's *Metropolitan Magazine*—to which Theodore Roosevelt was a contributor—and, finally, editor of *Town and Country* magazine.

Aunt Sibyl was born in 1871, and Uncle Charles in 1873. He became a director of one of the great international merchant banks, Morgan Grenfell, where he was instrumental in helping to negotiate the United States loan to Britain after World War I. Mr J. P. Morgan, of Morgan Grenfell, presented Uncle Charles with four George I silver cups, two of which I inherited. One of them is inscribed: 'Presented to Charles Frederick Whigham by his American partners in affectionate remembrance of his work for the common cause during the Great War, 1914–18'.

Next came Aunt Molly, and, in 1877, Uncle Gilbert, who became Managing Director of the Burmah Oil Company, a director of British Petroleum and, in the tradition of my grandfather, Amateur Golf Champion of both India and Burma.

The fifth son, Walter Whigham, was born in 1878. He became the richest of all the brothers. He was a director of the Bank of

England, and Managing Director of the old London and North Eastern Railway, and held numerous other directorships. He was High Sheriff of the counties of London and Kent, and during World War I, in which he served with the North Staffordshire Regiment, and later on the staffs of the Fifty-first Highland Division and Fourth Corps, he was three times cited in despatches.

Finally, in 1879, came the youngest of the ten children—my father, George Hay Whigham, born at Dunearn, the family home at Prestwick in Ayrshire.

My grandfather's income as a wine merchant was just enough for him to live comfortably—but not grandly. He loved to hunt, however, and hunting was expensive. My poor grandmother had a constant struggle to bring up ten children on very little money, and my father told me that the crowning humiliation of his childhood was being sent to school wearing his sister's cast-off boots.

The story was told in the family that my grandfather, in the good old British tradition of male chauvinism, once gave my grandmother material to make curtains for his bedroom as her birthday present.

Since a university education was completely out of the question for the four younger Whigham sons, my father left school at seventeen and began his career earning thirty shillings a week as an apprentice in the civil engineering firm of Formans & McCall in Glasgow. There he shared a flat with his brother, my Uncle Gilbert, who was also earning thirty shillings a week. They pooled their resources, knowing that if their weekly expenditure exceeded three pounds they would be in serious financial difficulties.

In 1902, when he was twenty-three, and his apprenticeship completed, my father was appointed Resident Engineer on the Lanarkshire and Ayrshire Railway. He was responsible for the design and execution of all the stations, bridges and tunnels on that line, costing in all £750,000. Throughout his apprenticeship he also went to night school to study accountancy, and by the time he was twenty-five he was not only a fully qualified civil engineer but also a chartered accountant.

My father and Uncle Gilbert, both of them good looking and

personable young bachelors in their early twenties, were much in demand in Renfrewshire society. They were invited to all the big houses owned by such as Lord and Lady Inverclyde, the Earl and Countess of Wemyss, the Sainsburys and the Coats families. At one of these houses, during 1904, my father met and fell in love with a charming and vivacious girl called Helen Hannay. She was the daughter of a Scottish cotton magnate, Douglas Mann Hannay, and she lived with her parents at a house called The Broom at Newton Mearns in Renfrewshire, then a village about an hour's drive from Glasgow.

My father was planning to leave for Egypt, where he had been offered an appointment as a civil engineer on what became the Aswan Dam project, and he hoped to win the consent of Helen's parents to marry her before he left. My mother was a pampered girl whose dresses came from Lelong and Worth in Paris, and she had a lady's maid to look after them. The Hannays were, therefore, understandably far from enthusiastic about their daughter marrying an impecunious young man with uncertain prospects. Nor were my father's parents very keen on this match with a rich man's daughter. Although they liked Helen very much, they felt that a wife would prove too big a drain on the pocket of a young man who had yet to establish himself financially.

When my father asked for Helen's hand, Douglas Mann Hannay replied, 'You may marry my daughter if and when you can come back to me and tell me that you are earning five hundred pounds a year.'

My grandfather did not expect to see him ever again, for five hundred pounds was a very considerable sum of money in 1904. But my father, nothing daunted, set off for Egypt intent on earning it.

Early in 1905 word seems to have come from Egypt that my father hoped, as manager of the Wardan Estate Company, to win the necessary rise in salary by January 1906. But my grandmother, Ellen Whigham, was sceptical, and felt that my father was always apt to paint things 'a little too strongly *couleur de rose.*'

She was also, on the strength of her own past experiences, beginning to worry about her son's budget—especially about the expensive team of thoroughbreds he was keeping in Egypt. 'He counts a great deal on horses,' she wrote. 'True, they are certainly a pleasure and I suppose out there a necessity, but they don't help the ordinary household expenses.'

But my father was set on marrying Helen, and she on marrying him. I can remember my grandfather telling me how his heart sank on the day he came down to breakfast at The Broom to find a letter from Egypt waiting on his plate. He knew then that George Hay Whigham was coming to claim his daughter.

Both families seem to have accepted the inevitable, for we find my father's father writing the following letter to his prospective daughter-in-law:

> Dunearn,
> Prestwick.
> 10th March, 1905.

My dear Miss Hannay,

(I am quite willing to address you in the more familiar way as soon as you give me the order). I must write a line to you to say that I wish you and my dear boy George every possible happiness.

I have written to him also to the same effect. I said I would like to see his increased salary, which is promised I understand very shortly, on a sound and safe basis. Beyond that I am dead against prolonging any engagement. It would ill become me to do so, for I married 41 years ago on a portion that was very little if any bigger screw than George has or should have at the beginning of next year. I cannot wish you better happiness than God has given me for the long period I alluded to—and I am pretty well a pauper *now*.

I had a very nice letter from your father today, and I quite reciprocate his sentiments. I think George is a very lucky fellow, and to add to that I may say that he is and always has been a very worthy and good son.

> I am,
>
> Yours very sincerely,
> D. D. Whigham.

As a result, eighteen months later, while my father was home on leave, the marriage took place at Thornliebank Parish Church,

Renfrewshire, on August 8th, 1906. Directly afterwards my parents left for Egypt, and my mother always told me how much she loved Egypt, and that she considered her years spent there with my father the happiest of her life.

For some reason my grandfather had stopped my mother's allowance when she married—perhaps as a test of their love. I was a 'luxury' they could not afford for many years, and my mother could buy only two hats and dresses a year for some time. Within six years, however, through thrift and business acumen, my father had saved £10,000. At the suggestion of my uncle, Walter Whigham, my parents then went to New York, where my father undertook to help Sir William Van Horne with the building of the Canadian Pacific Railway and the Cuban Railroad. Soon after they arrived, my mother found she was expecting a child. To make sure there could be no question of their child's nationality, my parents decided to go home to Scotland. So it was at my maternal grandparents' home, The Broom, on the Hannay estate at Newton Mearns in Renfrewshire, that my life began—on Sunday, December 1st.

Five weeks afterwards, at St Margaret's Church, Newlands, Glasgow, the Rector baptised me into the Scottish Episcopal faith with the names Ethel Margaret Whigham. Ethel, which must have been chosen in a moment of madness, was after two aunts—my father's sister, Ethel Tennant, and my mother's sister, Ethel Tod. Margaret was after my maternal grandmother, Margaret Richardson, the wife of Douglas Mann Hannay, in whose house I had been born.

One week later I made the first journey in a lifetime of travelling. I was taken back to New York by my parents on the *Lusitania*, and my American childhood had begun.

Chapter 3

New York always will be 'home' to me. No city can compare with its magic. The towering skyscrapers of Manhattan, many of which grew up around me during my childhood, always give me a strange feeling of 'belonging' whenever I return there. My love of America possibly explains why I find American men so attractive, and also why so many of my closest women friends are American.

By the time of my birth my father was a rich man. Through unremitting hard work his fortune steadily increased, and when I was two years old he became President of the Cuban Railroad after the death of Sir William Van Horne. Much later in my life, Gilbert Beyfus, QC, described me in open court as 'a dazzling figure ... high in rank, the possessor of great wealth and famous beauty. ... As one contemplates her,' he told the jury, 'one thinks back to the fairy stories of one's youth when all good fairies assembled for a christening and showered their gifts upon the infant.'

Like the rest of his excessively histrionic advocacy, Mr Beyfus' description of my childhood advantages was overstated. There was nothing very dazzling about me. I had no 'high rank', nor indeed any rank at all. Far from being the possessor of 'great beauty', my photographs show me to have been rather a plain little girl.

My parents and I lived in the centre of Manhattan, in a duplex (two-storey) apartment at 1155 Park Avenue, and Central Park was my first playground. My earliest memory is of lying awake at night in my big brass bedstead on the fourteenth floor and listening to the mournful hooting of the ships' horns as they passed up and down the Hudson and East rivers on either side of Manhattan. Although I must have been very small at the time, the haunting sound filled my mind with strange thoughts of dying and of death.

I have never had such thoughts since, even at moments when I have actually been close to death.

This childhood memory always puzzled me, until I was told recently that it is quite common for very young children, not long out of the womb, to have these morbid thoughts.

At the outbreak of World War I, my uncle, Jim Whigham, did his utmost to urge America into the war through his editorials in New York's *Metropolitan Magazine*. So outspoken were his views that the *Metropolitan* came under censure from President Woodrow Wilson himself, and his administration attempted to suppress it under the Espionage Act because of an article entitled 'Is America Honest?'

In 1915, my Uncle Walter, who had gone to France with the 51st Highland Division, was badly gassed at Ypres and invalided home to England. This put an additional strain on my father, who was torn between a natural desire to go home and join in his country's struggle and his obligations to his business partners and shareholders in America. My Uncle Bob wrote to urge my father to remain in the United States, and this was what made my parents decide, rightly or wrongly, to stay put. My father felt much relieved when America finally entered the war on April 6th, 1917.

One of my earliest memories of World War I was hearing the American war song, 'Over There', being played on our HMV phonograph, with its promise that 'the Yanks are coming, the Yanks are coming. . . .'

I must have been a strange child, and I was always a 'loner'. I was in many ways a rebel, and a streak of stubbornness showed itself early on. From the age of two I was known as Margaret, having resolutely refused to answer to my first name, Ethel, which I loathed.

I spent most of my childhood longing to grow up. I was not too interested in playing with other children—they disarranged my toys. Even at that age I was irritatingly tidy and orderly, and I have never changed. I preferred to be on my own, or else with grown-ups. I loved being an only child, and if I misbehaved the one thing guaranteed to bring me to heel was my mother's threat to produce a 'little brother' or a 'little sister'.

There was nothing of the tomboy in me. I loved pretty clothes, and the peak of my ambition was to wear high-heeled shoes and my mother's taffeta petticoat.

My mother was very pretty and petite, with tiny hands and feet. She had a lovely figure and a nineteen-inch waist. Her sister, Ethel Tod, was considered to be the beauty of the family, and my mother always regarded herself as the ugly duckling, though she was anything but. She was known for her alabaster skin and enormous, twinkling blue eyes. She was elegant, beautifully dressed, and I longed to be like her, and every evening, when she came to say goodnight to me in a cloud of perfume and glamour, I would envy her, thinking that she was on her way to some glittering ball. She always left me wishing for the day when I could escape from my nursery life into the excitement of the adult world.

My mother was an amusing woman whose humour was often directed at herself. To her nothing was sacred, and she always spoke her mind with devastating directness. Rome, for instance, would be dismissed as 'very cold, and a boring pile of old stones.'

I never really understood my mother; she could be changeable and capricious.

My father, on the other hand, was more reliable and predictable. He rarely lost his temper, but when he did I quailed. So did every one else in the vicinity. Throughout my life, my father's temper was something I preferred not to arouse.

One of our few clashes concerned my teddy bears. I never liked dolls, but lavished all my devotion on three teddies— Brownie, Blackie and Teddy. At least one of them was always 'in hospital' being mended because his fur had been kissed off. At night I was usually found hanging on the edge of my bed because I insisted on the three bears sleeping in the middle of it. They had their own wardrobes filled with clothes that I had knitted for them—woollen outfits, booties, caps and gloves in every colour. They also had their own chest of drawers and innovation trunks with hangers, as well as a pram complete with blankets and covers. After the war ended my parents took me to England every summer, and I used to insist that my bears and all their belongings went with us.

One year my father put his foot down and flatly refused to take 'those damned bears and their luggage' on board ship. There, on the dockside, my father and I had an eyeball to eyeball confrontation.

'If my Teddies don't go,' I announced, 'then neither do I.'

On that occasion, rather than drag one small child screaming up the gangplank, he admitted defeat. The bears and all their 'luggage' came with us.

This episode makes me sound like a spoiled brat. In fact, because I was an only child my parents were extremely strict with me, especially when it came to punctuality. If I was even a minute late for a meal there would be trouble, and it would be pointed out to me that I was the merest amoeba in the household and far less important than the staff. This habit of punctuality is still ingrained in me.

One of the friends I used to meet every day was a pretty, rather plump little girl with blonde hair, dark eyes and thick black eyebrows.

Her name was Barbara Hutton.

I had no idea that she was the heiress to the Woolworth fortune. I only knew that I liked her very much, but my Nanny was puzzled by her sad expression, which seemed strange in such a child.

Much later I learned that at that time her mother, Edna Woolworth Hutton, had killed herself by jumping from the window of her suite in the Plaza Hotel.

Barbara and I have remained friends all our lives, although now we see each other very rarely. I went to her wedding reception at the Ritz Hotel in Paris in 1955 when she married her sixth husband, Baron Gottfried Von Cramm.

At one time she considered marrying Robert Sweeny, my first husband's youngest brother, and could therefore have been my sister-in-law.

My parents worried over my lack of a sense of humour. They persistently took me to see Charlie Chaplin's films, and became increasingly anxious as they watched my small, unsmiling face. I am told they even consulted a psychiatrist about it. I still consider Charlie Chaplin a very unfunny man. What I did love was reading—anything from the Thornton Burgess animal stories to Thackeray, all of whose novels I read before I was ten. My reading eventually had to be rationed, to prevent my eyesight from being ruined. The worst punishment that could befall me was to have my books confiscated.

By this age I was faced with a very real problem. I was born left-handed, and, as was usual in those days, my parents insisted that I use my right hand. As a result, I developed a stammer which proved to be a considerable handicap during my young life. When my parents realised what they had done—however unintentionally—they were most upset, and immediately consulted specialists. One suggestion was to immobilise my right arm, thereby forcing me to revert to being left-handed, but for some reason this was never attempted.

My mother's attitude to the problem was rather impatient. Instead of making light of the whole thing she once said to me when I was in my teens, 'No matter how pretty you are, Margaret, and however many lovely clothes we give you, you will get nowhere in life if you stammer.' I was amazed at her insensitivity.

Later, when I was fourteen and we had returned to live in England, my parents took me to see the London speech therapist Lionel Logue, who was at that time treating the Duke of York—the future King George VI—for his stammer. Mr Logue's treatment, which was based on controlled breathing, failed, but he did give me one invaluable piece of advice.

'Margaret, you have a hard road ahead of you,' he warned me. 'You are faced with two alternatives. You can run away from life because of your stammer, and if you do you will find yourself seeing fewer and fewer people and answering the telephone less and less. In the end you will become almost a recluse. Or you can face the world and fight this handicap in every way possible.'

Needless to say, I chose the second alternative, but it was not always easy. Ironically, I often heard of people—usually women—

saying that my stammer was an affectation. Men often told me that they found it most attractive, but this was cold comfort to me.

The person who came closest to curing me was a remarkable Scotsman, Sir John Weir, physician to the Royal Family. He was a homœopathist, and his treatment consisted of two white powders taken daily. Many people said that these were merely a placebo, but they were wrong, for when he changed these powders—without my knowledge—my stammer became noticeably worse. I realised that I had finally conquered it on the day in February 1963 when I stepped down from the witness box in the Edinburgh Court of Session during the Duke of Argyll's divorce action against me. After undergoing the most gruelling cross-examination for ten days, five hours a day, it dawned on me that I had been too angry to stammer even once.

I remember coming out of school one autumn afternoon to find the sidewalks jammed with people dancing and cheering.

I asked my mother when I got home what was happening.

'People are celebrating because the war is over,' she said with tears in her eyes.

But, sadly, the war was not over—this was what became known as the 'False Armistice'.

The real Armistice came quite soon afterwards.

In the summer of 1919 my parents were able to make their first trip to England in seven years.

One of my mother's chief reasons for returning to England was to find me a fully qualified English nanny—then, as now, a treasure in any household anywhere in the world.

In London, where we stayed at the Ritz, my mother telephoned a number of agencies specialising in nannies. Since the position carried the chance of a work permit in America, which was El Dorado to many people in those days, the response was enormous, and my mother spent days interviewing what seemed an interminable procession of highly unsuitable women, while I watched anxiously through a gap in the curtains.

Finally a fresh-faced young girl of about twenty-five, with a sweet expression and lovely blue eyes, came into the room. After a few minutes I ran out from behind the curtain.

'She's the one, Mummy,' I cried, 'please take her.' My mother had little option but to engage the young woman, whose name was May Randall. So it was a very much happier and more secure little girl who returned to New York with Nanny Randall in September 1919. I felt that at last I had a real friend who understood me and upon whom I could depend.

May Randall was to become one of the most important influences in my life, and she remained with me permanently until after the birth of my daughter Frances in 1937. As I grew up she became my chaperone and maid.

To this day we correspond regularly, and in one of her recent letters she wrote, 'I am worried to read about all these bombs in London. Do be careful darling if you go out.'

Chapter 4

At this time I was attending a school which my father and several other fathers had helped found. It was called 'Miss Hewitt's Classes' and was run by a remarkable Englishwoman. Miss Hewitt was a motherly woman with red hair and pince-nez and we all loved her. She was quite advanced in her teaching methods and had been the first headmistress in New York to introduce the Dalton Plan, whereby pupils were required to complete a fixed amount of work each week but were left free to spend the rest of their time on the subject or project of their choice. This suited me very well, and now, with Nanny Randall's encouragement, I made rapid strides under Miss Hewitt's expert guidance.

I distinguished myself by winning a first prize two years running for my albums on such exotic subjects as Egyptian and Greek history. These albums consisted of a series of essays for which we were supposed to provide illustrations out of newspapers and magazines.

It was the third album—on medieval history—that brought about my fall from grace.

I badly wanted to win the first prize for the third year in succession, and I was therefore anxious that my album should have better pictures than those of the other girls. One day I wandered into the school library and saw a set of fine leather-bound books. In one of these I discovered some illustrations that seemed to be just what I needed. I could hardly believe my luck. Without hesitation I cut them out very neatly, replaced the book on its shelf, and pasted them into my album. It never occurred to me that these books were valuable, nor that I had done anything wrong.

My album was completed and handed in, whereupon I was summoned to Miss Hewitt's study. There she sat, looking surprisingly stern, and beside her sat my mother—looking stunned. The interview was brief.

'You have mutilated valuable property that does not belong to you,' announced Miss Hewitt stonily, 'and although I know you did not mean to do wrong, your album will be withdrawn from the competition.'

A great black cloud descended upon me, and I felt that my life was finished. My mother certainly did not help. For the next three days before our departure for Europe she lay on her bed in a darkened room, prostrate with shame over my disgrace. Young as I was, I was irritated by her reaction, which I thought silly and melodramatic.

Nanny, who had become a much-needed buffer between my mother and myself, calmed her down and did her best to restore my morale.

My mother seemed to resent Nanny and to be strangely jealous of my affection for her. She also resented the close relationship I had with my father, and the long talks and discussions we had together on many strangely adult subjects.

I came to dread going into my mother's room to say good morning to her, for I never knew, from day to day, what mood I would encounter—bright and loving, or complaining and bad-tempered. Yet, in spite of her bewildering changes of temper, I know that she loved me and was proud of me.

She always wanted me to look my prettiest, and when I was about six, with straight lanky hair, she decided that a permanent wave was what I needed. I was therefore taken to a hairdresser and put in a tall chair, where for hours I sat with a strange array of wires attached to my head. Being a vain little girl I suffered all this gladly and was thrilled with the result. History does not relate what others thought.

As a birthday treat my mother took me and a party of my friends to see Jerome Kern's new Broadway musical, *Sally*, starring the blonde, beautiful Marilyn Miller. It was the first time I had ever been inside a theatre, and I was determined not to miss a thing. Despite my mother's protestations about good manners and consideration for my little guests, I firmly elbowed my way to the front of the box and sat spellbound throughout. 'Look for the Silver Lining' was the hit song of the show, and whenever I hear it I always think of that enchanting day. Later, when my mother mentioned casually that Marilyn Miller's hair was dyed, I was outraged and protested that she was the most beautiful lady and that her hair was natural, pure gold.

Every week, together with most of my young friends, I went to New York's smartest dancing class, held by a Miss Robinson in the Plaza Hotel. It was there that I met my first beau, Bruce Bossom (his brother, Sir Clive Bossom, is a friend of mine to this day). Bruce was about ten and I was eight, but we both thought that ours was a great romance.

Ouija boards were then the rage, and were supposed to have magical powers. You placed your fingers on them and they 'moved' towards letters on the boards and spelled out answers to your questions. Bruce and I consulted the Ouija board constantly, and our question always was, 'Are we going to get married?' With a certain amount of pushing and prodding we usually managed to make the answer come out as 'Yes'.

I thought this game was harmless fun, and had not realised that Bruce was becoming rather possessive. One afternoon at the dancing class a drama took place. Another boy came up and asked me for a dance. To my horror Bruce started a fight with him in the middle of the dance floor, and ended up minus two of his front teeth.

After that, the Ouija board was banned in the Bossom and Whigham households.*

My mother's unpredictable moods created great tension in our lives, and there were many times when Nanny Randall would have packed her bags and left had it not been for me. My mother was neither hard nor intentionally unkind, but she was extremely emotional. I later discovered that she and my father did not always get on too well.

My father's charm and great good looks made him attractive

* Bruce was killed in an air crash in 1932.

to other women, and this caused my mother to be jealous and unhappy. Sad to say, they sometimes aired their differences in front of me. At meals we would sit through agonising silences, and often I would be the only person making conversation. I was already highly-strung and sensitive, and this disagreeable atmosphere certainly did not help the problem of my stammer.

Once, when I was eleven, my mother packed up and left my father in New York, and went to Biarritz, taking me with her. However, my father soon came over to bring us home. For, in spite of all the difficulties, theirs was a life-long romance. During the last fifteen years of her life my mother was crippled by arthritis. My father was utterly devoted to her until her death in 1955. Although she was confined to a wheelchair all these years, he managed to take her on a cruise every winter, accompanied by nurses. When they were in London he insisted upon always spending his evenings with her and refused even to go to an occasional film with me.

My childhood Easter holidays were often spent at Hot Springs, Virginia, and there, in the Blue Ridge Mountains, my father took me riding on a pony called Peach. These rides took us along very beautiful trails banked by azaleas and rhododendrons. It was on one of these holidays that I met Winthrop Rockefeller, who was then about eleven. We were constantly together and I was very 'keen' on him but I am not at all sure that the attraction was mutual.

Another favourite resort of my parents was White Sulphur, West Virginia. We always stayed at the Greenbriar Hotel, and every Saturday night we watched the coloured staff performing their dance, the Cakewalk, in the dining-room. It was a great sight, and one that is now sadly burlesqued.

During the war my parents had rented various houses in Southampton, Long Island, each summer. After 1919, however, we spent the long American school vacations (four months) in Britain, and during these holidays we would visit my grandparents in Scotland at their house, The Broom, at Newton Mearns, Renfrewshire. I loved it there and used to get up at 6 o'clock in the morning just for the joy of being in the country. My grandparents' estate was about thirty acres and led down to a river. To my childish eyes the fields seemed enormous, and the weir in the river was Niagara Falls. I remember watching with amazement my grandfather, Douglas Mann Hannay, at breakfast. He always put salt on his porridge, and ate it standing up. This, I learned later, was—and still is—a strange Scottish custom.

Meanwhile the Whigham family fortunes were steadily rising. Uncle Bob had been knighted by King George V for his war services and was soon promoted to the rank of Lieutenant General.

Uncle Charles had been decorated by the Emperor of Japan with the order of the Rising Sun for his part in bringing about the Japanese Sterling Loan. He had also taken a major part in negotiating the Dawes and Young Loan, had been on the Reparations Commission at the end of the war, and in 1918 was the British Government representative of the Ministry of Munitions in the United States.

During our summer vacation in Britain in 1920 something of the utmost importance happened to my father and to all of us. Uncle Walter, who was still with Robert Fleming & Co. in the United States, sent a cable to my father urging him to return as soon as possible to New York to investigate a new process for producing artificial silk. In September, therefore, my father, my mother, Nanny Randall, the teddies and I all returned to Park Avenue.

Shortly afterwards my father met three brilliant Swiss brothers called Dreyfus. They were inventors and had been working on the previously unknown formula for viscose acetate. This liquid was the beginning of artificial silk, which was to revolutionise the fabric industry.

My father, who always had tremendous foresight, quickly realised that the discovery was of world-wide importance. But the Dreyfus brothers were not businessmen. He suggested to them, therefore, that they should concentrate on invention, and leave the business side to him.

Courtaulds also had the formula for viscose acetate at the same time, and a fierce rivalry developed between my father and the head of Courtaulds, Alfred Lowenstein. Out of this rivalry were born two trade names—'Celanese' and 'Milanese'—which were to be the forerunners of all the familiar household names, such as Nylon, Orlon and Terylene.

During the next six years, my father gambled all he had on the success of Celanese; and spent many sleepless nights over it. But his faith was to be rewarded. Even though I was very young at the time, I can clearly remember the day on which the front page of the London *Evening Standard* announced that Celanese shares had jumped from six shillings to six pounds.

Overnight my father had made his fortune. He was to become Chairman of the Celanese Corporations of Britain, America and Canada. He relinquished the chairmanship of American Celanese in 1940 because of the ban on British businessmen holding foreign directorships or chairmanships. The Canadian chairmanship he retained until his death, and that of British Celanese until 1957 when, before his retirement and much against his will, he consented to negotiate the merging of Celanese with Courtaulds. It has always been a great regret that my father never took me on a tour of the Celanese plant in Derby. I often begged him to, but he could not believe it would interest me.

With our yearly visits to Britain, I had made fourteen Atlantic crossings by the time I was twelve, but I had always considered New York my home, and had never thought of living anywhere else. However, unknown to me, my parents had been taking a hard look at life in America, and they did not care for what they saw.

This was the era of Prohibition. The sale of all forms of alcohol was forbidden, but suddenly America was invaded by bootleggers who smuggled it in from Canada and also from the West Indies. Many people brewed their own liquor in illicit stills. This was when 'bath-tub gin' came into existence, so called because it was often actually brewed in the bath. As a result there were some terrible drinks on sale. Masquerading as gin and whisky, they were so potent and so dangerous that they could blind or even kill. My mother had been appalled to see young girls in the cloakrooms at debutante parties dead drunk from drinking what was called 'moonshine', another lethal concoction of raw spirits. My parents naturally did not wish me to 'come out' in this atmosphere. Neither of them could know that I would drink nothing but water, nor smoke a cigarette, until I was thirty.

And so, on a summer day in 1926, I said a tearful farewell to Park Avenue. I, with my teddies and their luggage, embarked for the last time, leaving the fabulous Manhattan skyline behind us, to begin life in England.

Chapter 5

In London my parents initially leased a house in Charles Street, Mayfair, and I was sent to Miss Wolff's day school in South Audley Street. This was an ultra-conservative establishment, and Miss Wolff's pupils included many daughters of the British aristocracy. Fourteen years earlier, the Lady Elizabeth Bowes-Lyon—now Britain's beloved Queen Mother—had been a pupil there and one of her essays had won a prize for literature. My contemporaries included Cecil Beaton's sisters, Nancy and Baba.

The personality kid of the school, however, was Lord Birkenhead's daughter, Pamela Smith, who later married Lord Hartwell, and is the godmother of my son Brian. Pamela was enchantingly pretty in a gamine way, with a little heart-shaped face and enormous brown eyes. She looked as though butter wouldn't melt in her mouth, but poor Miss Wolff and her staff very quickly found that it would! Her favourite trick was to ask to go to the lavatory every half-hour and then to spend twenty minutes sliding down the banisters.

I was very happy at Miss Wolff's. At home, and in the country house at Ascot which my parents bought, I still played with my three bears. But the day came when Brownie, Blackie and Teddy were left out on the lawn overnight. And the next morning, when my mother discovered the three forsaken bears in the garden, soaked with dew, she realised that my childhood was over.

On leaving Miss Wolff's, I was sent as a day pupil to the famous Heathfield School. This was my first experience of a girls' boarding school and I did not like it. Although, as a day girl, I was not wholly subjected to it, I hated the regimentation and lack of privacy. The emphasis placed on athletics and games amazed me. I was an adequate tennis player, rider and swimmer, but girls playing hockey, basketball and cricket I could not understand. As for my sessions in the gym, these were a disaster, culminating in my being stuck upside-down on the parallel bars, purple in the face, with my gym tunic over my head.

I was certainly not the most popular girl in the school. For one thing I had an American accent, and in those days the English were inclined to regard Americans as some sort of Red Indians who lived in wigwams. Then there was the fact that I attended classes at Heathfield only until lunchtime, when the chauffeur came to collect me in the family car.

I regret to say that I was delighted to escape every day, and I used to call from the window of the car to the other unfortunate 'prisoners', 'Bye-bye girls! Enjoy your hockey and your lacrosse. I'm off to a matinee in London.' And under a rug in the back of the car I would hastily shed the detested school uniform and change into a dress.

Not surprisingly, my parents eventually received an ultimatum from the headmistress: either I must remain at Heathfield as a boarder, or leave, as I was upsetting the morale of the whole school. With immense relief I left.

I have been against boarding schools for girls ever since, and refused to send my daughter to one. I believe it is essential for girls to be individualists, and individuality is what boarding schools are apt to eradicate.

My mother then engaged a charming elderly governess called Miss Baker, under whose efficient tuition I learned more in two weeks than I had in months at Heathfield.

Our country home, Queen's Hill, adjoining Ascot race course, was large and comfortable. Every weekend about half a dozen boys from Eton school used to come over to Queen's Hill for the day, to play tennis and dance with my girl friends and me in the music room, where there was a gramophone. The town of Ascot was officially out of bounds to Etonians, but with my father's amused consent our family Rolls was sent over to fetch the boys, who climbed into the back and crouched on the floor under the car rug until they were safely out of Windsor. They would then be returned to Eton by the same method in time for the evening curfew.

These boys—now sadly all dead—were not only good-looking but tremendous fun.

They included David ('Winkie') Brooks, the nephew of Lord Astor; the Earl of Rosslyn's son, Hamish St Clair-Erskine; Desmond Parsons, brother of the Earl of Rosse; and the Duke of Roxburghe's nephews, Alistair and David Innes-Ker.

'Winkie' and I had one shattering experience together when he took me to lunch with his aunt, Lady Astor, at Cliveden. Viscountess Astor, who was then forty-eight, was already a legend as the first woman ever to sit as a Member of Parliament in the House of Commons. She was a powerful political hostess, and had gathered around her the famous 'Cliveden set' of Conservative politicians. She was considered to be a martinet, and meeting her would have been an ordeal at the best of times for a girl of fifteen. I remember being over-awed even at the sight of Cliveden and by the stone staircase that led up to the house and seemed to be never-ending. Once in the hall I met Lady Astor, looking just as formidable as she was reputed to be, and she did nothing whatever to put me at my ease. I did not know then that Nancy Astor disapproved of her nephew, nor that Winkie was regarded as the charming black sheep of the family. We went in to what seemed like an enormous and very formal lunch party, and had just sat down when I saw Winkie make a surprisingly hurried exit from the room.

In a few moments, to my astonishment, Lady Astor signalled to me also to leave the dining-room. I did so, to discover that Winkie, having had too much to drink before lunch, had been sick outside over Lady Astor's carpet. An arch-teetotaller, she was outraged, and we made our exit from Cliveden without lunch and in disgrace.

My father was annoyed with Winkie for involving me in such

an incident, but none of us could understand why Lady Astor had blamed me. As I never met her again I had no chance to find out.

At the time it seemed to be one of life's dark moments, but Winkie and I soon forgot it and continued to have a wonderful time together. He and his friends sometimes persuaded me to slip away from Ascot and dine with them at some glamorous restaurant in London, such as Sovrani's, Quaglino's or the Berkeley. We always returned to Ascot the same evening. So in spite of my parents' wishes that I remain unheard and unseen until I made my official debut, I was managing to 'slide out' much too young.

One event, sanctioned by my parents, took place during the Eton 'long leave'. We all had been to watch the Eton and Harrow match at Lord's, and Winkie had arranged for another aunt of his, Nora Phipps, the mother of Joyce Grenfell, to chaperone us. That evening we went to see *Show Boat*, which had just opened in London at Drury Lane, with Edith Day, Marie Burke and Paul Robeson in the cast.

To me it will always be the musical to end all musicals. How many shows can claim to have had eight 'hit' songs? And no one who heard Paul Robeson's rendering of 'Ol' Man River' is likely to forget it.

The song, 'Bill', which Marie Burke sang that night, was strangely prophetic. Although I never dreamed, as a carefree girl of fifteen, that I would ever need a champion to defend me, it was indeed a man called Bill who one day did become that champion.

But the night I saw *Show Boat* was full of laughter and gaiety, ending with dinner at Sovrani's. Nora Phipps turned out to be more fun than the rest of us put together, and no young girl could have had a more enchanting chaperone.

Easters, during this period, were often spent at Bembridge on the Isle of Wight, which was then a lively meeting place for teenagers.

One of my favourite friends there was David Niven, who looked much the same as he does now, and was just as funny.

I had a schoolgirl crush on him—natch!—but I doubt if he even noticed it, far less returned it.

After the holidays I used to drive down from London with a great friend of mine, Georgiana Curzon—Earl Howe's daughter

—to spend the day with David at Stowe. We were accompanied by our respective nannies as chaperones, unbelievable as this may seem today.

The summer holidays throughout my school years were spent at Baden Baden, where my parents took the cure. Although I was always among older people then, and leading a strangely sedate life for a young girl, I adored the Black Forest and loved to take long walks alone in the early morning before breakfast. In the afternoons my parents often took me sightseeing to the enchanting Bavarian towns and villages in the area. Once, my father and I, who both loved music, went to Munich to hear a new operetta called *Land of Smiles*. The leading tenor was unknown to us, but his voice and personality were electrifying. His name was Richard Tauber, and he was later to be godfather to my son Brian.

Another occasion I shall never forget was the day in 1929 when we motored to Nuremburg. We encountered dense crowds and were forced to stop the car. It appeared that some gigantic rally was taking place. Up on the dais was a small man, haranguing the people. Far away from us though he was, it was obvious that he had a strange magnetism. His name was Adolf Hitler, and this was the first of his annual Nuremburg rallies.

The first four winters after we had moved to England were spent in St Moritz, which to me has always had a fairy-tale quality. I used to love waking up to a clear, crisp, white world, to the sound of sleigh bells and the hotel band under my window playing waltzes for the ice skaters. For the first two winters my parents insisted on staying at Suvretta House, a hotel half an hour outside St Moritz, in the hope of keeping me away from the tea dances and the gala evenings at the Palace Hotel—the centre of the sophisticated life in St Moritz. Finally they grew tired of seeing only the back of a sleigh, with me in it, disappearing towards the town, so on our third visit, to my great relief, they gave up the unequal struggle, and we stayed at the Palace.

My mornings in St Moritz were spent trying to learn to ski. A number of kindly gentlemen volunteered to teach me, among them Gene Tunney, the former world heavyweight champion; Viscount Carlow, the Earl of Portarlington's son, whose death as a pilot in World War II cut short a brilliant career; and the Marquis of Donegal (known as Don), who had rivalled Lord

Castlerosse as the best gossip columnist of the day. (There was also Bobby Cunningham-Reid who married the late Countess Mountbatten's sister, Mary Ashley.)

They were all very patient with me, although I am afraid they soon got the message that I would never be a champion skier. But the lessons were great fun, and usually ended with our taking the funicular up the mountain to the Corviglia Club for lunch.

In those days St Moritz was filled with Argentines, all marvellous looking, very rich, and great fun. The tango was the rage at that time, and I tangoed with them all in turn in a haze of happiness.

One of the loveliest girls there was Clara Uriburu, whose father was the Argentine Ambassador in London for many years. I longed to look like her and all the other sophisticated American girls; in fact I longed to look grown-up and begged my mother to allow me to wear at least a little make-up. She, in her oddly indulgent way, gave in.

One of the regular visitors to St Moritz was an American called Billy Reardon, who had partnered Irene Castle after her husband, Vernon, had been killed flying in World War I. They had become world famous as exhibition ballroom dancers.

In the winter of 1929 Billy, in a moment of madness, asked me to partner him in an exhibition waltz at the Cresta Ball. This was to be held at the Palace Hotel and was one of the biggest galas of the season. I accepted with alacrity, and then told my mother. 'I don't mind your doing it,' she said, 'but if you are going to be flung around the ballroom by Billy I insist that Nanny buys you a pair of bloomers with elastic round the legs.' I protested, but to no avail, and underneath my beautiful yellow tulle dress I had to wear those bloomers.

I have always loved dancing of any kind, and Billy was a marvellous partner who gave me expert help throughout. I enjoyed every minute of it, and was so flushed with triumph when it was over that I begged Billy to let us do an encore. Fortunately he knew when enough was enough, and refused. I still have the pair of silver birds I was given as a memento of that evening.

After this particular winter holiday, I was taken straight to Paris to a finishing school run mostly for English girls. On my arrival there, fresh from the delights of St Moritz and feeling rather sophisticated, I was—much to my fury—smuggled in through a back door and not permitted to face the other girls until every vestige of my nail varnish and lipstick had been removed.

My parents had sent me to Paris for two reasons: to learn fluent French and to get me away from London and out of sight until I made my official debut in May.

Needless to say, I was not at all pleased with life at a boarding school, and it was not made easier for me by the fact that a brilliant first cousin, Ruth Nicholson, was there at the same time. While she was gaining top honours in Class A1, I was sitting in Class C3, learning painfully little and longing for the term to end. Everybody was amazed that we should come from the same family.

After three months in this finishing school, which was supposed to teach you, among other things, how to dress, how to walk, and how to comport yourself generally, I emerged feeling dowdier and shabbier than I had ever done in my life.

My mother must have realised that there was no holding me back, and to my great delight she allowed me to make my debut younger than most girls.

On my return from Paris, preparations to 'launch me' began. I remember my mother saying, 'This is the only time of your life that will be completely carefree. Be sure you make the most of it. Once you are married you will take on many responsibilities.'

I knew she was right, and I couldn't wait for the summer to begin.

Chapter 6

'Mr and Mrs George Hay Whigham and Miss Margaret Whigham have arrived at 6, Audley Square which they have rented for the season.'

That brief and rather pompous announcement in *The Times* proclaimed my official debut.

Looking back now on the glamour of it all, the first summer season seems like a dream. It belongs to another world—a world of manners and elegance that has now vanished.

As I did not wish to waste a second, we planned that my coming-out dance should be held on May 1st, the opening day of the London season. This was a calculated risk, for once all the other debutantes had been to my dance, it was possible that their mothers would not bother to invite me to theirs. The fear proved groundless, and for the rest of 1930 I received plenty of invitations.

In those days the build-up for a debutante's coming-out was really exciting. I was lucky enough to have an extremely generous father and a mother with impeccable taste. It was she who helped me to be both practical and economical in choosing the clothes I would need for the next three months. I was allowed to order a dozen beautiful evening dresses and many day outfits (awful word!) for the Derby, Ascot and the many lunch parties to which I would be invited.

Most of these clothes were made by two young men just down

from Cambridge—Norman Hartnell and Victor Stiebel—both of whom were later kind enough to give me credit for helping to launch them on their way to fame.

The morning of May 1st, *The Daily Telegraph* reported: 'Forget-me-not blue will form the very lovely frock of tonight's blue-bred debutante, Miss Margaret Whigham, for whom her mother, Mrs George Hay Whigham, is giving a coming-out ball this evening at No 6 Audley Square, which promises to be a very smart affair.'

The 'very smart affair', however, nearly didn't happen. Two days before it, my mother's mother, Margaret Hannay, fell dangerously ill. At one point she became so weak that her pulse was almost imperceptible, and it seemed inevitable that she would die. But just as we were about to cancel the dance, my grandmother summoned me to her bedside.

That wonderful old lady, after whom I was named, looked pathetically small and frail lying there propped up against her pillows.

'Come here child' she said, and her voice was scarcely a whisper. 'You are not to worry, dear. They all think I'm going to die and spoil your party.' Her lovely green eyes flashed defiantly and a small bony hand gripped mine. 'But they're wrong—because I'm not.'

And she didn't. Although her pulse flickered and almost failed on the night of my dance, Granny kept her word. She rallied, survived the crisis and lived on for another six years.

The evening of May 1st was an enchanting and outstanding success.

6, Audley Square was filled with spring flowers, and, wearing the turquoise-embroidered tulle dress that Norman Hartnell had designed for me, I stood with my parents to receive our guests while Ambrose and his band played in their best 'soft lights and sweet music' style.

Up to now I had never been mentioned in newspapers, except briefly by Lord Donegal in his articles, 'Almost in Confidence', during my visits to St Moritz. But on the morning following my dance I was surprised and flattered to find myself prominently featured in the social columns.

'Miss Whigham, one of the loveliest debutantes of the year,

shone out above everybody else, as is only fitting for the heroine of such an evening. . . .'

'The party' said another report, 'overflowed into the street where there sat, in his car, a peer's son who had been so hard at work all day that he had not had time to change and, therefore, could not enter the house. Instead he held court outside, people bringing food and drink to his car.'

From that moment on, life became a round of gaiety. Every night there would be a ball or reception, probably at Brook House, Londonderry House, Holland House, Sunderland House or Warwick House. Sadly, many of these no longer exist.

British women are renowned for looking their best in full evening dress. This they wore night after night, usually with beautiful family jewels. The men would always be in white ties and tails—plus their decorations if a member of the Royal Family was present.

The great hostesses, such as the Marchioness of Londonderry, wielded immense power, and their invitations were much sought after, even by diplomats and cabinet ministers.

In those days there would be sometimes as many as three or four dances held on the same evening, and I was fortunate enough to be able to pick and choose.

It was the era of the chaperone. Before each dance the mother of one of the debutantes would give a dinner party of young people, after which the other mothers would go to the dance, and sit out the evening on hard gold chairs, supposedly guarding their daughters' virtue. My mother and I soon decided that this routine was not for us. I much preferred to invite one boy friend to dine with my parents and me before going on to a dance. Also, my mother had no intention of spending the summer sitting on a hard gold chair every night. So we made a pact. If I promised to come home, however late, in the family car driven by our chauffeur, my mother would agree to make a brief and polite appearance at the dance and then quietly vanish. Very unconventional for the 1930s, but it worked.

On arriving at a dance, both men and girls would be given a numbered dance programme. The worst thing that could happen to any debutante was to have this programme unfilled. To combat this problem I devised 'the Whigham system'.

For the first half-hour I would agree to dance with any boy who asked me, however dim he might be. This obviated the danger of blanks in my programme. As my favourite beaux appeared later in the evening, I ruthlessly filled up the entire programme a second time. If someone on the original list complained that I could not be found for a promised dance, I would feign concern and surprise.

'But I didn't realise you said under the palm tree', I would protest. 'I thought you meant by the staircase.'

The 1930s have recently acquired a reputation for being wild. Nothing could be further from the truth. The climate in which I came out was severely moral, largely because of a strong reaction against the 'fast', hard-drinking decadence of the '20s, when the Bright Young Things had delighted in such pastimes as baby parties, at which gin was drunk out of feeding bottles. Life in the '30s was perhaps frivolous, but it was also very 'proper'. In spite of my mother's compromise in disappearing early from dances, during my first season I was never allowed to go out alone in the daytime unless she or Nanny accompanied me.

Months later, on the first day I was allowed to venture forth alone, a good-looking man with a Guards tie spoke to me as I was coming out of the Ritz. I thought I had met him and allowed him to walk with me as far as the Berkeley. Only then did he confess that we had never been introduced, and I realised that I was being *picked up*. I was so frightened that I ran into the Berkeley and sat in the cloakroom shivering for an hour.

In spite of the air of sophistication that I tried so hard to achieve, and in spite of being an outrageous 'flirt'—dated word!— I was essentially an innocent. The men around me seemed to sense this and treated me with chivalry and respect. I never had to fight my way out of any situation, and I have always suspected the women who boast of their battles for their virtue.

The rules of behaviour were rigid in those days, and people disregarded them at their peril. This I discovered to my cost on one occasion which took place during my first season. Viscount Selby, one of my young admirers, asked me to go with him to a ball that Viscountess Cowdray was giving in Mount Street. He told me that his invitation had been addressed to 'Lord Selby and partner' and that he would like me to go with him.

My mother was particular about which invitations I accepted, and she always made me refuse those from people whom neither she nor I knew.

Because of this I was not over-explicit about Tommy's invitation to Lady Cowdray's ball, in case my mother should forbid me to go. I did not know Lady Cowdray!

Tommy and I arrived at the house in Mount Street to find the ball in progress, and he led me straight on to the dance floor. We had been there only a short time when Lady Cowdray came up to us. Her daughter, Brenda, and her niece, Joan Pearson, had both been with me at finishing school in Paris, but there was no friendliness in Lady Cowdray's manner, and her voice was icy.

'Miss Whigham, do you have an invitation to my dance?'

I was dumbfounded and also acutely embarrassed.

'No, Lady Cowdray,' I replied. 'Lord Selby asked me to come as his partner.'

Our hostess turned her stony gaze towards Tommy, refusing to let him speak, and said, 'I don't remember inviting you to bring a partner, Lord Selby.'

I forget how the conversation ended. I only know that I felt so uncomfortable that I insisted upon leaving immediately. To my young and inexperienced mind, the incident seemed the ultimate in social disgrace. Tommy and I were so worried as to how I could break the news to my parents that we walked round and round Grosvenor Square until four o'clock in the morning. Next day, after a sleepless night, I told my parents what had happened. My father, as I had anticipated, was furious. Not with me. Not with Tommy. But with Lady Cowdray. He telephoned her immediately, and this time his was the voice that was icy. Listening with glee on an extension, I heard strangled noises emanating from the Viscountess, but my father was relentless.

'You put my daughter into a most distressing and embarrassing position,' he told her. 'I want a written apology sent round by hand. If I do not receive it I am afraid I must take advice on the matter.'

Lady Cowdray's note arrived within the hour and the incident was closed. But it taught me one important lesson. I never again accepted an invitation that was not issued in my own name.

Three weeks after my coming-out dance, I was presented at Court. Miss Vacani, my dancing teacher for many years, was the ultimate authority on the Court curtsey. 'The head must be kept absolutely erect,' she would insist.

I was to be presented by my mother, and I sat with her in our car, wearing another Norman Hartnell dress—of white tulle embroidered with silver and pearls—with the three traditional Prince of Wales ostrich feathers as a headdress. For more than an hour our car wedged its way at a snail's pace up The Mall, past crowds of excited, cheering people peering in through the windows and scrutinising us. At last we drove through the gates of Buckingham Palace and across the forecourt. My mother and I went up the Grand Staircase, through a succession of magnificent state rooms, and came finally to the gold and scarlet ballroom where a breathtaking sight met our eyes.

Everyone was in full court dress; the men with orders, decorations, swords, and a variety of different coloured tunics. The room was ablaze with colour—an unforgettable spectacle.

King George V was prevented by a bad attack of rheumatism from attending the Court, and when Queen Mary walked from the Royal apartments to the Throne Room, she was escorted by her eldest son, the Prince of Wales, who was in the scarlet uniform of a Colonel of the Welsh Guards.

The Royal procession was preceded by the Lord Chamberlain and his officers walking backwards. As they reached the dais, the Prince handed his mother up the steps and Queen Mary took her seat alone on the golden throne beneath the great canopy of state.

The Queen wore gold brocade, and the blue riband of the Garter. She had a coronet of emeralds and diamonds on her silver hair, and a matching necklace. Among those being presented that evening was Viscountess Furness, the dark-haired American beauty who was to be so much admired by the Prince of Wales. My mother made her curtsey first, and when I followed her I was surprised to find that I was not at all nervous. I made a very slow curtsey in order to give myself time to take a good look at the Royal party.

As I was rising, my attention was suddenly caught by an incredibly handsome young man standing behind the Queen. He was dressed in a white knee-length Indian tunic with a high military collar and a white turban glittering with an emerald the size of a large bird's egg.

For a split second our eyes met before I had to turn and walk away from the throne. I wondered who he could possibly be.

The next night I met him at Brook House at a ball given by Lord and Lady Mountbatten. He was introduced to me formally as Prince Aly Khan (the elder son of the Aga Khan). He was then nearly nineteen, dark haired, with magnificent brown eyes. We danced every dance together that evening. It was love at first sight. Three weeks later I spent my first Ascot race week with Aly, as he came to stay at Queen's Hill for the house party my parents were giving.

Then Aly took me to my first Derby. The Aga Khan had two horses running, and I backed them both. When Blenheim streaked past the post to victory I was as thrilled as if it had been my own horse! That night the Aga Khan had a celebration party at the Embassy Club in Bond Street. The Embassy was world famous not for its outstanding decor, which was quite simple— the banquettes being upholstered in red velvet and the walls lined with mirrors—but for its elegance, its food and wine, its music and its clientèle. All these were and still are unsurpassed by any other restaurant.

Of the four corner tables there was always one reserved for the Prince of Wales and the Duke of Kent, who often came with Mrs Freda Dudley-Ward and Edith Baker (Mrs d'Erlanger). At the second you would probably find ex-King Alfonso of Spain; at the third the Mountbattens; and at the fourth probably the Duke of Westminster—the famous Bendor—with some beautiful woman.

Everybody in the room knew everybody. The women all wore their best dresses, the men were in white ties—at least, until the Prince of Wales introduced the fashion of wearing the dinner jacket in restaurants. Until 1930 the Embassy had been thought of by the smart 'young married' set as their private property. As they were often dining with each other's spouses, they had no wish for little debutante eyes peering at them. However, nothing daunted, I managed to persuade the committee to make me an honorary member—the first unmarried girl to be so honoured. From then onwards, the Embassy became almost a second home to me. I lunched there every day, and danced to the music of Ambrose or Jack Harris most evenings. It was even suggested by a rude friend of mine that I should arrange for a camp bed to be put up there.

If my friends and I were not at the Embassy we would be at another of London's glamorous restaurants—the Café de Paris—watching the great cabaret stars such as Beatrice Lillie and the Yacht Club Boys from America. The Café's famous curved staircase to the dance floor was designed for spectacular entrances, and many women would make unnecessary telephone calls upstairs just to be seen descending it.

The image of Aly Khan later became that of a cynical playboy where women were concerned, but at nineteen his attitude towards me was utterly correct, possessive and distinctly Oriental. During the Ascot week house party at Queen's Hill we went to dances every evening. After one of them, my guests ended up in my bedroom, gossiping and giggling.

All except Aly.

The next morning I noticed that he was very silent and looked glum. I asked him what was wrong and why he had disappeared the night before.

He answered me in a voice of misery, saying that he had no right to go into my bedroom and that he hated the thought of anybody else—even women—being there.

We were very deeply in love and wanted to marry, and before leaving Queen's Hill, Aly asked for my father's consent. He met a firm refusal, on the grounds that at seventeen I was far too young to contemplate marriage.

After that my father forbade me to go on seeing Aly or to dance with him at parties.

My father's mind was made up. Aly and I were both very unhappy and seized every chance we could to meet secretly in the gardens of the houses where we were both invited to parties.

As we were forbidden to telephone each other, our only means of communication was by letter. But Nanny, who had been of the opinion that only the Prince of Wales was good enough for me, luckily approved of Aly and was in favour of our marriage. It was she, and Aly's Indian servant, who carried our desperate, frustrated messages of love to and fro between Audley Square and Aly's house in Aldford Street, just a few hundred yards away.

Aly's romantic letters, although obviously written by a very young man, are among the most touching and tender I have ever received.

On June 24th, 1930, he wrote:

My Love,

Your Letter has given me such happiness. I read the words you wrote and I can't believe you wrote them to me. I would just like to spend the rest of my life hearing you tell me that you love me . . . love me.

I dream of you, think of you. Every plan I make and every thought I have is with you. I can't manage to tell you of the love in me for you . . . all of you. I *never* want you to change from what you are now. You are infinitely too wonderful for this world. I am ashamed of myself when I think of you and wonder why God made you love someone like me.

Margaret, I love you but that word does not mean four letters, it means all the world and life to me. Write me please. I'm just living for tomorrow night and for you, and want to live forever if you love me and the day you stop I should like to die.

Ever yours,
A.

One of the last letters I received from Aly was written after my parents had made me break off our unofficial engagement. It seems strangely mature.

June 27th, 1930

'My Margaret,

When I saw you in the street just now, for a short moment I was alive again. I lived because till then I could have been cut to pieces without feeling anything. The moment that I passed you I felt like running back to you as fast as my body would go. When I left you yesterday I would have given anything to have been run over. I thought of killing myself but realised that you loved me and that everything was far from being impossible and that by dying I would forever lose you on this

43

earth; and that is the last thing I shall ever do if it is in my power to hold your love forever.

It is no use telling you of my agony and I know what you are also feeling. But I *will not* think of this as being the end of everything. We are both young and have many more years to live. I will trust in you till I die. My trust will never die. I will not give up seeing you either but I will have to see you very seldom.

I am going abroad for a week tomorrow morning and I may write to your father and ask him to listen to me for a few minutes when I come back as the other day I could not talk. My love, you mean my life to me and for nothing in the world would I give you up, so trust me and in time if you still love me everything will come right, it must while I live. Never stop writing to me at 12 Rue de Poincare, or the Ritz, Paris, will find me or in any case they will keep my letters till I come back which will be at the end of next week. When I come back if you trust your own maid she will have to bring me your letters and take mine back to you as mine to you would be seen.

You have my love and my life and I want you forever to keep both. A.

After we had been forbidden to see each other, Aly used to sit alone night after night at the Embassy Club, drinking orangeade, and asking the band to play our favourite song, 'I've Got a Crush on You', over and over again.

It was indeed a golden romance in a golden summer.

At the end of the season my parents took me to Europe in the traditional manner 'to forget', and Aly left for a long trip to the Orient. From Cairo he cabled me: 'My heart always with you'. I read the words with a sadness that took many months to fade.

I am grateful that I knew Aly then, when he was at his best. Later he became restless and spoiled, pursued by too many women. But he remained a staunch and devoted friend to me for the rest of his life.

I last saw him in May 1960, when we lunched together in New York at the 21 Club. He was delighted by his recent appointment as Pakistan Ambassador to the United Nations, and remembering his charm and intelligence I had every hope that this would lead to a new and successful career, marking the end of his playboy existence.

He returned to Paris, and one week later died in a car accident at the wheel of his own Lancia.

To me he will always be young.

Chapter 7

Until 1930, a debutante had been a person any man over the age of
twenty would run a mile from. The Bright Young Things of the
1920s had been regarded as an eccentric little group of society
enfants terribles, a law unto themselves, but the prevailing image
of the debutante was that of a painfully shy mouse, lacking both
make-up and conversation. Suddenly and unaccountably, all this
changed. The girls of 1930 not only had good looks; they knew
how to dress; and they had far more self-confidence than their
predecessors. All at once the well-known married beauties, who
had held sway in London society, began to feel threatened by the
appeal of the Young Girl.

The press were quick to swoop on this new development. Suddenly newspapers began to 'feature' us. For the first time, debutantes became front page news along with royalty, politicians and
actresses. The three girls in my coming-out year who were given
the most attention and coverage were two of my friends—Lady
Bridget Poulett, the sister of Earl Poulett, Rose Bingham, who
later became the Countess of Warwick—and myself.

'Miss Margaret Whigham', reported the *News Chronicle*, 'goes
everywhere, and photographs of her have appeared so often that
they are as well known as those of any film star'.

Our news value by no means faded after our first season. Two
years later, in 1932, one London columnist wrote a full centre-

page article headlined: 'Wanted—New Faces for 1933'. And there, underneath, were the faces of Bridget, Rose and myself.

Only three girls since that time have received the public attention we had: Brenda Frazier in the United States just before World War II; Sharman Douglas, while her father was the American Ambassador in London; and Henrietta Tiarks, who is now the Marchioness of Tavistock.

The social columnists were very kind to me.

According to *Bystander*, then a popular glossy, I was 'quite the smartest *jeune fille* London has seen for a long time. . . . Her clothes are original . . . do not depend entirely on their cost . . . and she wears them with great chic.'

'It is amazing', said the *Sunday Chronicle*, 'how she had leapt into the forefront of every social event of consequence during the past twelve months. A year ago, Margaret Whigham was little more than a name to me. Now I cannot go anywhere without meeting her. From being rather a shy and retiring little thing, she has suddenly become the most photographed girl in the country.'

The verdict of the *Sunday Graphic* editor was less delicate: 'She stood out from a row of debutantes like a thoroughbred in a field of hacks.'

Thoroughbred or not, I was more than fortunate to end that first season as Debutante of the Year, for Bridget and Rose were my equals in every respect.

The year had been a whirl through Wonderland. I can remember several times dancing with the Prince of Wales, and being startled by the intense blue of his eyes, and by the curiously wistful expression that was always in them. Though a small man, he had the presence and unmistakable aura of royalty—this he never lost. We met often, then and after the Abdication, and he was always his friendly, charming self.

Some of these early memories are bizarre. At the Westminster Ball, Lady Diana Cooper, that enchanting beauty who is still a dear friend of mine, appeared as a coster, distributing flowers from a barrow, while Douglas Byng, already a cabaret idol, came dressed as an English nanny with a pram full of toys.

One of the most successful hostesses was Madame Florence de Peña, known as 'Flo' to all her friends. She was the American widow of a rich Argentine and had a beautiful house in Charles

Street. Her parties were a mixture of all ages and nationalities and her invitations were much sought after.

She would begin by giving a cocktail party, which would last until about 9 o'clock. A further group of guests would then arrive, and some fifty people would sit down to dinner, and afterwards there was an orchestra to which we would dance until dawn. If you played your cards right you could be at Flo's house, having a wonderful time, from 6 p.m. to 6 a.m., which I frequently did.

At that time the London theatre was sheer magic. Gertrude Lawrence, Beatrice Lillie, Dorothy Dickson, Evelyn Laye, Gerald du Maurier, Adele and Fred Astaire, and Maurice Chevalier were all at the height of their fame. The first nights were exciting affairs at which the audience was almost as glamorous as the actors: Noël Coward's *Cavalcade*, when I sat between Somerset Maugham and Michael Arlen, to hear Noël tell the audience that it was 'still a pretty exciting thing to be English'; *Evergreen*, with Jessie Matthews; *Stand up and Sing*, with Jack Buchanan and a slim, unknown young blonde called Anna Neagle, who had the whole audience standing up to cheer her debut as a star.

Then there were the charity galas, the most spectacular of which was the Jewels of the Empire Ball, held at the Park Lane Hotel. £1,500,000 worth of jewels were worn by the women appearing in the parade, and sixty detectives were on guard in the ballroom. Much to our chagrin, Bridget and I were told to wear coral and turquoise respectively—not diamonds and emeralds as we had hoped. The second Jewel Ball in which I took part, two years later, was much more to my liking! I was laden with diamond bracelets up to my elbows, and wore an enormous diamond necklace and brooch—all loaned by jewellers for the occasion. The effect was startlingly vulgar, and when photographs of me were published some people thought that the jewellery was mine and that I had gone berserk.

It has often been said—even by Barbara Cartland, who knows me so well—that my father employed a press agent for me. Nothing could have been further from the truth; indeed, had anybody suggested such a thing to my father, he would very quickly have been shown the door.

No one promoted or paid for the publicity that Rose, Bridget and I attracted—like Topsy, it just growed. We seemed to fill a gap between the picture postcard beauties of World War I and the star models, such as Barbara Goalen and Fiona Campbell-Walter, who burst upon us after World War II. Much of the attention was due to our friendship with the three popular gossip columnists of the day: the Marquis of Donegal (known as 'Don'); the ubiquitous Viscount (Valentine) Castlerosse; and the originator of the William Hickey Column, Tom Driberg. They were invited to all the parties we went to, and they mentioned us daily in their columns, probably because they could not avoid us —we were here, we were there, we were everywhere.

My energy was boundless—and it came from nothing stronger than water!

If I had made a 'double date' one evening by mistake I was quite capable of having dinner with one young man, pleading tiredness and going home at 10.30, only to sally forth again to meet another beau at the Embassy or the Café de Paris, where we would dance until the doors closed at 2 a.m.

Then we would float on to the late nightclubs such as the Florida, the Silver Slipper, the Bat, or Uncle's, ending up by having eggs and bacon at dawn. My parents insisted that, no matter what time I'd got to bed, I should appear dressed for breakfast at nine—which I always did.

This was the era of the famous Big Bands—Tommy Dorsey or Paul Whiteman would come over specially from America to play at the Kit Kat Club; Roy Fox always played at the Monseigneur, and Carroll Gibbons at the Savoy. They were all a joy to dance to, and this kind of 'live music' is one of the things I miss most today.

Two establishments were 'out of bounds' to me. One was the 'Bag o' Nails', where the young men I knew 'picked up' girls, and they certainly did not want me or my friends poking our noses in there. The other was the Cavendish Hotel, run by the legendary Rosa Lewis, once the mistress of Edward VII. Rosa, whom I met several times, was the subject of great fascination to my generation, but I must admit her charms escaped me. She also had an irritating habit of pawing me all the time.

One story I heard about the Cavendish—and I'm not now certain whether it is as hilarious as once I thought—concerns Lord

Londonderry, father of the present Marquis. Robin Londonderry arrived at the Cavendish late one night, rather the worse for drink, and was given a room for the night. He staggered into it, collapsed into bed, and felt something very cold lying beside him. It was a corpse which had been left there for the night. Poor Robin shot out of bed and ran screaming from the room.

My mother was very strict about where I went and with whom. For instance, she did not approve of my going to the famous weekend parties given by Woolf ('Babe') Barnato; I was only allowed to go there for the day.

Babe was the intrepid South African millionaire who raced his (foreign) cars at Brooklands, hunted with the Whaddon, and played golf at Sunningdale. He was married and had also had a long and much-publicised romance with the actress, June, later Lady Inverclyde. Babe's reputation with women was rather suspect, and this was why my mother didn't approve of my staying at his house.

It was Babe who, in January 1931, introduced me to Lieutenant Commander George Pearson Glen Kidston, the millionaire sportsman and pioneer aviator. He was then 32, tall and extremely good looking. He had great charm, and the attraction between us was instant and mutual.

He owned Blackburne House in Culross Street, and had a large estate in Scotland. He and his wife had been separated for some time, and they had a five-year-old son called Archie. Glen and I began to go out together a great deal, and I often dined at Blackburne House, though the two of us were never alone because of my mother's rule that I must not dine alone with a man until I had been 'out' for one year. We would always invite another couple. Glen would ask Dickie Mountbatten, Lord (Lionel) Tennyson or Richard Norton (later Lord Grantley), and I would bring a girl friend.

For the next three months Glen and I were almost inseparable, and when we danced together he would always ask the band to play 'You're Driving me Crazy', which became our theme song.

Although it was obvious that he enjoyed my company he was strangely undemonstrative. The only positive signs of his affection were the masses of flowers that arrived daily and the parcels containing all the latest gramophone records.

I knew that Glen was no longer in love with his wife. I also knew he'd had many love affairs, including one with Pola Negri, the Hollywood film star. But as for his feelings towards me, he had given me no clue. I only knew that I was deeply in love with him.

My mother was also very fond of Glen, and my father often played golf with him. He was the man I think they would have been happy to see me marry.

Glen was planning to make a solo flight to Cape Town in an attempt to break Amy Johnson's record. This, of course, meant that he would be out of England for some time, and I was praying that before he left London he would give me some positive indication of how he felt about me.

But on the last evening we dined together, a few days before he set off, nothing of importance was mentioned. He took me back to Grosvenor House, where I was staying, gave me his usual chaste goodnight kiss and said goodbye. I went upstairs feeling puzzled and despondent.

On the morning he was due to leave, my first waking thought was that Glen was on his way. He had flown out at dawn, and I said a small prayer to ask for his safe arrival.

Minutes later the hall porter telephoned to say that two parcels and an urgent letter were being brought up to my room.

All were from Glen. The first parcel contained a beautiful diamond watch from Cartier's, which I wear to this day, the second a dozen records. They included 'With all my Heart', 'I Surrender, Dear', 'By My Side', 'Hello Beautiful', and 'When Your Lover Has Gone'.

When I showed the watch to my mother she said, immediately, that I must return it, that I could not accept presents from a married man. But I didn't hear her. I was too busy reading Glen's letter, which contained all the things I had been longing to know for weeks:

Blackburne House,
1a Culross Street
London, W.1.
Monday, 30th March, 1931.

Margaret,
    I write this letter the night before I fly off in my attempt at

the Cape record. I go in a few hours time, confident that I will succeed.

Margaret, you may have wondered why you haven't heard anything from me since the night we went out. Well, Margaret, I feel I must now tell you, and although I've done my best to conceal it from you in the past, I did not dare see you before my departure, as I knew I could not possibly withhold myself telling you.

Margaret, I am terribly fond of you. I've just been thinking of you the whole time and don't know what I should do or say because it is all so difficult—me married with a child and not even divorced.

This may sound a ridiculous letter but in times like this when I am all pitched up to a high key I simply must tell you of my feelings towards you.

I haven't the least idea how you feel towards me. I don't think you could ever accuse me of having made love to you, even though I may have been, or tried to be, kind.

Margaret, just think of me a little. Glen will be often thinking of you as he flies South to the Cape. I'd like to send you a cable now and again. It would encourage me. My address in Cape Town will be c/o Thomas Cook, but my secretary, Miss Williams, will always tell you of my latest movements.

Things are all very exciting. I am wondering how we will get on. I feel I will succeed, but the trouble is it's often those small little things that put you out of the running. Wish me luck, Margaret, when you go to your bed. I'd be so heartened to think you were wishing me good luck.

If you think all this just nonsense, Margaret, tear it up and I'll understand. If you do not, then I'll understand too.

A little watch for remembrance.

Glen.

I was stunned and overjoyed by the letter, but felt utterly helpless, as Glen had now gone. All I could do was to write a long letter back, cable my love to await him in Cape Town, and follow his flight by buying every edition of the evening papers.

On April 7th, a cable from him arrived at Queen's Hill: 'I've done it Margaret. Love my dear. Glen.'

He had broken Amy Johnson's record and become an international hero. His photograph was on the front page of every newspaper.

Glen and I wrote and cabled each other almost daily. The deep and very unusual love between us grew entirely through the written word. I was living in a dream of happiness waiting for his return.

On April 13th, my grandmother, Ellen Murray Whigham—my father's mother—died in her 91st year at Dunearn, the family home at Prestwick where she and my grandfather had raised their ten brilliant children.

At her funeral service three days later in the Holy Trinity Church at Ayr, they sang Psalm 103:

... The days of man are but as grass: for he flourisheth as a flower of the field.
For as soon as the wind goeth over it, it is gone: and the place thereof shall know it no more.

If I had possessed the gift of foresight, those words would have sounded a knell in my heart. Within three weeks I was to recognise their eternal truth.

After getting my first letter from England, and realising that his love was returned, Glen wrote at length from South Africa about the future:

> Carlton Hotel,
> Johannesburg.
> 22nd April, 1931.

Margaret my darling,
Today I am the happiest man on earth, just having received your sweet letter written on the day of my leaving England.
Margaret, I understand all you say. The last four years I've often thought I could never feel the way I do just now. ...
Darling Margaret, I just feel miserable at being so far away. I just think of you all the time. I have some wretched newspaper cutting of your photo which is kept so near to me. It heartens me and it makes me feel life is wonderful after all.
Margaret, I am a different man to read your letter, and to realise that you do care for me even just a little bit makes me so

gloriously happy, but at the same time it makes me feel rather a beast.

I know I was not really a tiny bit as nice as I wanted to be during our last days in London. I felt I should not let you know what I thought or felt towards you because I could not honestly come to you in the way my instinct told me I should.

Margaret, I am not a saint and I hope I do not profess to be. Apart from being married and having a sweet son, I have had affairs galore. Believe me or not, these have meant nothing to me. They have just come and gone and I have no lasting impression of them.

This may be and probably is all wrong and I despise myself on this account, but frankly if I professed I regretted them I would be a hypocrite because, at the time, for nothing better to do, I enjoyed them. I realised they meant absolutely nothing to me.

Margaret darling, I have never tried to make love to you because I knew deep down in my old heart that I did love you and that if I made any kind of love to you, you would think I was just doing the usual kind of thing. But it was not easy. I so wanted to tell you all kinds of things before I went away.

I blame no one except myself for my marriage . . . my sweet son is certainly the real difficulty. . . .

Margaret, you have the whole world before you, and you can choose the finest husband in the world, and lucky, damned lucky, fellow he will be.

I don't know what to say or do darling. I'm terribly fond of you and I simply cannot bear the thought of your ever being married to anyone else. . . .

I can of course fix things with my wife very easily. She is more than anxious, but up to the present I have never had a reason to wish to get my freedom, and for several reasons I thought it best that she should pause and consider before she got hers. . . .

Don't know what you thought of me dashing off down here the way I did. I'd love to stay in England up to a point, but I don't think, Margaret, you would care for me the least little bit if I just spent my life gadding around the dear old Embassy and places like that.

I've been bitten for years with an awful complex of ambition. Often I wished to God I had not had any ambition. It is a most disturbing instinct, yet I feel one is not made just to exist. Life, I imagine, is given to man or woman—more particularly man —to do something with. Mere existence to me is just wasting one's life.

Because one has means is, to my way of thinking, a greater reason why one should strive to do something. The fellow who has to earn his own living has an excuse for doing nothing.

At heart I am a bit of a socialist. Not that I despise money or that I do not appreciate its value—God forbid! But I feel one should try to do something and do it to the best of one's ability.

Sitting here in this dingy old hotel, I just think of you in the Embassy looking too radiant and beautiful for words. You'll never know what anguish I felt the night Lionel Tennyson kept on dancing that wretched 'You're Driving Me Crazy'. I was the poor fellow being driven crazy although I hope I did not show it.

Darling, how I wish I were with you now. It would just be too wonderful for words. I'm going to my bed with your photo in my pyjama pocket and your letter to keep it company. I'll just give both of them a little look and perhaps, yes, a little . . . before I go to sleep.

Darling, I feel so wonderfully happy although we're so far away. Sweetheart mine, I'll come back as soon as I am able. I want to see just one person and that one person my little Margaret waiting for me and not hundreds of awful people who, kindly as their intentions may be, I just don't want to be there.

I'll try hard to get back by June. Don't be annoyed with me if I try a record flight back from Kenya.

All the way out on my flight I wondered time and again what you were doing and if you ever thought of silly Glen trying to break his neck.

I loved your telegrams and was terribly thrilled to get them, but Margaret your letters were so much better. That I felt was your real self.

Do write me again as soon as you can. You do not know

darling how wonderfully happy I felt when I got your last one.

Goodnight darling, my own sweet darling Margaret. Had a long tiring day making a speech to the Chamber of Commerce —about a hundred and fifty to two hundred old men. You would have laughed.

Just off to bed. I'm dreaming of you darling child and longing to be near you again.

God bless you Margaret.
Glen.

P.S.: Glad you liked the watch but you *must* keep it.

With the help of the Master of Semphill, who controlled Hanworth Aerodrome, arrangements were made for me to be waiting on the tarmac to meet Glen on his arrival home.

I was to drive to the aerodrome in Glen's Rolls-Royce which he instructed me to 'use as your own'.

Afterwards, my parents and I were invited to stay with Glen at his villa in Le Touquet.

On the afternoon of May 5th, 1931, I was at the London Hippodrome taking part in a special charity matinée called *A Day in the Life of a Débutante*, in the presence of the Duchess of York, who is now the Queen Mother. It was in aid of East End youth clubs, and among those also appearing were Mrs Alexander McCorquodale, who is now Barbara Cartland, and Mrs Ronald Armstrong-Jones, now the Countess of Rosse and the mother of Lord Snowdon. I remember that I took the role of a modern débutante and wore a shimmering blue Norman Hartnell evening dress.

After the performance, I was standing in the foyer of the Hippodrome, watching the Duchess of York leave, when I caught sight of the front page of an evening newspaper.

Across the top of the page, in a great black headline, were three words: GLEN KIDSTON KILLED.

The words began to dance before my eyes. So did the room and the people around me.

Someone was leaning over me, and arms were reaching out to help me. (Next morning's newspapers reported that I had slipped on the stairs and had a nasty fall. The truth was that for the first time in my life I came near to fainting.)

'I'm all right,' I told anxious friends. 'I just became dizzy for a moment.'

I escaped alone into the night air and went to buy a newspaper. I looked at the words on the front page in horrified disbelief.

Glen had been killed at eleven twenty that morning when the plane he was flying from Johannesburg to Natal crashed on the Drakensberg Mountains sixteen miles north of the Van Reenen Pass and close to the mountain known as Tantjiesberg. There had been a high wind, thick dust and poor visibility. Why had he ever taken off in such conditions?

Local farmers who rushed to the scene found the aircraft smashed to pieces. Some of the fragments were lying among the rocks and in thick bushes. The rest were scattered across the veld.

The bodies of Glen and his co-pilot, Captain Gladstone, were unrecognisable. Glen himself was identified by a visiting card that had fallen out of his pocket during the crash.

I crumpled the paper in my hands and went home to my parents. For days, weeks even, I was numb with grief. It had to be a private grief, for I had told no one, not even my parents, of the real depth of my love for Glen.

On the day after the accident, a letter arrived from Glen by air mail:

My plans, Margaret, are something like this: Fly to Nairobi May 20th. Leave Nairobi early June. Attempt record flight to London. I hope to do it in 2½ days. . . .

I hope the return flight succeeds. It will be hard work as I shall be coming back just with my mechanic. But Margaret darling, if you'll be there to meet me it will just be too heavenly for words and I will think as I fly along that I am getting closer and closer every moment. I do so long to see you. . . .

Sweetheart I'm terribly in love with you. I never realised it until I got down here. Do meet me when I come home, otherwise I'll be in an awful state. All my love, I'm thinking of you always.

Glen.

Other letters continued to arrive by sea mail for several weeks afterwards.

Eighteen is very young to have to face tragedy, and each letter from Glen that I opened was a new agony.

I forced myself to go to the memorial service at St Mark's Church in North Audley Street.

Some word of my relationship with Glen must have reached his wife, and it was conveyed to me that I should not be welcome at the church. But Dale Bourn, the golfer and a friend of Glen's, took me to the service, and very quietly we slipped into a pew right at the back. I bowed my head and tried to accept what had happened as God's will. But I knew then, as I know now, that Glen Kidston was the man I should have married.

Had he lived, and had I become his wife, my life would have been happy, protected and with never a dull moment.

But Glen had gone, and the words of Alfred, Lord Tennyson, which we sang that day in the final hymn, were a bitter-sweet ending to my love for the man who found peace and freedom in flying:

> Twilight, and evening bell,
> And after that the dark;
> And may there be no sadness of farewell
> When I embark;
> For tho' from out our bourne of time and place
> The flood may bear me far,
> I hope to see my pilot face to face
> When I have crost the bar.

Chapter 8

My grief over Glen Kidston's death was of necessity a very
private one, and I threw myself into preparations for my second
London season, knowing that keeping busy would be a great
help.

One of the events of that summer was the Famous Beauties
Ball at the Dorchester, at which many of the most beautiful
women in England represented great beauties of the past.
Viscountess Castlerosse—the dazzling Doris Delavigne—
appeared as Madame du Barry; Lord Snowdon's mother, then
Mrs Armstrong-Jones, was Lady Hamilton; Gladys Cooper was
Helen of Troy, and I was Mrs Mary Robinson—Perdita—the
actress and mistress of the Prince Regent, in a dress modelled on
her portrait by Gainsborough.

Two weeks later my parents gave me another dance—this time
at Queen's Hill, our house at Ascot. Eight hundred people came,
and the gardens were lit by three thousand lights hung in great
festoons. It was a larger affair than my 'coming-out' party, as
by this time I knew many more people. In one of Norman
Hartnell's loveliest dresses, I danced with a succession of good-
looking, eligible young men until sunrise. Had Glen been there it
would have been the perfect evening.

That summer Simon Elwes, who was considered the best
portrait painter of women at that time, asked me to sit for him.

I always wondered why, because I soon discovered that he had a preconceived idea of me as being arrogant and spoiled—and this is how he began to depict me. What he did not realise was that my face was that of a very sad girl.

After several sittings, however, Simon and I became great friends, and he told me that I was much nicer than he had expected. He tried to soften my expression in the painting, but the result—as often happens when artists try to change their work—was a failure. The portrait was scrapped, and Simon told me that he finally painted a large female nude over the unfinished Margaret Whigham!

Meanwhile, I was the cartoonists' delight. They usually made me baleful looking, with large sunken eyes and a square jaw jutting out from an elongated neck. I was regarded as a trend-setter, and was apparently the first girl to wear pearl-coloured nail varnish that was luminous at night.

The press often made good-natured fun of me. When Britain went off the gold standard in October, 1931, the *Daily Express* made the following announcement:

> As an example to the girlhood of Britain, the lovely Margaret Whigham has decided, in the interests of economy, to have her hair re-set only once a fortnight in future, and to stop wearing stockings in the evening. On the other hand, to stimulate trade, she has just bought four new evening dresses.

Not surprisingly, this provoked numerous ribald remarks, and some not so good-natured fun. The left-wing *Daily Worker* commented:

> This should be a lesson to the wives of the unemployed, whose extravagant habits include setting their hair in curl-papers every day and buying no dresses at all.

The rebuke was apt and deserved. I would like to be able to say that my friends and I had done something serious and useful at this time, such as working for the poor of London's East End, as my daughter Frances did twenty-five years later. But I am afraid that my generation—the generation that was young between two harrowing wars—were butterflies, without a serious thought in our heads. I can only say for myself that, although

I may have been bird-brained, I was never intentionally unkind.

In the months that followed Glen's death, one man began to mean a great deal to me. He was Max Aitken, the son of Lord Beaverbrook. I had known him ever since I came out, but gradually we began to see more and more of each other. Young Max, who was then just twenty-one, had enormous charm and is one of the most attractive men I have ever known. Out of all the beaux I had in my youth, he is one of the few who have retained their looks and glamour.

Max and I became unofficially engaged, and I wore his garnet ring. Old Max—his father, Lord Beaverbrook—seemed to like me, but the relationship between him and his son was often strained. 'Daddy had a long long talk with me this morning,' young Max wrote to me at one point. 'He started off about my work and how we've got to make the newspaper the greatest in all the world, and how absolutely essential it is for me to be in absolute and complete partnership with him. Darling, he is frightfully jealous of you because he used to be the only person I would go to the end of the earth for. Now there's you, sweet one, and I feel like going to the end of the earth sixty million times and then flying to the moon.

'He went on and said that I would be God's biggest fool to get married. Oh Margaret darling I don't know where to turn. He is the loneliest man I know. Everyone is frightened of him because he has such unlimited power. And I seem to be the only person he will confide in and who he enjoys having around.'

In spite of Max's anxiety, his father seemed to like me, perhaps because I amused him and was never overawed by him.

One evening, when we were dining together, young Max was obviously upset and worried. He told me that his father and he had had a blazing row after which old Max had turned him out of the house and dismissed him from the *Manchester Daily Express*, on which he was then working. He begged me to go and see his father on his behalf. I promised to do my best to make peace between them.

Next morning I telephoned Stornoway House (the Beaverbrook residence) and was put straight through to the Great Man. 'Lord

Beaverbrook, I should like to see you as soon as possible, and alone,' I said with all the imperiousness of youth. Old Max betrayed no surprise, and invited me to dine with him the following evening at Stornoway House, assuring me that we should be alone.

I promptly arranged to fit this dinner in between two cocktail parties and a dance!

The next evening, in my ball dress, I trotted into the library at Stornoway where Max and his close friend, Mike Wardel, were having drinks. Mike left, and we went in to dinner.

My host and I sat at opposite ends of the table, which seemed a mile long, and I almost had to shout my various complaints about the cruel way he had been treating his son. I was listened to with courtesy and patience. Before I bustled off to my dance, Max thanked me and promised to consider my advice on how to deal with his son.

He must have been secretly amused, and I have always been grateful for his forbearance. He could have given me a sharp rebuff and told a foolish, though well-meaning, girl to mind her own business.

I left Stornoway House that night with the impression that Max would be by no means displeased to have me as his daughter-in-law. The 'Aitken row' was soon mended, but whether my part had any effect on the outcome I never found out.

Lord Beaverbrook remained a most loyal and staunch friend to me until his death in 1964.

In December my parents told me that I was going with them to Egypt, as my mother was suffering from arthritis and had been advised by doctors to get away from the British winter.

Because of my growing attachment to Max Aitken, I received this news with dismay. Max had asked me to marry him, but I needed time to get to know him better before making up my mind.

Before setting off I had a wonderful birthday party at the Embassy, at which there was an astrologer. When he came to tell my fortune he said, 'I see happiness, laughter . . . much love. But beware! There is danger.'

'Danger from what?' I asked.

'Treachery', he said. 'You will be betrayed by people you trust.'

I dismissed the incident from my mind. But thirty years later I was to discover the uncanny accuracy of that old man's prediction.

On December 17th, when my parents and I left on the boat train from Victoria, many of my friends turned up to say goodbye to me, and our compartment, which was full of flowers, soon turned into the setting for a cocktail party.

'Lord Reading was on the same train,' reported next morning's *Daily Express*, 'but nobody took much notice of him; after all he is only an ex-Viceroy.'

'The wires have flashed the information to the regimental messes of Cairo,' said another report of our departure. 'As yet there is no news of a native rising in her honour, though I hear the Sheiks are clipping their camels.'

Egypt was then still under British rule, and Cairo was at the height of its winter season. Parties were given every night by the British Guards officers stationed there. At one of these parties, on Christmas Eve, I met the young Earl of Warwick, whom I had known in London, and who was now in Cairo with his regiment, the 1st Battalion of the Grenadier Guards.

Fulke Warwick was twenty years old and very, very handsome, complete with military moustache. Good looks ran in his family. His uncle was Anthony Eden, and his grandmother was Frances, the Dowager Countess of Warwick. The Dowager Countess was still very much alive, and had been not only the most fervent Socialist in Edwardian society but also King Edward VII's 'Darling Daisy'. Her memoirs, published a year before our visit to Egypt, had created a tremendous stir in England. I always regretted not meeting her.

After a few days in Cairo my parents and I went up the Nile to Aswan on the de-luxe White train. I soon discovered that Fulke Warwick was also on board. He came to talk to us in our carriage, and told us that he was spending the weekend in Aswan.

The Cataract Hotel, where we stayed, overlooked the mighty Aswan Dam which my father had helped to build before I was born. The town seemed full of elderly people taking the cure, which involved burying themselves up to the neck in the hot sand that was supposed to help their rheumatism. My parents feared that I would be bored, but I was thrilled with my first taste of the East. I found myself a pet camel, and I used to take long rides on him far into the desert every day, accompanied only by an Egyptian bodyguard.

Many of the officers stationed in Cairo used to come to Aswan for weekends. We would go on our camels into the desert for moonlight picnics. In the daytime we would go sailing in native boats on the Nile, visiting the Temple of Philae and Coptic Churches nearby. The most regular of these weekend visitors was Fulke Warwick. In this Arabian Nights atmosphere he pursued me and finally proposed to me on New Year's Eve, while we were walking together across the Aswan Dam.

In a panic I realised what a mess I was making of everything, for I was still unofficially engaged to Max Aitken and was wearing his ring.

Max had been writing to me almost every day with accounts of his exploits. His car had caught fire outside Stornoway House, and three huge fire engines had raced up St James's Street to put out flames that leaped a hundred feet high.

He was miserable in Manchester. 'The office lights,' he wrote, 'have now been on for three days for the simple reason that a thick fog will not go away. I honestly shall go clean crazy if I don't see a bit of clear sky soon.'

He had also been upset by rumours in the newspapers. 'There was a paragraph in the *Sunday Dispatch* saying that on your return you would become engaged to a well-known peer. You were not mentioned by name but just as "a well known and much written-of debutante who is now on an extended holiday." I suppose the peer is my Lord Tennyson?'

But Max was wrong. The peer was Fulke Warwick, right on the spot and being very, very persuasive, while Max was thousands of miles away in Manchester. How important proximity can be.

In the end I gave in and accepted Fulke's proposal. With a heavy heart I wrote to Max to tell him that our engagement was broken.

The letter I got back from him was heart-rending:

'I guess it wasn't quite such a biff as it might have been for something has kept telling me for days that I was going to come a crack. . . . I do wish you just everything in the world Margaret. You deserve it because you are so wonderful. I feel like saying hundreds of things but I suppose I mustn't now. The old crazy tram driver has just gone screaming past. I reckon I'll start driving one soon and drive it all the way to Ascot flat out.

> Goodbye, darling.
> Max.

I may have *thought* I had made up my mind, but there followed two agonising months in which I vacillated between Fulke and Max.

Fulke had bought me a magnificent engagement ring, a large cabochon sapphire, and had written to tell his mother the news of our engagement. Lady Warwick, the sister of Anthony Eden, immediately came out to Egypt to meet me and talk to my parents. Like all the Edens, Marjorie Warwick was extremely handsome, but her manner was somewhat intimidating. Later, when I got to know her better, I liked her, and I believe she liked me. She was anything but encouraging, however, about the proposed marriage, telling my parents that she considered Fulke too young to marry and that she doubted whether he had the qualities to make a woman happy.

Her opinion disturbed my parents, who were themselves concerned over such practical problems as Fulke's having no definite job lined up for when he left the army. My father was particularly worried about money. The Warwick estate had been in financial difficulties for some years. On paper, Fulke's income was £18,000 a year. In reality, all he could expect to see in hard cash was £2,500, and my father did not consider we could marry on that sum and run Warwick Castle as well.

My diary for 1932 chronicles the almost daily changes of heart I went through over Fulke and Max. In February, for example, it reads:

15th February: Decide on Max. Get letter from him.
16th February: Get up and write to Fulke on verandah breaking engagement.
19th February: Get sweet letter from Fulke that upsets me terribly.
23rd February: Write to Max in evening finishing all.

To make things even worse, Fulke's brother officer and closest friend, Napoleon (Naps) Brinckman, chose this moment to fall in love with me as well. By a coincidence his father, Sir Theodore Brinckman, had been an ardent admirer of my mother's. Naps was tall, blonde, just as good looking as Fulke—and married. Fortunately I was not interested in him, although he was a wonderful person. Answer his letters sweetly, Fulke urged me, since his love was the most sincere tribute he could pay me. At the same time, Fulke himself bombarded me in Aswan with love letters from Cairo. One of them was written in an examination paper form:

Subject: Margaret.
Question: What do you know of her?
Answer:
  She has big grey eyes
  Mousy hair
  A big (but adorable) mouth
  A very funny kind of nose
  Pink fingers
  Nice feet
  A divine figure
  And I love her

In the end, against the advice of Lady Warwick and my parents, I settled on Fulke. Max's garnet ring came off for the last time and Fulke's sapphire replaced it.

Fulke cabled home to his Colonel, Viscount Gort, VC, asking permission for us to marry, and received a favourable reply. So on March 4th, Fulke's twenty-first birthday, my father, Fulke and I sailed from Cairo, leaving my mother behind in Aswan to continue her cure.

The engagement between Fulke and myself had been formally announced in *The Times* on March 3rd, and on March 9th we arrived back in London by boat train to face a battery of press and crowds of friends on the platform. Fulke, looking rather embarrassed, hovered in the background.

In the evening we dined at the Embassy, where Luigi had honoured our engagement by renaming all the dishes on the menu: Salmon Welcome Back, Caviare Suprême de Notre Happiness, Petit Pois Prosperity. It was flattering and absurdly delightful! On the following day we chose another engagement ring, a large square-cut solitaire diamond, and Fulke went off to Warwick Castle to accept the good wishes of his tenants.

That night I went alone to a large party that Max Aitken was giving at the Embassy. Seeing Max again, I was filled with terrible doubts. I seemed to be suffering an emotional schizophrenia and was unable to decide what and who I really wanted.

Also at Max's party I met again an American whom I had known well since the year before my coming out. Charles Sweeny and his younger brother, Bobby Sweeny, were then dazzling London with their Irish-American 'Kennedy' good looks and charm. They were both brilliant golfers, and Charlie had captained the Oxford team. As I danced with Charlie on that evening at the Embassy I realised two things. One, he was probably the best dancer in London; two, I was undoubtedly attracted to him, and he to me.

This made things even worse, but surely there could be no turning back now? My marriage to Fulke was to take place at Westminster Abbey in June. Victor Stiebel had started making my wedding dress, and I had chosen my eight bridesmaids, who were also to be dressed by Victor.

Meanwhile, from Warwick Castle, Fulke wrote in great excitement:

What a day darling—the whole of Warwickshire has gone mad! I was met by a mass of people at the station. The car could hardly get through the crowd at the gates. Thirty-two telegrams and I shudder to think how many letters. I've had a shorthand writer in attendance all day. Except for a short visit to the office I spent the morning dictating letters and giving interviews. In the afternoon a deputation from the tenants to offer their congratulations. At 3:30 p.m. the Mayor and Corporation, who stayed till five o'clock, and petitioned me on behalf of the town to persuade you to be married at Warwick. I said you would be coming to stay for the weekend next Friday. I'm afraid it means a certain amount of Public Appearances, but I'm sure *you* won't mind that.

On the following Friday, March 18th, I arrived in Warwick accompanied by the faithful Nanny Randall. I received a wonderful welcome. Cheering crowds lined the streets as I drove through the town and up the hill to my future home—the castle of Warwick the King Maker.

I was told that I would be the youngest countess in England, and after Fulke had introduced me to the Mayor and his tenants, he made a short speech:

'I very much look forward to the day, and I hope it will be as soon as possible, when my wife and I shall be able to come and live at Warwick and take as active a part as possible in everything associated with the town.'

Directly afterwards, however, I was dumbfounded and rather crushed when Fulke said casually, 'I am going to get the head guide to show you round. He knows the place so much better than I do.'

Later I was taken over the castle by Fulke's mother, a highly intelligent woman who knew every detail of Warwick and its history.

Otherwise Nanny Randall and I were left rather to our own devices. 'Well Nan,' I said to her despondently on our last night, 'I don't think I can see myself sitting around here.'

And I couldn't.

When I got back to Queen's Hill, my parents saw at once what I was feeling. One evening my father came into my bedroom and sat at the end of my bed.

'You're not really in love with Fulke, are you?' he asked me with his usual directness.

'No,' I admitted, 'I'm not.'

'Well,' he said, 'I am going to stay here in this room until you promise me that you will return Fulke's ring and break off your engagement tomorrow.'

We argued far into the night. 'But Daddy, everything is arranged. Think of the fuss and publicity there will be if I break it off now.'

'What does that matter,' replied my father, 'compared to your whole life and happiness?'

So, after three weeks of unhappy doubts, a sixteen-word announcement appeared in *The Times*:

The marriage arranged between the Earl of Warwick and Miss Margaret Whigham will not take place.

END OF WHIRLWIND COURTSHIP, said the headlines. MISS WHIGHAM DOES NOT CARE ENOUGH. 'She decided she did not love Lord Warwick sufficiently to want to marry him,' my mother was quoted as saying. 'They are both so young and it is one of the misfortunes of youth that it is liable to make mistakes.'

One paper, *The Daily Herald*, even applauded my decision:

We admire her courage. The younger generation are not *ashamed* to break their engagements. They face facts and admit their mistakes. Too many of our fathers and mothers were married because they feared public opinion and the wrath of their families. Unhappiness is too high a price to pay for 'respectability'.

Whether Fulke agreed with this is debatable. When, in floods of tears, I had broken the news to him, he took it quietly, but with obvious surprise, as if he couldn't understand how any girl could be so foolish.

We remained friendly and even continued to go out together. He seemed to resent any one else dancing with me, and one night at the Embassy we danced together so many times that the next day's papers were full of rumours of a re-engagement. My mother had to issue an official denial.

There was no doubt that Fulke wanted me back. But the only thing I was completely sure about was that I could never marry him. Now I just hoped that I would remain fancy free for a while.

Meanwhile, Charles Sweeny had come down from Oxford and was working in the City for his father's company, the Charterhouse Investment Trust.

I have always found American men attractive, and Charlie was the epitome of male glamour. His income was less than Fulke's, but we would not have to run a castle on it. And his job was a good one, which counted a good deal with my father.

Charlie told me that he had been in love with me for a long time, and he was very insistent that we should marry. I also knew that I was in love with him and soon I found myself engaged, and for the last time.

The Times, November 17th, 1932:

The engagement is announced between Charles, elder son of Mr and Mrs Robert Sweeny of Grosvenor House, Park Lane, and Margaret, daughter of Mr and Mrs George Hay Whigham, of Queen's Hill, Ascot.

When Fulke and I were engaged he used to send me a spray of purple orchids every evening. These continued to arrive for the next six months, but he at last accepted the fact that I would never be the Countess of Warwick and mistress of Warwick Castle. That honour fell to the beautiful Rose Bingham, who married Fulke the following year. Their marriage lasted only five years, but they had a charming son, David (Lord Brooke), who today is one of my friends.

Fulke was not the man to harbour resentment, and eighteen years later, after my marriage to the Duke of Argyll, he and his son were the first visitors we entertained at Inveraray Castle while we were in the process of making it habitable.

Chapter 9

The Sweenys were a Roman Catholic family, and this meant that I had to promise I would bring up any children of my marriage to Charlie in the Roman Catholic faith.

After long thought, and without any pressure from Charlie, I decided that I wanted to become a Catholic myself. I considered then, and I still do, that it is the only Christian Church with any strength.

Charlie was delighted, which is more than can be said for Mr and Mrs George H. Whigham! My parents realised, however, that this must be my decision alone, and my father said resignedly, 'Anyway, thank goodness you'll still be a Christian.'

For the next two months I went several times a week to Farm Street to receive instruction from Father Francis Woodlock, an Irish Jesuit. He soon discovered that I was taking the matter seriously and was by no means docile. Poor Father Woodlock had a tough time with me. Catholicism is a dogmatic religion, and since I disliked being told what to believe, I argued and questioned every inch of the way. In the end, I agreed to become a Catholic with two qualifying conditions. I would not accept the infallibility of the Pope, neither would I pray to any saint.

'When I pray,' I told the bemused Father Woodlock, 'it's going to be to the Head Man, and to nobody else.'

I was received into the Catholic faith at Farm Street church on

February 11th, the Feast of Our Lady of Lourdes. The occasion was not without comedy, for my parents, ignorant of Catholic procedure, chose to sit right up against the confessional in which I was then making an extremely brief first confession. Charlie finally went up to them and, after some urgent whispering, suggested that they move away. But my being received into the Church was a more emotional experience than I had expected, and when we returned home I fainted for the first and only time in my life.

I received my First Communion on February 12th, and was confirmed as a Catholic at the Sacred Heart Church, Westminster, on the day before my marriage.

Later that same day, at the final fitting for my wedding dress in Norman Hartnell's showroom in Bruton Street, the press were allowed in to see my trousseau. The wedding dress—ivory white satin, with orange blossom cut out of lace outlined and embroidered with seed pearls and tiny silver glass bugles—had been worked on for six weeks by two hundred seamstresses. The angel sleeves were of white tulle. The train, which had been specially designed for the exceptionally impressive aisle of Brompton Oratory, was twenty-eight feet long and nine feet wide. It also had a wide border of tulle.

The total cost of this beautiful dress was £52. Incredible as it seems, I was outraged by this, and said that I hoped the headdress would be included in that price! Today the cost of such a dress would be at least £3,000!

The design of my wedding dress must have lingered in Norman Hartnell's mind, for fourteen years later I was most flattered to see it repeated in the dress he made for the wedding of Princess Elizabeth, now our Queen, to Prince Philip.

Photographers followed me everywhere on the day before my marriage. I was photographed going in for my dress fitting, coming out, at the wedding rehearsal, and with my bridesmaids.

'The Whigham', as I had become known to columnists, was about to disappear from print for ever. In twenty-four hours I would be Mrs Charles Sweeny.

My parents had rented 55, Prince's Gate for the wedding, because of its proximity to the Brompton Oratory, and on the eve of the great day three large rooms were filled with over three thousand wedding presents.

There were gold cuff links for Charlie from his golfing friend, the Prince of Wales, sent 'with best wishes from Edward P'.

Fulke Warwick gave me a cocktail cabinet in green shagreen, and Cecil Beaton painted a charming portrait of me—it still hangs on my bedroom wall—in which he gave a special emphasis to the sparkle of my engagement ring, of which I was enormously proud.

Among the other presents were a silver teapot from the Earl and Countess of Dumfries; a glass cigarette box from the Countess of Dudley, formerly stage star Gertie Millar; brandy goblets from Gordon Selfridge; a silver table lighter from Lord Inverclyde, and a red and gold brocade cushion from the Ranee of Sarawak, embroidered 'For the loveliest head in London to lean against.'

My parents gave me a mink coat, two silver foxes, a six-skin sable stole, and an ermine coat.

Charlie's gift to me was a diamond solitaire ring, and his parents gave me a parure of aquamarines.

Before I went to bed for the last time as Margaret Whigham, my father took me on one side and made a little speech that brought a lump to my throat.

'Margaret, you are leaving us now to be married and start a new life,' he said. 'Just remember one thing: if you are ever in trouble or need any help I will always be there.'

He always was. And when trouble really came I found he was the one person in the world on whom I could truly depend.

My wedding day—Tuesday, February 21st, 1933—was an extraordinary day. To appreciate the sort of excitement it generated, one has to look back at the front page headlines.

2,000 'GATE-CRASH' A WEDDING. Crowds scramble over pews to see Miss Margaret Whigham Married (*Daily Mirror*).

CROWD'S RUSH STOPS WEDDING PROCESSION. WOMEN FIGHT THEIR WAY INTO CHURCH (*Daily Sketch*).

CROWDS AT WEDDING OF FAMOUS BEAUTY (*Daily Express*).

People started to queue outside Brompton Oratory at eight

o'clock in the morning. By 10.30, when the wedding guests began to arrive, the church was surrounded by thousands of people. Even the members of the Old Vic Company had taken a day off from the theatre to watch the spectacle. The pavements were jammed with onlookers. Traffic in Brompton Road and up as far as Hyde Park was brought to a standstill, and because of the crowds our car crawled along at a snail's pace. However, we arrived at the church two minutes before the appointed time— 11.15. As we got out of the car I became aware of a tremendous noise and a crush of people pushing towards me.

'Margaret, Margaret.' The women in the crowd were shouting my name. Some of them were cheering. The *Sunday Graphic* later commented:

> I discovered in the crowds that fought to see her married scores of young women who had obviously modelled their appearance on hers. They had long earrings, full, rich, cupid-bow lips, and tiny hats aslant, as 'the Whigham' wears them. I watched them scan her avidly to get 'confirmation', for few had actually seen her except in photographs. I think this imitation is certainly the highest form of flattery, and usually reserved for film stars. When the bride returns I must ask her if she has a fan mail!

While the cameras clicked and whirred, and dozens of police-men linked arms to hold back the crowd, my nine bridesmaids lifted my train. My mother had advised me against having either children or contemporaries as attendants. Children, she said, usually trod on the train, were sick, or else loudly demanded to go somewhere during the most solemn moments; pretty girl friends had been known to outshine the bride!

Over this, however, I made up my own mind, and chose nine of my loveliest friends as bridesmaids. They were Bridget Poulett—of course—Jeanne Stourton, Molly Vaughan, Baba Beaton, Dawn Gold, Sheila Berry, Pamela Nicholl, Angela Brett and Margaret Livingstone-Learmonth. Their dresses matched mine in design, but were made of silver lamé and tulle. They carried large bouquets of crimson roses, and they made a beautiful group.

If the scene outside the Oratory was extraordinary, conditions inside were even more so. Two thousand guests had been invited. A thousand more had somehow managed to gatecrash their way in. It is not surprising that the poor ushers—who included Lord Birkenhead, Max Aitken, Randolph Churchill and Michael Berry, now Lord Hartwell—were looking harassed and somewhat battered.

There was not an inch of space in the church, and I was told afterwards that people were standing on pews and clinging to the tops of the pillars which they had climbed.

As I moved slowly forward on my father's arm, the great organ of Brompton Oratory thundered out the Wedding March. Music always affects me and I hoped the congregation did not see my tears as I was going up the aisle.

I was steadied by the sight of Charlie, standing calm and smiling at the altar steps, with his brother, Bobby, who was Best Man, beside him.

Fortunately the organ drowned the worst of the commotion, for once I had moved up the aisle the main doors of the Oratory were literally stormed by hundreds more women who used their fists, elbows and even their umbrellas to force their way in. Finding no seats left, they stood at the back in a solid army, completely cutting off all means of entry for guests who arrived late. Poor Lady Mount Temple, I believe, never reached her seat at all.

The Nuptial Mass itself is still a vivid memory to me—our two journeys up to the altar and back to the priedieu, and the singing of the choir, which was glorious. (I invited all the choristers to the reception afterwards.)

As we came down the altar steps after signing the register, there was a sudden blaze of sunlight through the windows of the Oratory. Falling on Charlie and myself, it spread a radiant circle around us. People afterwards told me it had been a moment of magic.

Outside the Oratory excitement had risen to fever pitch, and as we came into view the cheers were deafening. Both of us were startled, but it was obvious that the people all round us were extremely happy. It was the darkest moment of the Depression, with millions of unemployed, but I think they felt our wedding had brought a flash of colour into a grey world. I hope it did.

As we got into the car to drive away, a short, fair young man with glasses pressed a single red rose into my hand. He murmured something I couldn't hear, and then vanished into the sea of faces. I was later told that my unknown cavalier was a twenty-four-year-old, unemployed clerk, living with his parents in Battersea. For three years, apparently, ever since my coming out, he had followed me around, standing on pavements in all weathers to catch a glimpse of me at various functions. Afterwards I tried to find him to thank him for his rose, but I never could. If he reads this book I would like to thank him now and to tell him I have not forgotten.

We spent the first two days of our honeymoon in Paris, after which we boarded the French Liner 'Colombie' for a six weeks' cruise of the West Indies. Going through the Bay of Biscay the sea was very rough and I felt very seasick. I spent that first day wearing a green dress, looking even greener, trying to pretend to Charlie, for the sake of romance, that I was suffering from a bad headache.

But being alone with Charlie was a wonderful relief from the frantic activity of the wedding, and I began gradually to learn what marriage was all about. As we got to know one another better, I discovered that Charlie had an almost pathological streak of jealousy in his make-up. Although he knew everything about my life, he began to make ridiculous scenes over the mention of any young man I had ever been out with. I was very young to face these early marital rows, and they puzzled me.

But altogether it was the happiest of honeymoons, and when I came back to London I was expecting a child.

We docked at Plymouth on April 4th, and were faced with a surprising complication. I was held up by the Immigration Authorities as an alien. Apparently upon marrying an American I had lost my British nationality without being allowed to acquire that of my husband. I was informed that I had become a 'stateless person', and could only enter my own country on production of some dreary document known as an affidavit. This, needless to say, infuriated me—the law, as it happens, was soon afterwards changed by the efforts of the redoubtable Viscountess (Nancy) Astor.

Back in London we had taken a furnished house at 39, Hans Place, Belgravia, for which my parents and in-laws, knowing that I'd had no time before the wedding, had thoughtfully provided silver, linen and china.

Charlie and I had £2,000 a year between us, and on that we managed with ease to run a household comprising a house-parlourmaid, a cook and, of course, dear Nanny. Those were the Good Old Days!

I was thrilled about my pregnancy and I felt well and happy, until one day, about seven weeks after our return to London. It was May 26th, and at 11.45 that morning I took my two poodles, Suzette and her daughter Gaby, into Hyde Park. Suddenly the dogs and I were startled by nearby gunfire. It was the Royal salute in honour of Queen Mary's 66th birthday. The dogs bolted in fright, and I raced after them. After searching in vain for an hour I returned to the house desperately worried about the dogs. Fortunately they had their addresses on their collars, and Suzette was brought back in the afternoon, while Gaby was eventually found in Eaton Place. Both were unharmed. By that time, however, I was in bed feeling far from well.

Four nights later, on May 30th, Charlie took me to the Capitol Cinema to see a film called *A Kiss Before the Mirror*. It must have been an opening night because I remember I was wearing a white satin evening dress and white satin shoes. During the performance I was again not feeling at all well, but I hoped for the best. Then, when we rose for the National Anthem, I realised I had started a miscarriage. Charlie acted with remarkable swiftness and calm; draping his overcoat around me, he somehow managed to get me out of the cinema without any fuss. Sad to say, my beloved Suzette and Gaby had caused me to lose my first child.

Miscarriages are frightening, unhappy experiences, and un-fortunately I have had many during my life. However, by the end of the summer the newspapers were able to announce that 'Mrs Charles Sweeny is once again expecting a happy event.' No one could guess that my next pregnancy was to end in near tragedy, or that it would bring about what I can only think of as a miracle.

Chapter 10

'You're the nimble tread of the feet of Fred Astaire,
You're Mussolini,
You're Mrs Sweeny,
You're Camembert'.

That was a verse from Cole Porter's song 'You're the Top', the big hit of his new musical *Anything Goes*. I did not care for being sandwiched between Mussolini and Camembert, but it was flattering to be included with the Louvre Museum, a Shakespeare sonnet, Mickey Mouse, the smile on the Mona Lisa, Garbo's salary, a dress by Patou, and the other things Cole Porter considered 'the top'.

Yet, ironically, the year in which those words were first heard—1934—could have been my last.

At this time our marriage certainly was 'the top'. One paper wrote, 'Margaret is happily, really happily, married and no one can make her leave her home fireside. She is the beautiful proof that the Bright Young Thing of 1931 can blossom into the perfect wife of 1933.' It was true, and Charlie and I were always known as the model of an ideal married couple for many years.

Oddly enough, although I was a Whigham I decided early in life that golf was not for me. Fortunately Charlie never wanted me to be a golfer. He believed that wives should be spectators only, and it was in that capacity that I went up to Hoylake in June to watch him and his brother, Bobby, compete in the British Amateur Golf Championship. A month later we were in Le Touquet for the first of many golfing weekends, and in mid-September I proudly watched Charlie set up a new amateur record for the Canterbury Golf Course with a round of 67. I was the epitome of the 'golfing wife', and happy to be so.

On December 1st I spent a quiet birthday—my first as a married woman. An astrologer noted that, having been born on this date, with Venus in the ascendant, I was destined to live my whole life in a blaze of unwanted publicity. How right he was!

Life in London went on. On January 24th I was at St Columba's, Pont Street, to see Peter Aitken, Max's youngest brother, marry Janey MacNeill. And early in February Charlie and I joined one of C. B. Cochran's supper parties at the Dorchester. Our fellow guests seemed to represent the 'in people' of those days: the glamorous Gertrude Lawrence, Douglas Fairbanks Jnr., the Earl and Countess of Jersey, Randolph Churchill, and Lord and Lady Plunket, an enchanting couple who were to die tragically four years later in America when the aeroplane in which they were travelling caught fire.

It was soon after Cochran's party that I caught a chill—or so I thought—and spent the day in bed. Late in the evening I began to feel as if I was suffocating.

'I can't breathe,' I told Charlie, and he spent most of the night sitting up with me. The doctor came early the following morning.

'You've just got indigestion,' he told me.

'It can't be indigestion,' I said, 'because I've eaten nothing for twenty-four hours. I feel as if there is a huge stone on my chest.'

During the weekend I got steadily worse. On the Monday Nanny Randall saw that I was turning blue, and a specialist was called to the house. He took one look at me.

'She has double pneumonia,' he announced, 'and we must get her into hospital at once.'

I was rushed by ambulance to a nursing home in Welbeck Street. On arrival it was found that my temperature was 104° and that, in addition to double pneumonia, I was suffering from a serious kidney infection.

For the next five days I was desperately ill and unconscious. 'Critical' was the word the newspapers used. Unknown to me there were daily headlines, and an *Evening Standard* placard announced in purple letters MARGARET WHIGHAM GRAVELY ILL.

In extremis, it seems that I reverted, in the minds of the press, to the name by which London had first known me.

On the Tuesday I was worse. All I can recall from my few moments of consciousness is a small oxygen mask being pressed over my face. In those days there were no oxygen tents, nor was there penicillin.

I was eight months pregnant and the doctors decided, in order to try and save my life, to induce the birth. They did so, only to discover that the baby was still-born, due to the pneumonia.

The child, a girl, was buried according to the rites of the Catholic Church, and Charlie attended the funeral while my parents kept vigil at my bedside.

In delirium I kept asking for the baby, and the nurses considered using another woman's child to pacify me. None of them dared tell me the truth.

On the Wednesday morning they gave me a blood transfusion, donor unknown. Man or woman, Jew or Gentile, prince or pauper, I shall never know.

Not that it seemed to matter, for my temperature now fell below normal and went on falling. Bulletins announced my condition as 'very grave', and every newspaper in Fleet Street was preparing my obituary.

One of my doctors, the King's physician, Lord Dawson of Penn, told Charles, my parents and my in-laws, 'I regret to say that there is nothing more we can do. If only her temperature would rise there might be a chance. But it isn't going to happen, and she has only a few hours to live.'

Charlie's reaction was immediate. 'I don't believe this,' he said, 'and I just won't accept it.' He went straight round to Farm Street church and fetched Father Martindale, the well-known Jesuit priest.

Father Martindale, apparently, gave me Extreme Unction, and sprinkled Holy Water over me and upon my bed. I was told later that this Holy Water had been sent from the Grotto at Lourdes by a person unknown to me.

All I can remember of that crucial Wednesday afternoon is the shadowy figure of a man standing at the foot of my bed murmuring prayers.

Three hours later, by which time, according to the doctors, I should have been dying, my temperature at last began to rise. Upon hearing this, Lord Dawson said, 'There is no medical explanation. I can only describe it as a miracle.'

By the following morning I had rallied sufficiently to pass the crisis, and on Friday I regained consciousness and was declared out of danger.

To this day I am convinced that it was indeed a miracle, and I shall always be grateful to God and the Catholic Church for my life.

Charlie had been at the nursing home day and night during the crisis, and there is no doubt that he was distraught with anxiety. Once the crisis was over, however, he wanted to celebrate. On the Friday I was not only very weak, but deeply depressed and in tears, having been told at last about the death of the baby. That night Charlie went out with a man friend to dine at the Embassy, which made my mother and Nanny Randall very angry indeed. He was not intentionally unkind, but being young he did not understand the black depression that follows a serious illness.

Every night as I was having dinner in my room at the nursing home he would visit me in evening dress. He would sit and talk for about half an hour, but he would never stay longer—not even on February 21st, which was our first wedding anniversary. All too soon he would look at his watch, kiss me and say, 'Well, darling, it's nice to see you looking better. I'll be in tomorrow.' And off he would go to the Embassy or to some party, leaving me feeling more depressed than ever.

After a month in the nursing home the doctors ordered me to go somewhere abroad for the sun, but I did not want to leave Charlie and I knew that he could not take time off from his work in the City. So, instead, I chose to go to Hove, hoping that he would stay there with me and commute to his office. On March 21st I left the nursing home in an ambulance, accompanied by a trained nurse and Nanny Randall.

Sadly, my hopes that Charlie would commute daily vanished; he only came down for weekends.

Hove in the winter was deadly, and from Monday to Friday our chief interest was to watch Princess Beatrice, Queen Victoria's youngest child, being wheeled along the sea front in a bath chair. She was then almost seventy-seven, and was recovering from an attack of bronchitis.

The long and dreary weekdays were not improved by my seeing photographs in *The Tatler* and elsewhere of Charlie and some bachelor friend, such as Sir Robert Throckmorton, dining together in various restaurants. I would wonder who they danced with *after* dinner. Charlie was very attractive, and the danger of having a good-looking young husband loose on the town minus a wife was only too obvious. After six weeks of uneasy convalescence I was thankful to leave Hove and return to London in time for the season.

On June 12th, in a dress of pale coral pink satin and with a train of darker coral velvet, I was presented to King George V and Queen Mary at the third Court of the season, this time as a married woman.

A letter from the Lord Chamberlain informed me that under Rule 8 of Court Regulations, 'Ladies of foreign nationality, either by birth or by marriage, can only be presented through the diplomatic representative of the country concerned, except in the case of ladies married to British subjects.' So, as I was now married to an American, I was presented to Their Majesties by Mrs Robert Bingham, the wife of the United States Ambassador.

By October I was back on the golf links to watch Charlie's success at Sandwich, where he set up a new record for that course by playing nine holes in 31, and won the Prince of Wales Cup into the bargain.

At the end of November we were invited to the wedding at Westminster Abbey of Prince George, the Duke of Kent, and Princess Marina of Greece. We gave them a silver cruet stand as a wedding present, and Prince George wrote, in his letter of thanks: 'I am very happy and very lucky to have found someone as sweet and lovely as Marina.' I understood what he meant on the night before the wedding, when Charlie and I attended the ball given by the King and Queen at Buckingham Palace in honour of the bride. I shall never forget the sight of the three Greek princesses—Princess Marina and her sisters, Princess Olga and Princess Elizabeth, Countess of Torrin-Jettenbach—entering the ballroom like goddesses, tall, statuesque and breathtakingly beautiful. Princess Marina's natural elegance outshone that of every other woman in the room, with the exception of Queen Mary.

In the autumn of 1934 Charlie and I took the Embassy for the night and gave a dinner dance for a hundred and fifty friends. The guest of honour was the Prince of Wales. I asked C. B. Cochran, who was a friend of mine, if he could suggest a new and exciting cabaret entertainer. He suggested a then unknown young man called Larry Adler, who played the harmonica. It was his first appearance in England, and he was a triumphant success, but he has often told me how nervous and overawed he was that evening.

About this time my father gave Charlie and me a home of our own—6, Sussex Place, Regents Park. It was a pretty Nash house with a large garden, perfect for children and dogs. My parents had decided, now that I was married, that they preferred to live in London, and they therefore sold Queen's Hill. In 1935 my father bought 48, Upper Grosvenor Street, an early 18th-century house overlooking Grosvenor Square. This is my home today.

My mother engaged Somerset Maugham's former wife, Syrie, then the most fashionable interior decorator in London, to help her with the new house. Syrie was the daughter of the philanthropist Dr Thomas Barnardo, and she was married first to Henry (later Sir Henry) Wellcome, of the firm of Burroughs, Wellcome, the chemists. She had met Somerset Maugham in 1913, when he was thirty-nine, and they were married three years later, after her divorce from Wellcome. The marriage was a failure, for Willie Maugham had already met Gerald Haxton—a handsome young American with whom he was to spend the next twenty-five years—even before he married Syrie. Syrie divorced Somerset Maugham in 1927, and she then concentrated on interior decorating. I had known her ever since our arrival in London, for her daughter, Liza Maugham—now Lady Glendevon—was a great friend of mine.

This was Syrie's 'white period'—white walls, white sheepskin rugs, white leather chairs, white or ivory satin cutains, and white camellias arranged in great sprays against immense mirrored screens. She would cheerfully 'pickle' or paint any piece of furniture, however valuable it might be. This rather appealed to my mother, who wanted a pretty and feminine house and cared little about period furniture being desecrated. My father, on the other hand, was aghast when he saw Chippendale, Hepplewhite and Queen Anne furniture being pickled or stripped and painted white. He was also aghast at the size of her bills. Syrie was a tough business woman and, knowing that he was rich, she milked my father mercilessly. But the results were worth it. Today, forty years later, I still take pride in the house, including the unique all-mirrored bathroom that Syrie designed specially for my mother.

One of Syrie's most interesting contributions to the house was a magnificent mirrored screen, which had stood in the drawing-room of her own villa at Le Touquet in the mid-twenties, when she was still trying to combat the attractions of Gerald Haxton and save her marriage to Willie.

In *A Case of Human Bondage*, his book about the Maugham marriage, Beverley Nichols writes:

Somewhere, perhaps in the cellar of a Parisian *antiquaire*, Syrie's mirrored screen is gathering the dust. 'A period piece, monsieur, and—as you will observe—of exquisite craftsman-ship. Shall we say ten thousand francs?' Or did she sell it to a cocktail bar in Detroit?... Or did she forget about it? Was it shipped back to London, with the sheepskin rugs and the white leather chairs and the pots of enamelled camellias, when the war clouds were gathering, when Willie and Gerald were finally deserting her, and when Fate was writing 'Finis' to the whole affair? One would like to know.

Inanimate objects into which emotion has been poured, one sometimes fancies, absorb the radiation of their owners' personalities.

I can answer Beverley's question, for the mirrored screen still stands today in the hall of my house, where Syrie herself put it. It must indeed have a tale to tell, for it has witnessed scenes of gaiety and sadness in my own life, as well as in Syrie's.

While she was decorating my mother's house I asked Syrie if she would do ours. Like most husbands, Charlie grumbled at the prospect of what he thought would be enormous bills, but Syrie had a very kind heart as well as a shrewd business head, and she knew that we did not have much money. 'I'll make your house as pretty as your mother's,' she promised, 'but much, much cheaper'. And this she did. My toughest battle with her was to keep a pair of Regency negro figures *out* of my drawing-room.

But however hard she worked, and for how many hours a day, she was always immaculately dressed, beautifully made up and with never a hair out of place. She was also a very amusing, vital person. For me the taste of Syrie Maugham has always been the ultimate in elegance. When she died in July 1955, one of the last remaining lights of the old London, and of those years of grace before the war, seemed to be extinguished.

Chapter 11

On the afternoon of January 20th, 1936, I stood in drizzling rain and a bitterly cold wind outside the railings of Buckingham Palace. There were people all around me, people of every age and kind. Beside me stood a young page boy with a raincoat over his hotel uniform. Next to him was an immaculate City gentleman with a rolled umbrella and a bowler hat which he held in his hand, so that blobs of rain glistened on his sleek brilliantined hair. Nearby an elderly woman shivered and pulled a shabby winter coat closer around her.

Old and young, rich and poor, we all stood there in absolute silence, united by a common sorrow. Our King was dying.

George V, that kind, dignified and courteous monarch, who had reigned in England since before I was born, was gravely ill and we were there to wait for the latest bulletin from Sandringham.

When it finally came, the words tore at our hearts. 'The King's life is moving peacefully to its close.'

As people pressed forward and saw the wording posted on the Palace gates, a deep but gentle sigh went through the crowd. To all of us there—those who knew him as a man, and those who knew him only through the wisdom and humanity of his Christmas broadcasts—King George was a beloved friend.

The silence of that waiting crowd outside the Palace was

broken only by a man's voice quietly reciting some familiar lines:

> The tumult and the shouting dies;
> The captains and the kings depart;
> Still stands thine ancient sacrifice,
> An humble and a contrite heart.
> Lord God of Hosts, be with us yet,
> Lest we forget—lest we forget!

The words were those of another great Englishman, Rudyard Kipling, who had died two days before.

Feeling very downcast, I went home to Sussex Place, and Charlie and I spent the rest of the evening listening to the radio bulletins. At five minutes to midnight King George died. For the whole of the following morning I was in tears. The BBC cancelled all its programmes and dance music stopped in the restaurants of the West End. A pall of sadness descended upon everything and it felt as if a whole era of certainty and convention had come to an end.

I had known the new King as Prince of Wales for six years, and, like many others, I was aware of the problems of his private life.

When I had first met him his constant companion was Mrs Dudley-Ward, a woman of wit, elegance and enormous charm. She also had dignity and discretion. For a time he had a brief, though not very serious, love affair with Lady Furness. By the time of his accession to the throne, however, both Freda Dudley-Ward and Thelma Furness had been succeeded in his affections by a woman whom very few people knew anything about until 1934.

I first met Wallis Simpson at a luncheon party given by my mother-in-law, Mrs Robert Sweeny—she and Wallis were close friends. She was not outstanding in any way, nor well dressed. Her hair was parted down the middle, arranged in 'earphones', and her voice was harsh. My impression was of quite a plain woman with a noticeably square jaw, and not particularly amusing. But she was a pleasant person, and we were to remain friends. But I cannot help marvelling how she changed after meeting the Duke. She became a witty, brilliant hostess, one of the best dressed women in the world, and a *femme fatale*. Neither I nor most of the people I knew could believe that our King Emperor, who had been so idolised as Prince of Wales, would let his subjects down by abdicating for any selfish reason. The fact that he was in love with a woman at that moment was relatively unimportant. Nobody was asking him to stop seeing her. Bachelor kings had been known to have mistresses, and Wallis Simpson would have been a far more important woman as the power behind the throne than she was as the wife of a king with no throne and no job to do.

For me, the Duke of Windsor changed, within a few weeks, from a Prince Charming of the world into a pathetic and desperately unhappy man.

Charlie and I spent the weekend immediately preceding the abdication at Leeds Castle, Maidstone, as the guests of the Honourable Lady Baillie, a powerful political hostess whose 'Leeds Set', to which we belonged, rivalled Nancy Astor's 'Cliveden Set'.

Two of the group at Leeds that dramatic weekend were able to give us the latest news of the constitutional crisis. They were Olive Baillie's two close friends, David Margesson, the Government Chief Whip, later the 1st Viscount Margesson, and Geoffrey Lloyd—now Lord Geoffrey-Lloyd—who had been Stanley Baldwin's parliamentary private secretary, and was then Under Secretary of State for Home Affairs.

Leeds Castle, one of the oldest inhabited fortresses in Britain, stood in a 350-acre park and was surrounded by a ten-acre moat. Charlie and I were first invited there through our friendship with the Marquis and Marchioness of Queensberry, who were regular visitors. Olive Baillie was the eldest daughter of the first and only Lord Queenborough. Her fortune came from her mother, who was a daughter of the Hon William C. Whitney, Secretary of State for the US Navy. By the time I met her she was already married to her third husband, Sir Adrian Baillie, MP. Though good-looking and charming, he was somewhat overshadowed by his undoubtedly domineering wife.

Before I went to Leeds Castle for the first time I was warned by Cathleen Queensberry that Olive was an eccentric woman, and so shy that she could take two or three days before meeting a new guest in her house. 'You might not set eyes on her the whole weekend,' Cathleen warned me. This did not happen, for on the day of our arrival I was bidden to have tea with Olive in her boudoir. She was a good-looking but forbidding woman in her mid-thirties, with a certain charm and the indefinable air of authority that rich women so often possess.

I am sure that many momentous decisions were made at Leeds, when Olive was closeted in her room having mysterious meetings with Very Important People. But although an undoubted power in the political world she was scarcely known to the public at large. She had written to all the newspaper owners informing them that she disliked publicity and wished never to be mentioned in the press. And she rarely was.

The weekend house parties at Leeds were luxurious and amusing, and seldom were there less than thirty guests. There were croquet lawns, tennis courts, a nine-hole golf course, and gambling at night. With both golf and gambling available, Charlie was in his element.

Olive also had a house in London, a beautiful home in Nassau, and every summer she rented a villa in the South of France, taking her entourage with her.

After the abdication, Charlie and I spent Christmas and the New Year at Leeds. By now I was pregnant again, and this time I was so cosseted that when my grandmother Margaret Hannay—after whom I had been named—died on December 23rd, 1936, I was not allowed to travel even from Maidstone to London for the funeral.

Life with Charlie was proving to be pleasant but narrow. He had two interests only—business and golf. We never explored either places or people. Our friends were exact contemporaries of ours, and we had all been married at about the same time. These young marrieds were attractive and successful, but never once did Charlie and I venture outside our right little, tight little group. If I ever suggested inviting a writer, an actor, a politician or a diplomat to dinner Charlie would say, 'What on earth do you want them for? They won't fit in.' Nor did he want me to have any interest in current affairs. If I commented on anything more ambitious than the newspaper headlines, his reaction would be, 'What's all this? You're getting to be quite a little intellectual, aren't you.'

In fact, all Charlie wanted for a wife was a pretty, brainless doll.

When I was ill, which happened all too often in those years, Charlie would go out to various dinner parties with my blessing. But if he was ill, or away, he forbade me to dine even with close friends of ours. I was up against the same old unreasoning and unreasonable jealousy.

However, he was the boss in our marriage and I complied, although with growing resentment. I began to feel like a bird in a not-so-gilded cage.

On January 19th, 1937, I was at home taking the chair at a meeting for a charity film premiere in aid of the London Society for Teaching and Training the Blind. In the middle of the meeting, Charlie's secretary, Miss Denham, telephoned to say that Charlie had left the office in obvious pain and gone straight to his doctor.

Leaving the Duchess (Loelia) of Westminster to take the chair at the meeting, I left the house and hurried round to the doctor to find that Charlie was desperately ill with a perforated ulcer. Throughout our married life he had suffered with an incipient duodenal ulcer, even though he was very careful in his eating and drinking. We had spent two months in the autumn of 1935, with Charlie far from well, in various well-known Swiss and German clinics, in search of a cure.

Now, however, in agony, he was rushed straight into hospital and operated on that same day. Bobby Sweeny came to the hospital, and together we sat for hours outside the operating theatre waiting for news. At long last we were assured that Charlie had come safely through the operation, but we were told he must remain in hospital for a month.

Worried as I was about him, and very pregnant, I went on with the job of arranging the charity premiere. The film was *Beloved Enemy*, starring Merle Oberon, and at the premiere, at Leicester Square Theatre, Bobby accompanied me, deputising for Charlie. I felt the effort had been worthwhile as we managed to raise £1,800 for the blind.

When he came out of hospital, Charlie and I went to the Princes Hotel, Hove, where I had convalesced after my own illness. We returned to London in time for the Coronation and took a box in Oxford Street to see King George VI and Queen Elizabeth drive to Westminster Abbey in their golden coach.

In my last month of pregnancy, on the morning of June 17th, while coming out of Swerlings, the milliners in Bond Street, I missed my footing and fell headlong down the stairs. My maternity nurse, who was with me, was very worried and put me straight to bed. Charlie, however, was unperturbed and spent the afternoon at the Ascot races.

Perhaps my fall was just what was needed. At three o'clock on the morning of June 19th I had to wake Charlie and tell him that labour pains had begun. I was taken into the nursing home Beaumont House, and at 9.30 that morning I gave birth to a beautiful little girl.

Charlie, never having seen a newborn baby, was very worried by her small, crumpled face. He had to be reassured about her by all four grandparents.

On July 21st Father Woodlock christened her Frances Helen, at Brompton Oratory, where Charlie and I had been married four years earlier. The Countess of Dumfries, Lady Bridget Poulett and the Marquis of Queensberry were among her godparents. Her family christening robe was long and very elaborate, unlike those of today.

Charlie and I then took a holiday. We went to the Schloss Mittershill Sports and Shooting Club, near Salzburg, run by Prince Alex Hohenloe and Count Hans Czernin. We had been the previous year for the opening, and we were among the thirty original founder members. Also at Mittershill were Mr and Mrs Gilbert Miller, Mrs Randolph Hearst, and Lady Mendl— the legendary Elsie de Woolf—Syrie Maugham's great American rival as an interior decorator. Always an eccentric, Elsie had turned up at Liza Maugham's wedding with her hair dyed bright blue.

From Mittershill we went on to Venice, where we had a glorious time at the Lido, and found that Barbara Hutton, Oliver Messel and the sinister Dr Goebbels were also there.

The last stage of our holiday proved disastrous. I was longing to visit Hungary, and persuaded Charlie, much against his will, to go to Budapest. We drove through Yugoslavia in our Rolls, and the very rough roads all but ruined the car. Charlie got sunstroke and retired to bed in the Hotel Duna Palota, while I went off alone by taxi to Lake Balaton, determined to see something of the country. We then left for London, with Charlie vowing never again to go to any of those 'God-damned places'.

Frances spent the first Christmas of her life in a setting of real grandeur, for we were all invited by the Earl and Countess Fitzwilliam to Wentworth-Woodhouse, their home in the West Riding of Yorkshire. The invitation came through the Fitz-williams' son and daughter-in-law, Viscount and Viscountess Milton. Peter Milton had been a beau of mine in my debutante days, since when he had married Olive Plunket, who also became a great friend.

Wentworth, the largest house in England, was surrounded by lawns black with coal dust from the adjacent mines. It had two hundred and forty rooms, one thousand windows and a frontage of two hundred yards.

Inside the house, the corridors were so long that when the footman showed us to our rooms he actually unwound a ball of string to enable us to find our way back to the reception rooms. When Charlie and I went down to the drawing-room before dinner, we found all the men in hunting pink coats or white tie and tails, and the women in full evening dress. We then proceeded formally in pairs through countless magnificent reception rooms opening into each other until we reached the vast green dining-room.

There was a liveried footman standing behind each chair, and everything on the dining-table was gold, including the knives and forks. Ornamental gold plates were also on all the tables around the walls underneath the Fitzwilliam family por-traits. It was an unforgettable scene of pre-war splendour.

Soon after our return from Wentworth I had to face the ordeal of losing Nanny Randall. At the age of forty-three she had decided to marry our chauffeur, Bertram Parker, and to have a family of her own. She had been my loyal friend and companion for nineteen years, and I missed her terribly after she had gone, but she always wrote to me regularly and still does to this day.

Although I had never aspired to be a leader of fashion, in 1938 I was voted ninth by Paris experts in the Ten Best-Dressed Women in the World list. 'Her hats inspire millions,' declared the announcement. Top of the list came the Duchess of Windsor, who had long since discarded the ear-plaits she wore at my mother-in-law's luncheon party.

In December 1938 I tried to repay my debt to Sir John Weir by supporting him in the Beau Geste Ball, held in aid of the British Homœopathic Association of which he was the treasurer. He was most anxious that I should appear in the '£500,000 Jewel Parade', which I did. This time, however, I was not wearing any dreary old turquoises, but a fortune in rubies and diamonds! My dress was a beautiful pink tulle crinoline made by (guess who!) Norman Hartnell.

That summer Charlie and I went to Vichy, where he was again taking the cure. While we were there I had another miscarriage—this time a serious one. It began when we were lunching at the golf club, which was situated on an island. So, sitting in a chair and covered with blankets, I was carried on to the ferry and taken to the 'Clinique Pergola,' run by nuns. They kept me there for several weeks, and the doctors warned me that if I attempted to have another child I would risk my life. I listened to them, but made a mental note to ignore their warning. I have always loved children and was determined to have a large family.

Ever since I had left America at the age of thirteen I had wanted to return. At last, in February 1939, I insisted that Charlie should take me there. The inducement was that we had been invited to stay with Mr and Mrs Stephen (Laddie) Sanford in Palm Beach. Charlie, who by now had become completely Anglicised, was anything but enthusiastic about the idea, but I think he realised that he was up against the proverbial 'irresistible force'. Luckily, he had business reasons for going.

We sailed for New York on the 'Ile de France', and as soon as we arrived and I saw that unmistakable skyline and heard those American voices around me, I knew that I had 'come home'. In fact I felt as though I had never left. Obviously one's childhood environment is very important. We spent five days at the Plaza Hotel, doing all the usual tourist things such as seeing New York from the top of the Empire State Building and going to the famous Radio City Music Hall. We were lavishly entertained by many friends, including Byron and Thelma Foy—

she was the Chrysler heiress—the Winston Guests, and William Paley and his beautiful first wife, Dorothy.

We saw all the latest Broadway hits, among them *Hellzapoppin*, *Stars in Your Eyes*, *The Boys from Syracuse* and Cole Porter's *Leave It to Me*, in which Mary Martin won fame singing the hit song, 'My Heart Belongs to Daddy'.

After each show we went on to dine at the Colony Restaurant, the Stork Club, El Morocco or the 21 Club. We were present at the glamorous opening of a new nightclub called Monte Carlo, run by Fefe Ferry.

We then took the 'Florida Special' night train and arrived next morning to face a blast of the intense and very damp heat of Palm Beach. I have been to most of the well-known resorts in the world, but I have never known anything to equal the sheer opulence of Palm Beach—it was also the greatest fun. There were dinner parties of forty to fifty people every night in houses that were mini-palaces. The women wore their most glamorous dresses and fabulous jewellery, and the evenings usually ended at the Everglades Club, where there was dancing under the stars to one of the famous orchestras, such as Paul Whiteman's.

Mary and Laddie Sanford were the acknowleged leaders of Palm Beach society—Mary still is—and they were the most wonderful hosts to us.

Charlie played golf every day on the famous Seminole Club course, and Barbara Hutton's aunt, Mrs Woolworth Donahue, invited us as her guests to the Hialeah Races. We travelled with her in her private railway coach, in which I was amazed to discover that the ladies' cloakroom had solid gold taps and fittings!

At Hialeah we watched the races from Joe Widener's box, looking down at the bright pink flamingoes in the centre of the track, and at the Seminole Indians in their colourful tribal costumes mingling with the crowd.

Back in New York, where we spent another two weeks, I lunched with my old headmistress, Miss Hewitt. I visited her school and found that the 'Classes' my father helped to found had by now grown into one of the largest and most important day schools in America, and occupied two blocks.

On March 17th, after watching the St Patrick's Day parade going down Fifth Avenue, we heard the news that Hitler's troops had occupied Czechoslovakia. We sailed for England on the 'Queen Mary' the next day. I hated leaving America, and I would have been sadder still had I known that it would be seven years before I was able to go there again, in spite of Chamberlain's promise of 'peace in our time'.

In that last summer of peace, Charlie and I spent some time in Monte Carlo, where we stayed with Douglas Fairbanks, Snr, and his beautiful wife, Sylvia, formerly Lady Ashley. Dapper, vital and handsome, with very white teeth and immense charm, Douglas loved clothes and used to order forty suits at a time from his London tailor. He was another pathologically jealous man and had always insisted on Mary Pickford, his first wife, sitting next to him at any dinner party. It was the same now with Sylvia, whom he would never willingly allow out of his sight.

Douglas and Sylvia had just come from Venice. While they were there they had met Goebbels. His last words to them had been ominous: 'I'll be seeing you in New York.'

During our stay in Monte Carlo the German–Polish crisis began. We went to a gala as guests of Norma Shearer and George Raft, doing our best to be light-hearted, but it was sadly obvious that the sands of Chamberlain's peace were running out.

Every day a group of us—Esmond and Peggy Harmsworth, David Margesson, Leslie Hore-Belisha, Geoffrey Lloyd, Douglas and Sylvia, Charlie and I—sat around the pool gloomily discussing the steadily worsening situation. We left for Paris, lunched with Elsie Mendl at her house at Versailles, and then hurried home to London just before war was declared on September 3rd.

Chapter 12

For twelve months we had what they called 'the phoney war'—a time of ominous quiet. Charlie and I had closed our house in Sussex Place. My parents had done the same with 48, Upper Grosvenor Street. Before they left, however, my father, with his usual methodical care, switched off the gas, water and electricity, stripped and boarded all the windows, and removed every telephone machine to a place of safety. Six years later I had cause to be extremely grateful for his foresight in doing all this.

My parents rented a house at Cooden Beach in Sussex, and it was there that I spent that first winter of the war.

The following March, Charlie and I moved into the Dorchester Hotel, which was one of London's few concrete buildings and was therefore considered safer than most places. It was there, on April 5th, 1940, that our second child—a son—was born.

In spite of the Vichy doctors' gloomy prognostications, I had been perfectly well throughout the nine months of pregnancy, and the birth was a normal one. He was christened Brian Charles at Brompton Oratory on May 7th, and his godparents included Lady Pamela Berry (now Lady Hartwell), Countess Haugwitz-Reventlow (Barbara Hutton), Richard Tauber and Viscount Milton.

Two months later France fell to the Germans, and panic set in among certain people in England.

One evening Charlie and I were invited to dine with the American Ambassador, Joseph P. Kennedy, and his wife, Rose— the parents of the future President Kennedy. At dinner I was astonished to hear Joe Kennedy say: 'This country is finished. It will be overrun by the Germans in a matter of weeks. All the roads will then be blocked with refugees, just as they are now in France.' He turned to me. 'You and your children must get out,' he said. 'As the wife of an American you would be crazy to stay here.'

I was disgusted by this defeatist attitude, especially coming from an Ambassador, and I said to him, 'This country will never be finished and I have no intention of leaving.'

Charlie, however, added his own arguments to those of the Kennedys. The children, he pointed out, were half American, and it was wrong to risk their lives.

He wanted to send Frances and Brian to America to be looked after by Charlie's parents, who had left London when war broke out. But I would not consider being separated from my children —who knew how long it would be for?

Many of my friends—all of them British and with no American connections—had decided to leave their country and go to America for the duration. They must have had rather guilty consciences, because they tried very hard to persuade me to take the lead in this flight and become their bulwark. 'If Margaret goes, it will be all right for us to go,' seemed to be their attitude.

The United States Embassy now began to send alarming letters to all American nationals in Britain. In large red letters we were constantly warned that a ship was being sent to evacuate us from 'this beleaguered island'; that we were STRONGLY ADVISED to take it, as it might be THE LAST CHANCE; and that if we chose to remain in Britain it would be at our own risk.

Every time one of these letters arrived my heart sank. The decision was an agonising one—it would have been so much easier if I had had no choice.

My father, however, resolved the matter for me in one sentence.

'Margaret, if you leave Britain, or if you send your children away, I shall never speak to you again.'

That made matters very simple. The red letters went into the wastepaper basket. My nervous friends went off to become expatriates without me. Charlie was silenced, and the matter was never discussed again.

Frances and Brian were now sent to North Wales to stay at Bodnant, the family seat of Lord and Lady Aberconway, at Tal-y-Cafn in Denbighshire. Christabel Aberconway had decided to take the children of her friends as paying guests at £10 a head, in preference to having the Liverpool evacuees forced upon her. An invasion of the East coast was rumoured to be imminent and Bodnant, which was on the West coast, seemed the safest possible retreat. With Frances and Brian went the nanny and the nursery maid, which meant £40 a week for Christabel. She also had as paying guests the children of Garrett and Joan Moore (now the Earl and Countess of Drogheda), Sir Paul and Lady Patricia Latham, and Sir Nicholas and Lady Cayzer.

Although I had read of the bombing of Warsaw and Rotterdam, the horror of a 'blitz' from the air only became real to me on September 29th, 1940. Coming out of the Regal Cinema, Marble Arch, on that evening, with Charlie and my brother-in-law, Bobby Sweeny, I looked up and saw for the first time the sky filled with searchlights under a full moon. In the distance, towards the direction of the docks, the whole horizon was a mass of flames. Only then, with a surge of almost uncontrollable rage, did I realise that London—my London—was being bombed.

Charlie had been urging me for some time to join the children at Bodnant, in safety. But to no avail. Having decided to stay here I had no intention of sitting the war out, uselessly, in the country. One night a bomb fell in Deanery Street. It shattered the windows of our bedroom at the Dorchester and black smoke poured into the room.

'Now do you see,' said Charlie, 'why you must leave London?'

The next day we lunched with General 'Hap' Arnold, head of the American Air Force, and he, obviously prompted by Charlie, also urged me to leave. 'Mrs Sweeny, you really must do as your husband says and get out of town. It's going to get much worse.'

Defeated for the time being, I packed and Charlie took me to Euston to catch the train for Wales. While we were waiting on the platform a bomb dropped on the station. We heard it coming, and I saw a woman in a blue feather hat dive underneath a stationary train. I stood rooted to the spot, paralysed with fright. Glass showered all around us, but when the woman emerged from under the train with her blue hat covered in soot—I had to laugh. I said to Charlie, 'It's all your fault. You nearly got me killed. If you had left me at the Dorchester I would have been perfectly safe.'

The train was crammed with evacuee children, all with tags round their necks. The journey took six hours, and as the train pulled out of Euston I began to cry with anger and depression. A kindly man sitting opposite me said 'Don't worry, little lady, we'll soon be out of London.' 'That's what I'm crying about,' I wailed, after which he lapsed into a puzzled silence.

The train was so packed that I finally gave up my seat to a woman with a baby, and ended my journey in the guard's van with a goat. During the trip I had made up my mind that Wales was not for me, war or no war. On arrival, therefore, I sent myself a telegram from the nearest post office to reach Bodnant the following morning. It said that urgent business necessitated my immediate return to London.

Bodnant was a large but uninteresting house, surrounded by famous gardens and orchid houses. When I arrived Christabel Aberconway descended the stairs carrying a candle and looking rather like Lady Macbeth. Next morning my telegram appeared and was duly shown to Christabel. Having never unpacked, I simply kissed the children goodbye and boarded a London train.

After another six-hour train journey, with air raid warnings every few minutes, I arrived back at the Dorchester beaming with joy. When Charlie saw me he groaned and said, 'I give up.' How wise he was. After that I stayed put in London, though I managed regular visits to the children while they were in Wales. Even that was not for long, because shortly afterwards my father rented from Sir Ian and Lady Bowater a large country house, Calverton Place, at Stony Stratford, near Bletchley, and the children were moved to my parents' new home.

Charlie's health had made it impossible for him to be considered for active service in any of the armed forces. He carried on with his work in the City as Principal of the Federated Trust and Finance Corporation. Then, shortly after the fall of France, he thought of a way to make his own contribution to the war effort.

He personally supervised the importation from America of sub-machine guns, automatic rifles and armoured cars to arm a hundred and fifty men. By January 1941 he had managed to equip and train a third of this number, whom he formed into the 1st American Motorised Squadron, which was composed entirely of American citizens and became a unit of the Home Guard.

When Winston Churchill inspected this famous unit, Mrs Churchill and I were the only two women present on Horse Guards Parade to watch a small piece of Anglo-American history in the making.

For Charlie, however, it was only the beginning. He now roped in his uncle, Colonel Charles Sweeny—'Sweeny of the Legion'—one of the most decorated and colourful soldiers of fortune in the history of the Foreign Legion. That autumn they formed what later became known as the Eagle Squadron. It was equipped at the expense of Americans, and young fliers were recruited from all over the United States to form the Squadron, which became a unit of Fighter Command. As the American pilots were not allowed to swear allegiance to the King, Charlie, with the help of Sir Archibald Sinclair (later Lord Thurso), who was Minister for Air and leader of the Liberal Party, succeeded in getting an Act of Parliament passed that enabled the American volunteers to fight for Britain without having to swear the oath of allegiance.

In November 1942, only fourteen months after the birth of Charlie's idea, Sir Archibald Sinclair was able to report to Parliament that there were three American Eagle Squadrons fighting alongside the Royal Air Force.

These were magnificent achievements for which Charlie deserves lasting credit.

Soon after Brian was born I went to work at the Beaver Club, near Admiralty Arch, which was run for the benefit of Commonwealth troops. I had volunteered for washing up, but it was waitresses they needed, and I found myself waiting at table and on my feet for long hours every day. Evidently it was too soon after the birth of the baby to undertake this sort of work, and my doctor insisted that I give up the job. I was then transferred to the RAF Benevolent Fund, where I worked less arduously under Lady Portal of Hungerford.

At the beginning of December 1941, when British morale was at its lowest and we were all longing for America to enter the war, I met Averell Harriman, who had succeeded Joe Kennedy as American Ambassador in London.

'I'm afraid America will never come into the war actively,' he told me, 'although we will keep on sending all possible aid to Britain. I have just been over there and the mood throughout the country is getting more and more isolationist.'

Precisely one week later the Japanese bombed Pearl Harbour and America entered the war! On the day this happened I went to see Harvey Gibson, the head of the American Red Cross, who was then in London.

'How do I join?' I asked him, and I became the second woman to wear the American Red Cross uniform in London, the first being the late Mrs Anthony Biddle, who was to be my boss. A wealthy woman, and the wife of Anthony J. Drexel Biddle, who was US Ambassador to eight countries, she was charming, and with a man's mind—she had been trained by her oil billionaire father. Margaret ran the women officers' club in Charles Street, Mayfair, and was determined that it should be the finest Red Cross club in London. If she was unable to get some such luxury as asparagus, or strawberries out of season, from the Catering Corps, she simply bought them at her own expense. Our food, therefore, was better than any in London, the result being that we were patronised not only by the WACS and the WAVES but also by the men officers.

Margaret made me Entertainments Officer, and I was responsible for providing the club with a good dance band and cabaret one or two nights a week. I arranged for stars such as Bob Hope, Jack Benny, Sid Field and Marlene Dietrich to appear. One night Bing Crosby sang to us for two hours and Vera Lynn gave us several marvellous evenings. Fred Astaire's sister, Adele, was assigned to the Red Cross Rainbow Corner which was run for the GIs, and she used to tease me, 'You're such a snob, Margaret, working for all those officers.'

One evening we were told that a shipload of coloured officers and nurses were coming to the club for dinner. This was long before the days of the Race Relations Act, and a directive came from Mrs Eleanor Roosevelt, through General Eisenhower, that there was to be no discrimination whatsoever. The coloured officers and nurses duly arrived and Mrs Roosevelt's orders were faithfully carried out. I sat with a charming coloured doctor and two American coloured nurses for dinner. But the moment the dancing began, all the Southern officers very pointedly got up and walked out. It was an embarrassing evening.

As soon as I joined the American Red Cross I had to wear the uniform, which consisted of an RAF-blue suit and an overcoat lined with red. With this we wore either a white jersey or blouse. As Margaret Biddle always wore a pearl necklace when in uniform I assumed I could do the same. Unfortunately Dorothy Wilding photographed me in uniform, plus pearls, and displayed the photograph in her Bond Street window. It was seen within an hour by Harvey Gibson—the Big Boss—who demanded, 'Who the hell is that dame wearing pearls with her uniform?' I was ordered to remove the pearls at once, and Margaret had to follow suit.

Meanwhile, at Calverton, my mother's health had suddenly broken down. A pain, starting in the soles of her feet, moved from her legs and up through her entire body. From being an active woman who loved golf, tennis and dancing, she became bound to a wheelchair within a matter of weeks, unable to stand or walk. The illness was belatedly diagnosed as severe osteo and rheumatoid arthritis, which made her helpless and in constant pain for the last fifteen years of her life. During all this time my father's devotion to her never wavered. Neither did her own courage. Her legs withered and her beautiful hands became twisted and deformed. But she would never take morphia, although she sometimes begged her doctor to give her a pill to end her life.

The war brought my marriage to a crisis. Charlie's possessive jealousy, which had always been a problem, now became a nightmare. He could be embarrassingly rude to any man who was merely saying a polite 'Good evening' to me.

After I began to work for the American Red Cross, the scenes between us became more frequent and were noticed by my parents and our friends. I decided, however, to put up with this—everything has its price, and in many ways Charlie was a devoted, faithful, almost model husband.

Every Friday I would leave London early for Calverton to spend as much time as possible with the children before returning to London on Monday. Charlie never came with me. He would arrive at Calverton late on the Saturday night, or sometimes just come for the day on Sunday. Because of this he barely saw the children at all, but I never questioned his explanations of 'business meetings' or 'exercises with the Home Guard'.

It was a woman staying at the Dorchester who dropped the first bombshell on our marriage. 'It's none of my business,' she told my parents, 'and you must decide whether to tell Margaret or not, but while she is away in the country at weekends, Charlie is making a fool of her with a series of girls.'

My parents did tell me. They had become increasingly angry at the unhappiness Charlie was obviously causing me. My reaction surprised me even more than it did them. There were no tears, and after the initial shock I felt a curious sense of relief. Charlie was now proved to be certainly no paragon of virtue, and I did not have to put up with those nerve-racking scenes any more. Calmly, I confronted him with the information I had received. He made no attempt to deny it. He admitted it all and begged me to forgive him. 'Please come with me to Mass on Sunday,' he said. 'I will pray for forgiveness and we will start afresh.' We went to Mass.

Next weekend Charlie did not come down with me on Friday to Calverton, saying that he had to dine with an American General in London. Unfortunately for Charlie, I discovered the following week that the 'General' had long blond hair and was very pretty!

This pattern of life continued until Charlie was briefly posted to Warrington, the supply depot of the American Army. He was most insistent that I go with him, but I refused. I had a job in London, and the children to see at weekends. I was also very disillusioned.

Three months later, when Charlie returned from Warrington, I had made up my mind. I moved out of our room at the Dorchester to a room on another floor. This sounds almost farcical now, but given the problems of wartime accommodation it was the only thing I could do.

I was then deluged with calls and letters from Charlie begging me to return, but I stayed where I was. Once my eyes had been opened, they could never be closed again.

One morning in July 1943, I went to Mr Wiberg, my chiropodist in Bond Street. I was late for my appointment, and I hurried into the dark hall to the lift in the corner. The lift gate was open and I stepped inside. The trouble was that there was no lift. I had stepped into space, and I fell forty feet to the bottom of the lift shaft. The only thing that saved me was the lift cable, which broke my fall. I must have clutched at it, for it was later found that all my finger nails were torn off. I apparently fell on to my knees and cracked the back of my head against the wall.

The caretaker, hearing strange noises, thought it was the cat, and mercifully stopped the lift coming down. If he had not I would have been crushed to death. I was in such a mess, unconscious and covered in blood, that the poor caretaker, who eventually rescued me, was ill for six months with a nervous breakdown.

I was rushed to St George's Hospital where thirty stitches were immediately put in my head. They did not dare risk giving me an anaesthetic while doing this, but luckily I was practically unconscious anyway. They also discovered that I had broken vertebrae in my back, and, due to the olfactory nerve being badly damaged, I had lost all sense of taste and smell.

After three days I was moved to the University College Hospital, and Mr Robert Burns, the orthopaedic specialist, was called in. He told my parents that I might be paralysed down one side and never walk again. Anyway, I would have to stay in hospital for at least three months.

Nobody told me of this diagnosis, but I was already getting restless. I managed to persuade the doctors to let me get out of bed. When I tried this I nearly collapsed, and then I was really frightened, but I persevered and insisted upon leaving the hospital after three weeks.

On my first 'night out' I was taken to the Four Hundred Club and there I saw Robert Burns. I tapped him on the shoulder and said, 'Remember me?' His face when he saw me dancing was a study.

A prominent American in London throughout the war was David Rose, head of Paramount Pictures, and a great friend of mine. He used to give parties at which he showed private previews of films. All the British and American 'top brass' were invited. One memorable evening David was showing *The Road to Morocco*, and in the audience were General Eisenhower and General Spaatz, head of the US Air Force. They left rather hurriedly, and within forty-eight hours I read that the Americans had made a landing in North Africa. David heard afterwards that the two Generals were convinced that he (David) had some inside knowledge.

Another evening that I shall never forget was that of May 14th, 1944, when I was invited to a cocktail party at the American Naval Headquarters in Grosvenor Square. It was given by Admiral Stark, head of the US Navy. When I arrived I saw that the party consisted of five or six other women and a roomful of American Admirals. Only one man in the room was a mere Commodore! In my naïve way I thought nothing of all this. Only on June 6th did I realise that these were the Admirals who were going to lead the American invasion of Europe.

I vividly remember the Normandy landings being announced by General Eisenhower at eight in the morning. I went out soon afterwards and discovered that an uncanny hush seemed to have fallen over London. It was as if the city was holding its breath. All the churches were full; the restaurants and shops were empty. There was no traffic. People stayed at home, glued to the radio. As King George VI said in his broadcast, 'The spirit of the people, resolute, dedicated, burned like a bright flame, lit surely from those unseen fires which nothing can quench.'

When victory came at last on May 8th, 1945, I took some American friends to join the crowds outside Buckingham Palace. I was wearing my Red Cross uniform, and I was most touched to notice how the people, thinking I was American, made a path for us through the crowd and pushed us forward to the railings so that we could see the King and Queen, the two Princesses and Winston Churchill on the Palace balcony.

In these four years the myriads of Americans based in Britain had formed close friendships with the British, and on VE Day, overjoyed as we were, there was considerable sadness over the inevitable partings to come.

After Winston Churchill, General Eisenhower was probably the most popular man in Britain. I well remember one evening, soon after VE Day, when I was dining at Ciro's Restaurant. Suddenly the whole room rose, everyone was cheering and clapping, the band was playing 'The Star-Spangled Banner'. I turned to see General Eisenhower and General Omar Bradley take their places at the table next to mine. It was a moment I shall never forget.

Much later that year I was most gratified to receive the following letter:

AMERICAN RED CROSS
General Headquarters
Paris

28th November, 1945.

Mrs Margaret Sweeny,
c/o American Red Cross,
London, England.

Dear Mrs Sweeny,
It gives me much pleasure to present you with the enclosed American Red Cross Theatre Ribbon. The wearing of this ribbon by qualified American Red Cross personnel has been approved by the Military Authorities of the US Army in the European Theatre of Operations.

This ribbon is given for meritorious service and in presenting it the American Red Cross thanks you for the long and devoted services you have rendered as a volunteer worker without remuneration. You offered your services in September, 1942 and for more than three years you have unselfishly given of your time and energies to assisting this organisation in carrying out its mission in this theatre. I hope that you have found a measure of reward in the grateful appreciation of those thousands of Americans who have been so dependent for their recreation upon the type of service you have rendered during their stay in the British Isles.

We are deeply indebted to the women of Britain who, like yourself, have cheerfully and generously given so much of their time to assisting the American Red Cross. Without this invaluable help it would have been impossible for us to carry out our programme successfully.

I trust that this Theatre Ribbon will often remind you of the deep gratitude of the American Red Cross.

Sincerely yours,

(Signature illegible)

Acting Commissioner.

On account of my mother's ill-health, my parents decided to remain at the Dorchester, and they offered their house at 48, Upper Grosvenor Street to me. I accepted with delight, and moved in on VJ Day, August 15th, 1945. I was also fortunate in inheriting my parents' loyal and efficient staff—Mr and Mrs Duckworth, the butler and cook, and Gertrude Giltrap, the housemaid. I also had my personal maid, Isabel Bennett, and Deta, the children's governess.

Thanks to my father's precautions at the beginning of the war, I had only to switch on the gas and electricity, turn on the water and plug in the telephones, and the house was in working order.

I sent Frances to a day school in London, as I do not approve of boarding schools for girls. I also preferred that she always lunched at home with me, and I arranged that she should have special tuition in French, Italian, painting, music, riding and tennis every afternoon. All this stood her in good stead in her future life when she became Duchess of Rutland and mistress of Belvoir Castle.

Brian, who was now five, was going to a kindergarten in Queen's Gate, and I, wishing to put my life in order at last, started proceedings against Charlie for divorce.

Chapter 13

Once I had settled Frances and Brian into their new schools and had got the house running smoothly, I began thinking of a trip to New York. It was seven years since I had last seen Manhattan, and I longed to return there, but this was almost impossible to arrange. To travel anywhere out of Britain one either had to be a VIP or have business of national importance. Unfortunately I was in neither of these categories.

Eventually I approached a charming man who was one of the heads of the Ministry of War Transport, called Mr Maby. He gave me two alternatives. Since I was still the wife of an American I could go on a liner as a GI bride, sharing a cabin with three other women, or I could sail in a banana boat called the SS 'Rippingham Grange', of the Furness Line. I chose the latter, and discovered that I was to be the only woman among the twenty-five passengers—at least this meant that I would have a cabin to myself.

In a February blizzard, my father came to Tilbury Docks to see me off. We both gazed in astonishment at a small ship of about 5,000 tons sitting high above her water line, obviously sadly lacking in ballast—even with my luggage on board! This was the SS 'Rippingham Grange'!!

My father, who had crossed the Atlantic more than a hundred and fifty times, was anything but encouraging. 'Well, my dear,' he said as he kissed me goodbye, 'have a good time, and give America my love—if you ever get there.'

We set off down the Thames in a thick fog. On the third day the fog cleared and I looked out of my porthole to find we were opposite Brighton!!

'Captain dear,' I said at lunch that day, 'I've got a date in New York on March 10th. Surely we can do better than this?' When, two days later, we had just reached Land's End and I again remonstrated with the Captain, he said, 'Why don't you talk to the Chief Engineer?' So I did.

'Lady,' he said, 'forget March 10th. This ship is neither insured nor seaworthy. If we run into a March gale you'll be lucky if you ever see New York at all.'

He was not joking. The March gale duly hit us, and the decks were awash for the next ten days, making it impossible to get any fresh air, even by opening a porthole.

My fellow passengers—who included Texas oil men, Norwegian sailors, Dutch merchant seamen and British sales representatives—and I sat around the lounge all day, and the days seemed endless. We lived on tinned food, and after ten days of this my skin was looking most peculiar. The ship's doctor told me that I was getting scurvy, and I began to wonder if the health officials in New York would let me off the ship.

At long last we arrived outside New York Harbour on the evening of March 9th, too late to go through Immigration. The pilot came on board at 5 o'clock the next morning. I was already dressed, and I have never been so glad to see anyone in my life. We then sailed up the river and watched the wondrous sight of the sun rising behind the Manhattan skyline.

As we docked I heard my name called first on the list to disembark. I came down the gangplank and was astonished to see Admiral Luis de Flores—a wartime friend of mine—waiting for me with a huge bouquet of flowers, two aides, an official car and a naval lorry for my luggage. He had often promised to meet me on my first postwar trip to New York and, learning of my arrival, he kept his word. I was given the Freedom of the Port, my luggage was whisked through Customs, and I drove to the Plaza Hotel to the accompaniment of wailing police sirens.

After seven years away, it was a wonderful welcome back.

Once in New York it struck me how fresh and healthy the American women looked, and in comparison I felt thoroughly bedraggled. After I had been there a few weeks I looked and felt a different person.

I sailed home on the 'Queen Mary'. She was making her first civilian crossing after being a troopship, but she was still painted battleship grey and was a 'dry' ship, which did not help the passengers' morale.

The following August I decided it was time that Frances and Brian had their first trip to Europe, and I planned to take them to St Moritz. As I was on friendly terms with Charlie I asked his advice about how to get the children and myself on to a plane. He said that our only chance was to charter one, and he offered to arrange this for me. When we landed at Zurich, Charlie, much to my surprise, was there to meet us. This made me slightly uneasy for I had already begun the divorce proceedings. Moreover, for some time Charlie had been constantly in the company of a lady called Isabel, the sister of a peer.

But on this August day in Zurich he turned on all his Irish charm and begged me to dine with him that evening. It seemed churlish to refuse and I agreed, although with misgivings. We dined on the terrace of the Baur-au-lac Hotel, overlooking the lake. Charlie plied me with caviar and champagne, and the orchestra played Strauss waltzes in the background. It was an evening Charlie did not mean me to forget, and I never have forgotten it. All the time he was begging me to stop the divorce and return to him. It was a very emotional and difficult evening. The combination of Strauss, the stars and the Sweeny charm were hard to combat. However, I did put one leading question to Charlie—'What about Isabel?' 'That's nothing,' he replied. 'It doesn't mean a thing.'

After this reply I thought it only fair to give us all another chance, so I told Charlie that I was taking the children to St Moritz the next day, and that, if he liked, he could come with us. I pointed out that we would then have ten days away from everything to see if there was any chance of our starting afresh. He hesitated, and said, 'I can't come with you tomorrow because I have a very important business meeting in London, but I'll join you in a day or two.'

The next morning he saw us off on the train to St Moritz, where a mass of flowers from him awaited me. I decided to telephone my lawyer in London and ask him to delay the divorce proceedings for a while.

The next news I got from Charlie was a call from Cannes explaining that he was going to London with a friend in his private plane; they had run out of fuel and had to stay the night in Cannes. The following day I rang his office, in all innocence, to find out when I could expect him in St Moritz. His secretary, Miss Denham, who had worked with him for years, said that he was away on holiday, that she did not know of any business meeting, and that Charlie definitely was not expected back in London.

I put the telephone down, feeling strangely cold, realising that Charlie had never intended to join us. I cancelled the call I had booked to my lawyer, and tried to give the children a happy holiday.

When we arrived back in London, there was Charlie to meet us at the airport. 'This is wonderful,' he said, hugging the children. 'We'll all go back together to your house.' I quickly disabused him of this idea.

That evening I dined at Ciro's with Paul Warburg, a dear friend of mine, and found myself at the next table to Bridget Poulett. 'I have just come back from Cannes,' she said, 'and guess who had the next room to me at the Carlton? Charlie and Isabel!'

I now knew that I had given my marriage every chance and that I need have no bad conscience about proceeding with the divorce. Mercifully for me and for my future with my children, even my worst enemy could not say that any other man was involved. In fact it was quite a long time after I left Charlie in 1943 that I became seriously interested in anybody else.

In February 1947—fourteen years after our wedding at Brompton Oratory—my marriage was dissolved on the grounds of Charlie's 'constructive desertion'. Five days later, in my Molyneux 'new look' outfit—I was one of the first to wear it—I sailed to New York on the 'Queen Elizabeth' and began a new life of freedom and many years of happiness. I did my utmost throughout the years after I left Charlie to save Frances and Brian from the tension and unhappiness of divided loyalties between their parents that I had suffered. I included Charlie in every family event possible. I invited him to the children's tea parties; he came with us to pantomimes and cinemas—he even helped to decorate the Christmas tree every year. I always begged him to take Brian out for the day at weekends and teach him to play golf. Brian was very proud of his golfing father.

The result was that the children did not seem in the least upset that he was not living with us, and they never asked me any questions.

From New York I flew to Los Angeles, where I stayed with the Ray Millands. I had a wonderful time there, meeting all the Hollywood stars and watching the films being made.

During the next thirty years I made numerous visits to America. One of the most amusing was long ago when I sailed on the same ship as Sir Cecil Beaton. We were each of us travelling alone, so we had all our meals together.

Cecil happened to have a deadly loathing for one of the other passengers—the wife of an Irish Peer. He asked me to warn him any time I saw her approaching. One evening, as we were dining in the Verandah Grill, I said 'Here she comes, looking lovely in a black cape with a chartreuse-green lining.'

Cecil replied, 'And a chartreuse-green lining to her mouth, no doubt?'

I remember one winter being invited to New Orleans for 'Mardi Gras,' and there I was asked if I would curtsey to the traditional kings and queens of Mardi Gras. Apparently Mrs Truman, as the wife of the American President, had refused. But the Duke and Duchess of Windsor had paid their homage, and I was happy to follow suit by making my curtsey, too. The British Ambassador, Sir Roger Makins, had come from Washington for the carnival. So had our Royal Navy, which meant a round of parties both ashore and on board ship. The officer who set most female hearts a-flutter was one of the youngest but most senior—Rear-Admiral Keith Campbell-Walter, the father of the beautiful model, Fiona Campbell-Walter, later Baroness Thyssen.

Just after the war had ended, another American came into my

life. He was Theodore Rousseau, the son of a wealthy banker. Ted, besides being good-looking, was highly intelligent, witty and self-confident to the point of arrogance. At the incredibly early age of thirty-five he had become Curator of Paintings at the Metropolitan Museum in New York. He was engaged on one of the most fascinating quests in art history, tracking down the treasures stolen by the Germans from occupied countries during the war. I went with him to Rome, Milan and Florence while he was on this job. Later on he met Herman Goering's banker in Spain, who was coaxed into giving valuable information over several lengthy, brandy-laced meetings.

Ted asked me to marry him and I hesitated for a long time. I loved him very much, but his future was at the Metropolitan in New York. Marrying him would have meant uprooting the children from London, which hardly seemed fair to them, and I also feared that Ted was not 'stepfather material'. So after much heart searching I told him that it would be better if we did not marry. But we continued seeing each other constantly. Ted died in November, 1973, when he was only 61.

In 1948 I began a brief career as a reporter. Mr R. J. O'Connell, the editor of *Woman's Illustrated*, commissioned me to go to Berlin and write an article about the conditions under which the wives of the soldiers in the British Army of Occupation were living. I jumped at the idea, received a Press pass, and it was arranged that I go in on the Berlin air lift. I stayed for a week at the only hotel left standing, the Savoy, which was reserved for the Press.

A great friend of mine, Anthony Marreco, met me at the Templehof Airport. He was then Chief Staff Officer to Sir Christopher Steel, the Political Adviser to the British military government in Germany. Anthony had arranged that I should lunch in Potsdam, in the Russian sector, and that I should meet a number of the Russian, French, American and British officials. I also managed to dart into the Russian zone and take many photographs, which was risky but, as it turned out, worth while.

The sight of devastated Berlin shocked me, and walking home at night in the light of a full moon is a memory that will always haunt me.

I received thirty guineas and generous praise from Mr

O'Connell for my article, and I continued to write weekly articles for *Woman's Illustrated* for the following eighteen months.

Shortly after this Berlin trip I got a cable from New York, that read, 'You are the loveliest thing ever brought back by the Berlin air lift.' The sender was Joseph Thomas, a Texan charmer who was one of the senior partners of Lehmann Brothers, the New York banking house. He had been married to an old school friend of mine, Eleanor Bangs, but they were now divorced.

A self-made millionaire, Joe was a complete extrovert and wonderful company. I owe my life to him, for while we were bathing together at Easthampton, Long Island, in August 1948, an enormous wave 'rolled' me and was carrying me out to sea. Joe, searching for me, saw my head bobbing up a long way away. He swam out and dragged me to the beach, half drowned.

We also stayed one weekend with Mrs Barclay Douglas, the Atlantic & Pacific heiress, who is now Mrs Ivor Bryce. She had a house in Vermont, and we all went over to the Saratoga Races. Miss Elizabeth Arden was there, and she sent a note across to our box asking what make-up I used, to look so cool in the intense heat. I replied, 'Elizabeth Arden, Miss Arden.'

After that she invited me to dine with her in her apartment on Fifth Avenue. Everything in this apartment reflected her impeccable taste. She was not only a charming woman but a perfectionist. When she asked for my opinion of the Arden products I told her that I found her lipsticks too greasy. The next day a sample box of drier lipsticks arrived at my hotel. Miss Arden had immediately informed her factory and had them made up especially for me. No wonder she was the founder of an empire.

On the same trip I also lunched with Helena Rubinstein. She, too, had an apartment on Fifth Avenue. There I met for the first time an attractive, well-known young photographer called Anthony Armstrong-Jones.

I then returned to London, followed by Joe Thomas, who asked me to marry him. I accepted with joy. He met my parents, who welcomed the idea of our marriage. I gave a big dinner for him, then took him to Leeds Castle for the weekend, as Olive Baillie was most anxious to meet him. She, also, thoroughly approved. We planned to spend half the year in London and keep my house. Everything seemed wonderful, until Joe said, 'There's one thing I must do, Margaret. I have to go and see Poppy in Switzerland to break the news to her myself.'

'Poppy' was Poppy de Salis, a Swiss lady with whom Joe had been much enamoured. It was now over, he said, but he felt it would hurt her deeply if she read the news of our marriage in the newspapers. A shiver of apprehension ran through me at this moment. 'Could you not write to her, or telephone?' I asked. But Joe was adamant. He said he would call me that evening, and asked me to meet him at the airport the following day.

Joe telephoned as promised. His voice was hesitant, and my instinct warned me what was coming. 'I'm terribly sorry, Margaret. I really don't know how to say this, but I have decided to marry Poppy.' I put the receiver down and cried for a long time. Joe's decision was a blow to my heart and to my pride; but perhaps it was for the best, for Poppy has certainly made him a wonderful wife.

When I moved into 48, Upper Grosvenor Street, another golden age began for me. I had a lovely 18th-century home and financial independence, all thanks to my father. I also had the opportunity of entertaining in the way I had always wished to do. This was made much easier for me by my incomparable housekeeper, Mrs Duckworth (now a widow), who was acknowledged to be one of the best cooks in London.

I had never even ordered wine or cigars before, so it was a big experiment, but my parties seemed to be a success because the guests usually stayed late.

Many evenings the then American Ambassador (Lewis Douglas) and his wife, Peggy, Brendan Bracken, Hector McNeill (Labour MP and Lord Provost of Glasgow), Edward Tomkins (now British Ambassador to France), Marshal of the Royal Air Force Viscount Peter Portal and his wonderful wife, Joan. Cynthia and Ben Welles (son of Sumner Welles and head of the London Bureau of the *New York Times*) would sit talking brilliantly into the small hours. I listened—fascinated. Other frequent guests at my house were Stavros and Eugenie Niarchos, Walter Pidgeon, Mary Lee and Douglas Fairbanks, Jr., Loelia, Duchess of Westminster, David Selznick and his wife Jennifer Jones.

I began to formulate my own rules for a hostess: (1) It is not necessary that you enjoy your own party—in fact, if you do, it will probably be a failure. The hostess is the stage manager putting on a show and must keep a constant eye on everything. (2) The women guests must be pretty or at least amusing, and one has to be ruthless about never inviting what I describe as 'dead wood'. Men are just not amused at sitting next to one's old school chum if she is not attractive. (3) People of high intelligence always mix well, however diverse their interests may be—diplomats, actors, artists, politicians, businessmen. It is only the mediocrities who will slow down a party. (4) The best reason of all for entertaining is to have foreign guests. They are always a new and interesting element. Sad to say, the British have a very poor reputation about returning hospitality received abroad. (5) Never allow the men to stay in the dining-room for longer than twenty minutes after dinner.

Many amusing, embarrassing and even important incidents have taken place under my roof. One evening I had the American Ambassador (Jock Whitney), the German Ambassador (Johnny von Herwath), and the Lord Chancellor (Lord Kilmuir) to dine. I automatically placed the two Ambassadors on my right and left. Next morning Sir Henry (Chips) Channon called me and said, 'Margaret, do you realise you have made the most ghastly *faux pas*? The Lord Chancellor precedes even Ambassadors in rank, and you placed him below the salt.' I could only write to David Kilmuir apologising and pleading ignorance. His answer was understanding and light-hearted.

Whenever I entertained Noël Coward and Elsa Maxwell together it was amusing to watch them fighting for the limelight and striving to cap each other's stories. These battles usually ended with each of them thinking they had won.

Elsa's remarks in her New York gossip column could be merciless, and for some reason she was constantly attacking Paul Getty at this time. I feigned ignorance of this, and asked them both to one of my dinners. Elsa was the first to arrive, and when Paul Getty was announced I saw her jaw drop.

After dinner I noticed, with surprise, Paul and Elsa engaged in deep and friendly conversation. The next morning Elsa said to me, 'Blessed are the peacemakers. I have completely misjudged

Paul Getty; he is charming.' She then retracted her earlier remarks about Paul in her column, and gave me the credit for their reconciliation, adding that I had 'a genius for inviting the right people, to my parties.

It was in my house that John Olin, the American small arms tycoon, was converted from his political bias against Britain. Knowing John's views, I invited him and his wife, Evelyn, to a dinner with Anthony Eden. I explained the position to Anthony, and after dinner, when the men were left in the dining-room, he used all the charm and diplomacy for which he is famous. When they came upstairs John Olin told me that his ideas were now entirely changed and that he would give his full support to Britain in the future.

In September 1949 I took Frances and Brian up to Dunrobin Castle, where we were the guests of the Duke and Duchess of Sutherland. While we were there, it was announced that Niall, the 10th Duke of Argyll, had died at Inveraray Castle, to be succeeded by his second cousin, Ian Campbell.

'So at last Ian has become a duke,' remarked Clare Sutherland. 'He's been waiting for it for years.'

'He'll make a very attractive duke,' I commented, for I had met Ian two years earlier.

Coming back from Paris on the Golden Arrow, I had found that Georges, the concierge at the Paris Ritz, had booked me a seat opposite an elegant man whom I recognised as Ian Campbell, and we had a very pleasant journey back to London. In the course of it Ian told me that he and his second wife, Louise, by whom he had two young sons, were then leading separate lives and that she had asked him for a divorce in order to marry her Russian admirer, Prince Dmitri. We parted when the train reached London, and it was two years before I next saw Ian, this time in Paris at the home of a friend of mine, Mrs Norman (Rosita) Winston.

Many years later, Ian told me a strange story. Apparently he had seen me in 1932 while dining at the Café de Paris, with his first wife, Janet Aitken, to discuss their pending divorce. He said he watched me come down the famous curved staircase, and said to Janet, 'There's the girl I'm going to marry one day.'

A few months after our meeting in Paris I found myself one man short for a lunch party I was giving for Baron Alexis Rede, a friend of the Chilean millionaire, Arturo Lopez. I had met Ian (now Argyll) at Claridge's the previous day, and I invited him to the lunch.

So it was that Ian Douglas Campbell, 11th Duke of Argyll, Chief of the Clan Campbell, Hereditary Master of the Royal Household in Scotland, Keeper of the Great Seal of Scotland, and Hereditary Keeper of the Royal Castles of Dunoon, Dunstaffnage, Tarbert and Carrick, entered my house for the first time on Friday, January 13th, 1950.

If I had been superstitious, the date would have been a warning to me.

Chapter 14

Momentous encounters in life often pass by without our realising their importance. My invitation to Ian Argyll to my lunch for Alexis Rede had been the result of a last-minute impulse, and I attached no particular significance to it at the time.

However, something about him must have lingered in my mind, for soon afterwards, when I went to New York to stay with the Gilbert Millers, I found myself thinking about the attractive Duke of Argyll and wondering whether his new life in Scotland would bring him and his wife closer together.

After my return to London I went to Paris to see the spring collections. There I unexpectedly met Ian again in the bar of the Ritz. I learned that his marriage had not improved. Louise, his wife, had left Inveraray Castle after spending only four months there as Duchess of Argyll and had returned to her home in Biarritz. Ian was obviously lonely, and also depressed by the burden of debt and mismanagement that he had inherited from his elderly cousin, the 10th Duke.

I also was alone, and felt drawn towards this troubled man who had so much charm. According to my diary, on March 25th, 1950, we spent the entire day together, having lunch in the country at an old mill house, dining at Maxim's that evening, and going on afterwards to the Lido.

I met him the next day, and the next, but this was my 'Merry

Widow' period when I was determined never to be a one-man woman again.

Ian was not the only attractive gentleman around me. There was Roberto Caracciolo—the Duke of San Vito—a vital, intelligent Neapolitan, one of Italy's most eminent diplomats in Paris. Roberto Caracciolo was also taking me out a great deal in Paris, and it was he who saw me off at Orly on my return to London.

Once home I found myself missing them both, and in a capricious moment I decided to send cables to Ian in Biarritz and to Roberto in Paris, saying 'Bored and missing you. Wish you would come to London.' I then sat back to await results.

Roberto replied that he could not leave his office. Ian did not answer; he just turned up unexpectedly at 48, Upper Grosvenor Street.

I can still see him standing there that evening in front of the fireplace in the library, hands in pockets. 'Well,' he said with a quizzical look, 'you must know why I have come. I'm here because of your cable, and I was very glad to get it.'

It was April 4th, 1950, and that evening marked the turning point in our relationship—I was no longer the Merry Widow.

On April 12th Ian took me to see Jean Anouilh's comedy, *Ring Round the Moon*. We sat in a box, and I noticed that the sadness had left Ian's eyes. He now looked happy, and the final lines of the play seemed entirely appropriate:

> Joshua: Ah, it's a happy day for me, Sir,
> to see you taking such a pleasure
> in life again.

The curtain fell and we got up to leave, only to find the door of our box jammed. It took twenty minutes to free it, and during that time Ian had asked me to become his wife if and when he could persuade Louise to give him a divorce. I didn't hesitate for a moment, and I told Ian that I would marry him if and when he was free. We then went off to celebrate at the Four Hundred, and danced until four in the morning.

If anyone had told me on that night that I was steering a course towards tragedy I would have thought them crazy.

Ian went to see my parents at the Dorchester. As the past had shown, they were not socially ambitious for me, but if there was

My mother and my father

I was about eight when I had my
first perm

Right Me as a debutante

My wedding to Charles Sweeny.
I leave for the church with my father

Coming out of Brompton Oratory after the ceremony

Daffodil time at Inverary

June 1953. The coronation of Queen Elizabeth II

With Frances and Brian (and Marcel!) at Brian's
21st birthday party at Claridge's, October 1960

one name that might mean something to their Scottish blood it was the dukedom of Argyll. They also liked Ian as a man. He was then forty-seven, exceptionally good-looking, and at least partly Scottish. My father also admired Ian's honesty in warning us that Inveraray Castle was almost a ruin, and that until the estate was put in order he himself had only £1,000 a year to live on.

'Before you really make up your mind,' Ian told me, 'I think you had better come and see Inveraray for yourself. It is quite a task you will be facing.'

We went on the night train, taking Frances with us, and arrived at Arrochar very early on the morning of June 1st. It was one of the most glorious summer days I can remember. We motored to the castle, and for the first time I went over the Rest and Be Thankful Pass, and saw the breathtaking beauty of Argyll. We passed the peak of Duniquaich, turned in at the lodge and drove up the tree-lined avenue. At the end was the romantic grey-green castle that was to be my home for nine years.

It may sound trite to say that I fell in love with Inveraray at first sight, yet that is what happened. From the moment I stepped out of the car an almost tangible feeling of peace and happiness seemed to come over me. The gardens had become an overgrown, tangled wilderness, but in that lay their beauty. It was, for me, an enchanted place, and Frances and I were soon busy exploring the woodland paths that had been cut for Mary Queen of Scots.

For thirty-five years the castle had been hopelessly neglected by the 10th Duke, a bachelor and a dedicated scholar who had spent all his time in the archives. As a result, the house had become shabby and dilapidated, and the estate had fallen greatly into debt. Even during that first weekend at Inveraray I was aware of anxious and acrimonious meetings going on between Ian and his trustees about the future.

Niall had left death duties of £357,000, plus a legacy of debts amounting to £82,000. Unpaid timber duties and other outstanding bills brought the black total to over half a million pounds. During that summer Ian was, understandably, a desperately worried man.

We were far from sure that Louise would ever agree to a

divorce, but that weekend in June, after seeing Inveraray and its heart-rending deterioration, I decided that, marriage or no marriage, I was going to help Ian clear his Augean Stables and try to make order out of chaos.

But events seemed likely to overtake my good resolutions. Later that summer, a tour which Ian and I made with friends round the chateaux of the Loire was interrupted by an urgent call from the Argyll trustees. Ian rushed back to Scotland and then went off to Rome in search of Paul Getty in a desperate attempt to raise money by selling him a Louis Quinze desk, which was one of the most valuable of the Argyll heirlooms. He failed to find Paul, nor was he able to sell the desk.

Finally Ian came to me one day in London, his face grim, and said that he would have to close Inveraray and take the roof off it. This meant that it would be officially no longer a residence and, therefore, not liable to tax.

Knowing how devoted he was to the castle, I felt desperately sorry for him, and I, too, was crushed by the news. After some thought I decided to go round to the Dorchester and tell my father about the crisis. He listened very carefully, saying little, and then arranged for Ian to see him.

The result of that meeting was that my father eventually agreed to provide about £250,000 towards paying the Argyll death duties. Later he was to give Ian a great deal more to help save Inveraray, and would not accept anything in the nature of a promissory note or an IOU.

This was strangely uncharacteristic of my father with his tough, businesslike mind. But he was convinced that Ian was a gentleman and, as such, would surely repay me if and when he came into any money.

Neither my father nor I was ever to see that money again, and Ian's manifestation of gratitude proved odd, to say the least.

Despite all that happened, however, I am pleased and proud that Inveraray Castle has survived, thanks to my father, who I am sure would echo this sentiment. I am also delighted that my stepson, Ian, the 12th Duke, and his wife Iona, whom I have known since she was a child, are now in residence there. Inveraray is a house that needs to be lived in and loved.

During my first visit Ian and I made a tour of inspection of the castle's eighty-eight rooms. This was no simple matter, for many rooms were too full of furniture and bric-à-brac for us even to open the door. The whole house was cluttered with possessions accumulated by many generations, and nobody had ever thought of getting rid of anything. Victoriana reigned supreme, and we finally turned one room, in which Queen Victoria had slept, into a public apartment called the Victorian Room.

A fire in one of the turrets had left the roof on that side of the house gaping open—and Argyll has one hundred and eighteen inches of rain a year. Dry rot was creeping inexorably through the house, and in another ten years would have demolished it. The very fine display of armour in the hall (eighty feet high) had not been cleaned or polished for sixty years, and it looked like lead. The pictures and family portraits were covered in dust, and many of them had been damaged by the liquid from the fire extinguishers. We discovered that the staff were using odd pieces of Crown Derby china and Waterford glass in the servants' hall, quite unaware of their value. Ian and I were using plates and glass from Woolworth's.

On going through the rooms we came upon beautiful pieces of china and glass in the attics, and it became a fascinating treasure hunt to find a dish in one room, a cup in another, and the matching saucer in the basement. We even had to gather the crystal stoppers and try to fit them on to the fine old decanters.

Once the china, much of it Crown Derby, Sèvres, Limoges and Meissen, was finally mustered and matched, it was arranged for display in the Adam cupboards of one of the turret rooms— known now to the public as the China Room.

After looking at the antiquated stone-floored kitchen and the endless stone passages of the basement, I understood why our meals always arrived lukewarm. Yet that kitchen is now one of the chief attractions to the public, and is filled with shining copper, all of which we discovered in anything but shining condition.

There was no telephone—an instrument distrusted by Ian's eccentric cousin—and there was only an ancient private electric generating plant, which conked out completely and finally the day I arrived, leaving us to rely on paraffin lamps and candles.

It was strange to come into a house that had been lived in by a woman and to find literally no trace of her presence—not even a woman's coathanger. Louise apparently never liked Inveraray and had taken no interest in it.

After the 'Grand Tour' Ian and I returned to the library—the one habitable room in the entire castle—and burst out laughing over the sheer horror facing us. Eventually, Ian asked, 'Where do we start?' I answered, 'We start by you giving me eight of your strongest men at nine o'clock tomorrow morning.'

This he did, but having little faith in my knowledge of valuable furniture (I wonder why?), he accompanied me and my henchmen with boxes of red, green and blue labels. Red meant that the item was to be removed from the house, green meant it had to stay, and blue meant 'Maybe'.

This method at least ensured that I didn't hurl out priceless Chippendale and Hepplewhite furniture that I might not care for.

But even after I had cleared out all the red-labelled junk, the difference was barely noticeable, which is an indication of how overcrowded was every room.

Our biggest headache was a room we christened 'The Nightmare'. It was almost impossible to enter because of two gigantic fourposter beds wedged against the door. When we finally battered our way through, we discovered every inch of space filled with black tin boxes containing hundreds of documents. The 10th Duke, a scholarly recluse with a masterly command of the English language, had kept copies of every letter he had written or received for sixty years. I wanted to burn the lot, but Ian, who had inherited his cousin's respect for history, painstakingly went through the mountain of documents, reading every one. His patience was rewarded, for he found manuscripts of great value, and some hilariously funny ones. Niall Argyll had a rapier-like wit, and his letters to poor Dean Inge and Sir Alfred Mond are masterpieces of verbal annihilation.

Those two weeks at Inveraray were the most physically exhausting I had ever known, and the happiest. For the first time in my life I felt that I was helping someone to do a constructive and important job.

The only break from our labours came when Ian took me to the Gleneagles Hotel Ball for the annual reunion of the 51st

Highland Division. In those days the women were segregated from the men at dinner and dined separately. I considered this an uncivilised custom, and dined upstairs in my room. This may not have endeared me to the other women there, but I hear that these Gleneagles dinners are now integrated.

Ian had been to see Louise in Biarritz to ask again for his freedom, but she was still procrastinating. In January 1951, however, she finally agreed, and the divorce became final on March 10th. Ian and I heard the news at Claridge's where we were lunching with Lady Jeanne Campbell, Ian's daughter by his first wife, Janet Aitken. Ian seemed thrilled and delighted by the news. So was Jeanne—and so, of course, was I.

The day after the celebration lunch, Ian arrived to dine with me, looking surprisingly bad-tempered. Before I could say anything he had launched into a tirade against Frances and Brian, calling them spoilt brats and saying they were hopelessly badly brought up. He went on to vilify my father, my friends, and me. He then announced, for no apparent reason, that he was not going to dine with me and was going to his club, whereupon he marched out, slamming the door after him, and leaving me dumbfounded.

For the whole of the past year Ian and I had not had a cross word between us and he had shown me nothing but gentleness and love. He had also seemed genuinely fond of my children, and they of him. His extraordinary change appeared only a day after his divorce had come through, which was the one thing he had been longing for. I could only put it down to pre-marital nerves. So the next morning I asked him quietly what had caused his outburst the night before. He again became unpleasant and bad-tempered, and remained so for the next forty-eight hours. It soon became apparent that during these evenings he was rather the worse for drink, and it was the first time I had ever seen him like this. I was very worried, but the wedding arrangements had been made (we were to be married quietly at Caxton Hall on March 22nd) and it seemed too late to back out. Or was it?

On the third evening, in great distress, I went to the Dorchester with the intention of seeing my father and asking his advice. It was late, and through the glass door I could see the light shining in his bedroom. I paced up and down the corridor for more than an hour wondering what to do. In the end I did not go in. I knew that if I did, my father would insist that I break off the engagement as he had in the case of Fulke Warwick. I also knew that Ian had given up custody of his two sons in his divorce action, and I thought it would be unfair to him to have allowed him to make that sacrifice if no marriage was to follow.

What I did not realise was that, for almost a year, Ian Argyll had been putting on a great performance worthy of Henry Irving, and that he just could not keep up the act for the last twelve days before our marriage. Mr Hyde had taken over from Dr Jekyll.

Much later, a mutual friend of ours—Air Vice-Marshal (Bill) Thornton—told me of a remark Ian had made to him on the day his divorce became final. 'Now I'll get all my bills paid,' he had said. If only Bill had told me this at the time it might have been the last straw that would have made me change my mind and call the whole thing off.

The one person who did try to warn me, however, was my ex-husband, Charles Sweeny. Just before I married Ian, he wrote to me:

I'll never forget you or love anyone else. I know that now and I also know that nothing I can say or do will change your mind. Therefore . . . I do wish you luck and I hope you'll be happy. I only hope you're not deluding yourself that Campbell is inspired by any great love, because he's not. He couldn't be and you'll be making your crowning mistake if you think anything else. He married his first two wives for money and you're no exception . . .

I hope you wouldn't be so foolish as to contemplate having a child by this alliance. Campbell has never paid any attention or contributed to the upkeep of his children. He didn't even send his son a Christmas wire to St Moritz this year. Therefore, his only interest in a further child would be as an insurance for his old age. Believe me, honey, it's sad but true—so be smart about something for once. . . .

I'll always treasure the love we had for each other and the

happy times we had, and nothing can take that or our children away from me.

My love and hopes for you, darling.

Charles.

It was a sad letter and one that would have wrung my heart had I not received many others from Charlie that had proved meaningless. I later learned that he had been to see Ian's ex-wife, Louise, and it was she who had given him much of the information in his letter about Ian and his children. Even then I did not pay too much attention to his warnings because, obviously, any conversation between an ex-wife and an ex-husband is not apt to be very complimentary about their respective spouses.

So, worried as I was, I resolved to go ahead with the marriage for better or for worse.

A few weeks earlier I had again been voted one of the ten best-dressed women, this time coming third, after the Duchess of Windsor and Princess Marina, Duchess of Kent.

'Mrs Margaret Sweeny,' it was said, 'underplays a beautiful effect instead of overplaying it. Whatever the occasion, you never see her wearing too much jewellery, too many colours or the wrong accessory. She believes in basically simple styles and good materials, beautifully tailored.'

For my wedding I chose a very simple short dress of grey chiffon, with a cloche hat of lime green feathers. I arrived with my father at Caxton Hall on March 22nd to marry Ian, but not looking the traditionally 'radiant bride', I fear.

Frances was at the wedding, and Brian came back especially from Gstaad where he was now at the Marie Jose School.

Ian's cousin, the Earl of Carlisle, was his best man, and my mother managed to come to the wedding in the wheelchair to which her arthritis had now confined her.

The reception was held at my house, and there were about eighty guests including Olive Baillie, Henry and Joan Tiarks, Mrs Magda Buchel and other close friends. Afterwards, Ian and I caught the night train to Glasgow, and breakfasted there next morning at the Central Hotel.

So at about 3.30 on the afternoon of March 23rd, 1951, Duncan MacArthur piped us into Inveraray to the strains of 'The

Campbells Are Coming', and Ian, wearing his Campbell kilt, carried me across the threshold of the castle. I was the first duchess to arrive at Inveraray in this fashion since 1895, when the 8th Duke had carried Ina Erskine McNeill into the castle as a bride.

In the Great Hall were assembled the Provost and Town Council of Inveraray, Ian's chamberlain, his tenants and household staff, and the officers of HMS 'Reclaim', the Admiralty's deep sea diving training ship anchored on Loch Fyne.

The traditional barley bannock was broken over my head, 'for luck and everlasting happiness', and Provost Robert Morrison proposed our health.

'I love coming home,' Ian said in his reply. 'I always love coming back to Inveraray, but I can assure you that I have never loved it as much as I do this time.'

He said this as if he really meant it, and I suddenly felt much happier. Perhaps, after all, the last twelve days had been only a bad dream, and I could now look forward with optimism to the future and to our life together.

Chapter 15

The twelve years of my marriage to Ian Argyll—nine years actually living with him—were explosive, nerve-racking and sometimes terrifying. They were often very, very happy; they were certainly never dull.

It did not take me long to find out that my husband—born on June 18th, 1903—was a true Gemini. He was two people within one body. Each day, from the moment I woke in our bedroom, which looked out over Loch Fyne, I was never sure what his mood would be, and his mood could change within an hour. At his best, no one could radiate more charm or be better company than Ian. He also had the gift of making anything and everything seem interesting—when he felt like it.

Later, when our life together had been poisoned by other people and torn apart by acrimony and jealousy, I still could not forget those first days at Inveraray when we were working hard and perfectly happy to be together in that isolated, beautiful castle.

During my years with him I grew up. He was a man of culture, well informed and with natural good taste. He taught me a great deal about beauty, about art and about life. He was at heart an idle man who had never made use of his many gifts. He was also a brave man, and this was proved during the five years of hunger and cold he suffered in German prisoner-of-war camps.

Since our marriage was to end by making Scottish legal history, it was not inappropriate that we began our life together with a writ. Two writs, in fact. The first, for £4,000, came from Worth, the Paris fashion house. It arrived just before we were married, and may have had something to do with Ian's strange behaviour at that time.

When he finally told me what it was for, I almost laughed. Eighteen months earlier, in a state of euphoria at finally becoming duke, he had agreed to buy his wife a mink coat that he could not possibly afford.

My father was no more pleased than I at the idea of our married life starting off with Ian being publicly sued. He therefore agreed to pay for Louise's fur coat, but this time he wrote out the cheque with some reluctance.

Meanwhile, Ian was convinced that he was sitting on a fortune. In Tobermory Bay, off the Island of Mull, it was said that there lay the remains of a sunken Spanish galleon. Ian firmly believed that the wreck was the payship of the Armada, and had carried aboard all the money to pay the Spanish troops invading Britain. It was also rumoured to have been carrying the crown intended for the Spanish-nominated king of Scotland.

The hoard was said to be worth £40,000,000 in 1951, and, as it was sunk in Argyll waters, Ian intended to lay claim to the lot.

The Royal Navy were constantly dredging Tobermory Bay in an effort to locate the galleon, and the intrepid frogman, 'Buster' Crabbe, was also searching under water.

According to Ian, the Navy were doing the dredging as part of their naval exercises and out of interest in the story. I marvelled at their altruism until I discovered another long brown envelope, hidden by Ian under a cushion in the library at Inveraray. It contained a writ from the Royal Navy for £3,000—the cost of the dredging. This time it was I who wrote out the cheque, again to avoid unpleasant publicity.

The mythical treasure ship was never found in Tobermory Bay, and I deeply resented wasting money that was so badly needed for the upkeep of the castle. For Inveraray was still barely habitable, and I spent the first three weeks of my marriage in overalls. Neighbours who called on me were startled to be told, 'Her Grace is in the attic and is in too much of a mess to receive anybody.' I was busy clearing out the third lot of junk ('red-labelled') and was at last making a noticeable impression on those eighty-eight rooms.

After three weeks of hard work Ian and I left for a belated honeymoon, and motored through France to Madrid. From there we went to Seville for the Feria, a spectacular annual festival which is always held after Easter. The Duke and Duchess of Alba (he is the Premier Duke of Spain) entertained us, and so did Stanton Griffiths, the American Ambassador. In fact there were parties every day and every night. Seville was packed, and the only hotel that we could get into was the Hotel Madrid. There we were given a basement room with a grille above our heads for a window, from which we looked up to watch a constant procession of feet passing along the pavement. None of our friends could get us a better room. Nevertheless, we spent a delightful week in our basement 'pad'. We went on to Granada, Cordoba and Burgos, then motored home via Biarritz. It had been a very happy honeymoon.

On June 29th we were invited to a large dance given by Lord Beaverbrook at Stornoway House for his granddaughter, Lady Jeanne Campbell—Ian's daughter. It was our first public appearance in London since our marriage, and many eyes were upon us. After dancing the first dance with me, to my astonishment Ian danced with his first wife, Janet (Jeanne's mother, now Mrs Thomas Kydd), for most of the evening.

As Ian had never referred to either of his former wives in very complimentary terms, I could only conclude that he was doing this deliberately to humiliate me in public. When I taxed him with it afterwards, he simply said that I was making a fuss about nothing.

Ian changed in many ways. He even seemed to have lost interest in the theatre, films and the opera, all of which he knew I loved. For example, I managed to get a box—no easy matter—for Kirsten Flagstad's farewell performance in *Tristan und Isolde*. Frances and Brian came with us. In the box Ian suddenly said, 'I've never liked the second act,' and went off to spend the rest of the evening at White's. Such incidents became quite commonplace, and it seemed that Ian was only happy in his clubs—in London, White's and St. James's; in Paris, the Travellers'.

During the summer of 1951 I went into the London Clinic for quite a serious operation on my sinus. Ian was in the room when I came to, and his first words were, 'It's going to be a bloody nuisance having to come up here every day. It's miles from the club.' The London Clinic is ten minutes by taxi from either White's or the St. James's.

I soon realised that the people of the Royal Burgh of Inveraray welcomed the idea of having a young and active duchess in their midst. The last Duchess of Argyll to have spent any appreciable time in the castle had been Queen Victoria's daughter, Princess Louise, forty years earlier. Her husband became Governor-General of Canada. One of the first things I did was to call a meeting of the Town Council, and I discovered that lack of entertainment was a serious local problem.

The people's only diversion in that beautiful, isolated highland town was a mobile cinema that came once a fortnight and showed very old, flickering black and white films. With Ian's permission I converted the local drill hall into a permanent cinema, providing all the equipment myself. I also undertook to arrange the bookings from London and ensure that the very latest West End films were shown at Inveraray four times a week.

All five hundred and twenty-one residents of the town seemed delighted by this innovation, and the Argyll Cinema was officially opened in the first week of September. Everyone was at the drill hall for this occasion—Ian and myself, of course; the Provost and his wife, the Town Councillors, Frances and Brian, and Ian's elder son, the fourteen-year-old Marquis of Lorne.

While young Ian and my children were with us, I invited some other children of their age to stay. Jean-Luis Faucigny de Lucinge (son of Princess Faucigny de Lucinge, who was Brian's godmother), Derry Moore (the Droghedas' son), and others visited us. I gave Frances a dachshund puppy, Ian a spaniel puppy and Brian a labrador puppy, which I thought would be a great joy to them. I also gave myself a poodle puppy called Gaston, who is now buried with a very fine headstone in the gardens of Inveraray.

This was our first summer together and I was most anxious to make it as happy as possible, but Ian. Lorne was sullen and obviously resentful of both his father and myself.

Ian discovered letters in his son's bedroom that showed only too clearly how he was being poisoned against us both. This worried us very much indeed, so one afternoon I took young Ian out alone for a drive, and tried to put things right. I pointed out that I realised he didn't like me, but that I was not the cause of his parents choosing to live apart, since this had begun long before I met his father.

He looked away from me and did not answer.

I then said, 'I suggest we make a pact. You needn't like me, but I do think it very important that you spend a lot of time at Inveraray with your father—he needs you. If you would rather not come while I am here, just write to me saying when you are arriving, and I will go to my house in London so that you can be alone with your father.'

He turned to me in tears. 'That wouldn't be very nice of me, would it?'

After that I hoped so much that we could be friends from then on.

In spite of my father's generosity, and an important sale by the trustees of farms on the Kintyre part of the estate which raised £200,000, money was still urgently needed to restore the castle. It was I who suggested to Ian the possibility of opening Inveraray to the public, and he was full of enthusiasm. The trustees, however, opposed the idea, but we finally persuaded them that it was the only way to make the castle pay for itself. It was a gamble, but one that proved to be most profitable. (In 1974 I read with delight that 119,000 tourists had visited Inveraray Castle.) Forty workmen moved in, and remained with us for eighteen months.

In February 1952, Ian and I left for the Bahamas. We had been invited by Olive Baillie to stay as her guests at her house in Nassau. It was this trip that brought my marriage to its first real crisis. Ian was in a vile temper from the first day to the last. He was simply not recognisable as the man I had married a year before. He was openly rude and sadistic towards me. Olive was horrified, and two of her guests, who were dear friends of mine (David Margesson and Geoffrey Lloyd), were so angered by what they observed that they took Ian aside and remonstrated with him. But by now Ian had become very arrogant, and no one could mediate. After ten days in Nassau we went on to stay with friends of his in Havana, Cuba, where things got steadily worse. From Cuba we flew to Kingston, Jamaica, to stay with Bobby (now Sir Robert) Kirkwood. There followed one night of acute embarrassment when Bobby had to come into our bedroom and intervene to prevent Ian from beating me up.

When we returned to London I went immediately to see my parents and told them of Ian's extraordinary behaviour. My father showed no signs of surprise, saying, 'Do you really not know what's causing the trouble? It's drink. Whenever I see Ian at White's he is never without a glass in his hand at any hour of the day or night. I'm afraid you have married an alcoholic, and your only hope of saving your marriage is to get him off the bottle.'

When I heard this I felt almost relieved. At least I now knew what I was facing, and understood the cause of all those unreasonable and unpredictable changes of mood.

Bill Thornton, a close mutual friend of ours, later told me that Ian had always started drinking every morning at ten o'clock, usually with a tumbler of neat gin. I asked Bill why he had not told me of this. 'I didn't want to upset you,' he said, 'and in any case I thought you already knew.' But I had not known, because I had never had to cope with a drink problem before, and Ian rarely looked or sounded drunk. From then on I watched his drinking with an eagle eye, and, strangely enough, things began to improve between us.

On April 25th, 1953, with the daffodils in full bloom, Inveraray at last opened its doors to the public. It was a glorious spring day, and the pipe band of the Argyll and Sutherland Highlanders played in the castle grounds under the command of a handsome young captain called Colin Mitchell. Fifteen years later, as 'Mad Mitch', he was to become the scourge of the Aden terrorists, a leader of the campaign to 'Save the Argylls' from disbandment, a Member of Parliament, and a great friend of mine.

Once the castle was opened, Ian and I went to London to prepare for the Queen's Coronation. There are no jewels in the Argyll family, since Princess Louise had left them all to the Duke of Kent on her death in 1939. But my parents had given me a diamond tiara, and I was lucky to have other jewellery of my own. There were no Argyll Duchess's robes, either, as the last ones had been made for Princess Louise in Royal purple, and these were worn at the Coronation by Princess Marina, Duchess of Kent. My robes, therefore, in red velvet and white ermine, were specially made for the occasion by Victor Stiebel, who also designed the silver dress that I wore under the robes.

I believe that I was the only Peeress in the Abbey who had to buy a new dress and new robes for this 'once in a lifetime' occasion.

I also had to borrow a coronet from Clare, Duchess of Sutherland, who luckily had two.

Coronation Day, June 2nd, 1953, began very early for us, for we were told to be in our places at Westminster Abbey by six a.m. To my delight I found that my seat—next to the Duchess of Portland, and at the end of the front row of the peeresses—was the best in the Abbey. It was within a few feet of the Queen, and I had an uninterrupted view of her throughout the entire service. By coincidence Ian was seated next to the Duke of Rutland, my future son-in-law.

We had been advised to come fortified with malted milk tablets, and these I chewed constantly, unaware that the television cameras were upon me. I fear my busy jaw must have been quite a talking point in many homes.

The Abbey was a scene of perfect splendour, but my most vivid recollection is of the Queen's humility at the moment of her anointing when, wearing only a simple shift, she bowed to the four corners of the Abbey, dedicating herself to her people. She looked so young, so feminine and so full of dignity.

That evening Ian and I were invited to an official dinner at the French Embassy given by the French Ambassador and his wife, Madame Massigli. The day had been a perfect one until Ian began dressing for dinner. My heart sank. It was obvious from his expression that his mood had changed drastically for the worse. I kept very quiet, and cheered myself up by thinking that this was one dinner that Ian would not dare to 'chuck'. The traffic was chaotic, and when we were forced to make a detour Ian suddenly said, 'I'm not going to sit in this damned car any longer. If you want to go to the Embassy you can go by yourself.' He then got out of the car, slammed the door and stalked off to spend the evening at White's.

Odette Massigli was most tactful when I made the same old excuse of 'a sudden cold' for Ian, but not having him at the dinner ruined what should have been a perfect day.

I was beginning to realise that this last-minute 'chucking' of engagements was a pattern that would run all through our marriage, becoming worse as time went on. It was only one of the many twists in the character of the strange man I had married.

Chapter 16

After the opening of Inveraray Castle to the public, my life with Ian became much happier.

In the first eighteen months of our marriage, apart from some spasmodic and rather dilettante research among the castle archives, Ian had done little beyond lying on a sofa smoking a cigarette in a long holder. Now, at last, he had an interest in life, and as thousands of people came (paying half a crown a time) to see the castle, Ian worked very hard to help make Inveraray's first open season the great success it was.

Once the castle was closed again, in October, his lethargy returned and he resumed his drinking. He became so trying to live with that I finally felt I must have a break, so I accepted an invitation to stay with mutual friends of ours, Mr and Mrs Ben Kittredge, in Charleston, South Carolina.

On February 2nd, 1954, the eve of my departure for America, Ian and I were in London and we had arranged to go out for dinner together. At about 6.30 that evening, however, he came back to the house from White's Club rather the worse for wear. He announced that he was not taking me out to dinner anywhere, and went out again. David Rose, head of Paramount Pictures in Britain, was in the house for cocktails at the time, and after hearing Ian's outburst he at once offered to take me out to dinner himself. We returned home at about 10.30 to find the police and a crowd of reporters outside the front door. The police inspctor told me that the house had been broken into. A cat burglar had shinned up the back of the house, over the roof and into my bedroom where he had taken every piece of jewellery that I owned, none of which was insured. I went into the house followed by several of the newspaper men, who were asking, 'Where is the Duke?' I said that he was at a business dinner and would be returning shortly. At that moment Ian appeared from the library upstairs, very drunk, and fell down the stairs, landing in the hall in the middle of the police and reporters.

The *Daily Express* and *Daily Mail* representatives helped him to his feet, showing no surprise. Later, when Ian had gone upstairs, the reporters assured me that they would not mention the incident, and they kept their word, for which I was truly thankful.

Early the next morning, much to my surprise, Ian was up and dressed, insisting on coming to see me off on the boat train. I spent a happy ten days in New York as the guest of the Gilbert Millers, and then flew to Charleston, where I had an enchanting visit. I was most interested to be shown the plaque dedicated to a former Duke of Argyll who had been the last Governor of South Carolina.

After my return to London Ian's behaviour continued to be erratic and unpredictable. Although I consulted him about every invitation we received, the answer he gave me never had any bearing on his ultimate decision.

The most bizarre example of this was over a dinner dance which the Duke and Duchess of Sutherland gave at Sutton Place. I had refused the invitation, since Ian had said that such evenings did not amuse him. He then heard from his friends what a good party it was going to be, and told me to call Clare Sutherland and tell her that we would like to come after all. I asked Ian if he was quite sure, and pointed out to him that Clare would have to rearrange her entire dinner table. But Ian was adamant. So I called Clare, who was extremely understanding about the whole situation. The day arrived, and one hour before we were due to leave for Sutton Place Ian refused to go. Once again I had the embarrassment of having to invent excuses for my absent husband.

Even more difficult to cope with was the uncertainty as to

whether Ian would turn up at our own dinner parties. Sometimes he didn't.

In the week of the Queen's Coronation, Perle Mesta, the famous American hostess who had been the US Ambassador to Luxembourg, gave a ball in London, at Londonderry House. I had arranged a dinner party beforehand at 48, Upper Grosvenor Street for eighteen guests. The dinner was due to start at eight o'clock. While I was dressing, Ian returned from White's saying that he did not intend to come to the dinner. After some persuasion on my part he reluctantly appeared at the head of his own table, dressed in a grey flannel suit. After dinner he changed and came with me to Perle Mesta's ball, where he thoroughly enjoyed himself. By the time we got home he had forgotten all about his tantrum of a few hours earlier.

In February 1955, while Ian and I were touring in Morocco, I received a cable from my father saying that my mother was seriously ill. Her condition had been gradually deteriorating for several months. We hurried home to London, and soon afterwards my mother passed into a coma from which, mercifully, she never emerged. She died peacefully on February 27th, and I was thankful for her release from the constant pain she had suffered for so many years. Although my mother and I had not agreed on everything, I loved her and was as proud of her as she was of me. I miss her to this day.

Her death left my father distraught and lost. They had been married for almost fifty years, and during the last fifteen years of her life he had scarcely left her for more than a few hours. Now that she was gone he was desperately lonely.

It has always been my regret that I was not able to stay with him and look after him during this time, but I was already torn between trying to run Inveraray and a London house, coping with Ian and bringing up two children.

Soon after my mother died I took Frances to Buckingham Palace for her presentation at Court. As I was in mourning I had to wear black. I also had to be presented to the Queen myself as Duchess of Argyll—by one of my dearest friends, Lady d'Avigdor Goldsmid, whose bridesmaid I had been at her first wedding to Peter Horlick.

As I once more entered the white and gold State Ballroom, it was brought home to me how the splendour of the 1930s had vanished for ever. Gone were the beautiful evening dresses and jewels of the women and the dress uniforms of the men. Debutantes were now presented at afternoon parties, and it was therefore in a short dress that Frances made her curtsey to the Queen, the Duke of Edinburgh, the Duke and Duchess of Gloucester and the Princess Royal.

At eighteen my daughter had become an enchanting beauty. She had completed her education in Florence and Paris, and spoke perfect Italian and French. At the coming-out ball I gave for her that summer she wore a dress designed for her by Norman Hartnell. It was held in the ballroom at Claridge's, which I transformed by turning out the overhead chandeliers and masking the wall lights with pink. There were pink candles on the dinner tables, pink table cloths and pink flowers. A hundred guests were invited for the dinner, and seven hundred for the dance afterwards. I engaged the Deep River Boys as a cabaret, and our piper from Inveraray, Ronnie McCallum, was there to play Highland Reels, which were then very popular with the young, even in London.

The dancing went on until I stopped the band at five a.m. Later, as we sat gossiping on my bed, Frances said, 'What a marvellous party it was, Mummy. I wish we could have another one tonight.'

Frances had a very gay season, and during it she and Charles (Viscount) Chelsea fell in love and wanted to become engaged. His parents, the Earl and Countess Cadogan, were against this for the sole reason that she was a Roman Catholic. Frances was obviously upset over this, and I was very angry. To cheer her up I said, 'It's their loss and not yours. You'll get over it if you just give yourself time—in fact it may all be for the best.'

In a short time I was proved right, for Frances made a very happy marriage.

During that summer I was much impressed to learn (not from her) that Frances was going once a week with her priest to do welfare work among the poor of London's East End. I could not help but contrast this with the butterfly existence my friends and I had led as debutantes. My daughter's generation was obviously more serious and less selfish than my own.

That summer Queen Frederika of Greece asked Stavros Niarchos to arrange the famous VIP cruise whose aim was to show off the glories of Greece—then comparatively unknown—to foreigners. Elsa Maxwell, who was arranging the guest list, invited Ian and me to join the one hundred and eight people on board the ship 'Achilleus' on its cruise among the Greek islands.

When I showed Ian Elsa's letter I expected him to refuse immediately, but to my amazement he was thrilled at the idea. 'I've never been to Greece before, and I would love to go,' he said. I therefore accepted for both of us, and asked if I could bring Frances and Brian as well. They were now eighteen and fifteen respectively, and I had a feeling that there would not be only the 'jet set' on board. I had heard that we would have four archaeologists on the trip to lecture us and be our guides. Altogether I felt it would be a wonderful experience for both the children and for us.

Ten days before we were due to join the 'Achilleus' in Venice we came down from Inveraray to prepare for the cruise. I said, 'Aren't you going to start packing, Ian?' 'Pack? What for? If you think I'm going with you on that cruise you must be out of your mind.'

This time I was reduced to tears, which I believe was exactly what he wanted. Ian had a markedly sadistic streak in his character. Things like this were done deliberately to hurt me, and hurt me they always did. I realise now that if I had not given him the satisfaction of knowing this, Ian would have been deprived of much pleasure.

Finally the children and I left without him, and the joy had already gone out of the trip for me. But the cruise was beautifully organised, with museums and palaces opened specially for us, and picnics arranged on the various islands we visited. These picnics were often accompanied by the playing of local musicians. As a highlight of the trip we were presented to King Paul and Queen Frederika, who were most charming and hospitable.

Stavros and Eugenie Niarchos accompanied the 'Achilleus' in their own yacht, the 'Creole', throughout the cruise, and invited us on board almost every day for caviar and champagne.

Ian had neither written nor cabled me during the entire three weeks of the cruise, but he was at the airport in London to meet us on our return. I soon learned that Inveraray was once again in trouble. In spite of my father's help, and the thousands of tourists coming to the castle, the estate was still badly in debt to the tune of £100,000 and in danger of being closed.

I did not dare approach my father again for, generous though he was, he was getting tired of paying out for Inveraray. In fact, I think he began to wonder where the money was going and if I was squandering it on mink coats and diamond bracelets for myself.

Later on I had to explain to him that it was I who was paying for the redecoration and running of the private part of the castle in which we lived, as well as for my London house.

I was also paying for my children's upbringing and education, though Charlie paid for Brian's fees at Oxford.

So I, too, was nearing the end of my resources, and one terrible day we decided that Inveraray would have to be closed and that we should live in the London house.

This was a real tragedy, for I knew that it would be well-nigh impossible to reopen the castle, and that without the interest of Inveraray Ian would go to pieces.

Ian had always regretted that there was no Argyll House in London lived in by a Duke of Argyll, and early in our marriage he asked me if I would object to calling 48, Upper Grosvenor Street 'Argyll House'. I readily agreed as I was most anxious that he should feel that my house was now 'our' house. I have always hated the word 'my', and forbade the children ever to use it.

Being only too well aware of my gullibility, my father kept the lease of 48, Upper Grosvenor Street in his name until he died, even though he had given the house to me to live in for as long as I chose.

Although he was most displeased at his property being called 'Argyll House', he understood the reasons for my decision.

On the afternoon of February 27th, 1956, I received a telephone call in my London library. It was from a solicitor, a Mr Attenborough, asking to speak to the Duke of Argyll. Ian was out, and I asked Mr Attenborough if he could please tell me what the matter was about. After he knew who I was he did tell me, and it was a miracle. A Miss Campbell, whom Ian had never even met, had died and left him £40,000 to be used for the good of the Clan Campbell.

I immediately telephoned Ian at White's and said to him. 'Get yourself a chair and sit down on it.' I then told him the news. Like me, he could hardly believe it, and was absolutely thrilled.

It would still be a struggle, but with the £40,000 we could save Inveraray and keep it open to the public. Our troubles, I thought, were over. I was wrong. Within a year they really began.

Chapter 17

Ian had never shown much interest in visiting his farms in Kintyre or the islands he owned off the coast of Argyll. In May, 1956, however, I managed to persuade him to visit Tiree, one of his islands, where he had not been since becoming Duke.

Ian wanted to make it a very cursory tour, but before we went I told our factor that I was most anxious to visit as many cottages and meet as many people on the island as possible; otherwise I saw no point in going.

The islanders were obviously delighted to see us, and there was one dear old man whom I especially remember. He lived alone, bedridden, in a 'black house' (a thatched cottage with rounded corners) and had never left Tiree in his life. I sat and talked to him for a long time, and he was thrilled when I told him about flying the Atlantic in a jet plane. He asked me many questions about life in America.

By now, Inveraray Castle looked very different from the neglected place I had first entered six years earlier. Ian had tamed the wilderness of the garden into Victorian neatness and order. I rather regretted this, but when the azaleas and rhododendrons were in full bloom, and the ground was a carpet of bluebells, it was one of the loveliest places in the world.

Inside the castle the impressive armour in the hall was now clean and polished, and all the china was well displayed in one of the round turret rooms. The fireplaces, which had been specially designed for the castle by James Adam, were magnificently restored to their rightful place. For Princess Louise, who never liked Inveraray, had spent little time there. She preferred to live at Rosneath, another Argyll residence, on the Clyde, and she had transferred the fireplaces there from Inveraray to Rosneath. The year after our marriage Ian heard that there was to be an auction of the contents of Rosneath before it was demolished. We motored over the day before the sale, and Ian charmed the auctioneer into selling us all the twenty Adam fireplaces for £50. And that is how they returned to the house for which they had been designed—Inveraray Castle.

The Argyll Cinema, instigated by me five years earlier, was proving a great success. I had many other dreams for renovating the town of Inveraray, one of the most beautiful in Scotland. I would have liked to see all the Georgian houses painted white, baskets of flowers hanging from the lamp posts, and the church steeple—knocked down in the war—replaced. Much of this work was too expensive for me to realise personally, but I did make a start by donating a church clock, and the church was repainted inside from the proceeds of the cinema.

I was invited to become a member of the Inveraray Town Council, and I was anxious to accept, but Ian vetoed the idea. He said that no duchess had ever been on the Council and that it was 'beneath me'. I totally disagreed with him, but he was 'the boss'.

At about this time there was a grave danger that the 18th-century town of Inveraray, designed as an entity by Robert Mylne would be pulled down and replaced by modern Council houses Ian and I were most concerned about this, and he called up the Earl of Dundee, former Secretary of State for Scotland, to ask for his help in saving the town. Thanks almost entirely to Jim Dundee, and Ian's determination, the Government provided a grant of £100,000 to the Royal Burgh, which is now preserved because of its ancient and historic interest.

At the request of Lord Malcolm Douglas-Hamilton I had become the London 'Appeals President' of the Highland Fund, an important project designed to re-people the deserted glens by lending poor farmers and crofters money to encourage them to return to make a living in the Highlands. Ian showed no interest in this admirable scheme, and it was only by cajoling that I persuaded him to head the Committee in a titular capacity. Later it took me ten days to get him to sign the short word 'Argyll' on a hundred appeal leaflets.

We visited Alwyne, the Farquharson of Invercauld and his wife, Frances, an old friend of mine. I was most impressed to see how much they had done to revive the home industries on Deeside, and I became fired with enthusiasm to do the same for Inveraray. The old craft of clockmaking, for which Inveraray was once famous, had unfortunately died out, but the local tweed industry was still very much alive. Captain Alexander McIntyre and his wife, May, ran one of the finest tweed shops in Scotland. (It was there that I bought all my tartans.) I suggested that with my help they could begin exporting these tweeds. I then went to Paris, armed with bundles of patterns, and returned with surprisingly large orders from Dior, Balmain, Molyneux and Balenciaga. I thought that this could be the start of a thriving trade between Inveraray and France, but my Lowland mind had reckoned without the Highland psychology. On my next trip to Paris I was told that none of the tweeds ordered had arrived. Returning to Inveraray I discovered that nobody there had known how to fill in the export forms, and they had just abandoned the whole idea. So much for my plan for 'Inveraray exports'!

On August 12th, 1956, Ian and I went to Iona for the visit of the Queen, Prince Philip and Princess Margaret. I felt sorry for Ian on that day. Iona was one of his islands and the honour of receiving the Queen and showing her round should have been his. But Ian's two divorces, in each of which he had been the guilty party, barred him from being the Lord Lieutenant of Argyll. Sir Charles ('Chips') Maclean—now Lord Maclean, the present Lord Chamberlain—instead held that office, and it was he, not Ian, who escorted the Queen around Iona.

I had a busy summer in London that year entertaining for Frances. Also, as President of the Royal College of Midwives, I was present when the Queen Mother laid the foundation stone of the College's new headquarters in Mansfield Street. Being as busy as I was, and knowing how lonely my father must be, I was hoping that he would remarry. I also knew a charming woman who was not at all averse to the idea, and who would have given him just the life he enjoyed. When I suggested it to my father his reply was, 'I can't marry her. She's got too damn much money.' An unorthodox answer, perhaps, but typical of him.

So, when on October 31st that year I received a telephone call at Inveraray from my father to say that he had married again very quietly at Caxton Hall, just that morning, I was startled. I had only met the lady in question once with my father. My new stepmother was Mrs Jane Brooke (a name she had taken by deed poll), who was thirty-five years younger than my father.

My mother had been dead for almost two years, and I certainly did not begrudge my father any chance of happiness, but I was worried about the age difference. Moreover Jane was not the person I would have expected him to marry. On the morning after his marriage—which was not made public for nearly two years—I received a letter from him:

You must have been surprised when I phoned you this morning but as I told you I have been pretty lonely and aimless since poor Mummy died and I feel I need a companion and someone who will pull me up and take care of me in my old age and I think Jane Brooke (as she was) is the one to do it. There is not a trace of romance in the whole thing . . . I purposely kept it quiet as I did not want publicity at my age, so don't feel hurt on that score. I would have liked you and Ian to have been there but that would soon have leaked out. My marriage will not in *any* way affect my love for you or anything else as far as you and I are concerned—no one can ever take your place in my affection.

Daddy.

As a PS he had written, 'I want you very much to like her.'

I, too, wanted to like Jane—for his sake—and I gave a celebration dinner party for them both in London two weeks later. I then invited them to stay at Inveraray, and did everything possible to welcome Jane into the family. My only wish was that Jane should make my father happy for the last years of his life. Sadly, this was not the case.

Soon afterwards Ian and I went to dine with Judge John Maude and his wife, Maureen. She and I had known each other for many years—she was a guest at my wedding to Charlie, at which her first husband, the Marquis of Dufferin and Ava, was an usher. Her sister, Aileen Plunkett, was also an old friend of mine. On the night we dined with the Maudes, almost the first question I asked was how they were getting along with their new secretary.

The secretary in question was Yvonne MacPherson, widow of Ian's fellow prisoner-of-war, Brigadier Clunie MacPherson. As he died after the war and not in action, Yvonne's pension was very small indeed, and Ian suggested that she become my secretary and also do any work necessary for him while he was in London. This seemed to be a good idea and I agreed. Yvonne proved to be an excellent secretary, and I liked her. It was arranged that Ian should pay her for any work she did for him, while I paid her for all the rest.

After about five months I was horrified to learn from her that Ian had paid her nothing at all. I tackled him about this, which put him in a very bad temper. When he still gave her nothing I paid Yvonne for what Ian owed her, and she was extremely grateful. I also tried to make Yvonne feel as if she were part of the family, and invited her to Inveraray and to several of my dinners in London.

After Frances had made her debut in the summer of 1955 there was almost nothing for Yvonne to do. When I told her, as tactfully as I could, that I had no further need for a full-time secretary, she burst into tears saying, 'I shall never be able to find another job like this. What am I going to live on?' She upset me so much that I promised to keep her in my employ until I could find her another job—yet another drain on my finances.

The following year I met Maureen and John Maude at a cocktail party and they mentioned that they were looking for a secretary. I told them that I had the ideal person for the job, and gave Yvonne the highest possible recommendation. I prayed that the Maudes would engage her and relieve me of the responsibility. They did, and now, while we were dining with the Maudes, they told me that Yvonne had proved to be most satisfactory.

In the autumn of 1956 Ian had a bad attack of influenza, which left him feeling weak and depressed. On the recommendation of our mutual friend, Bill Thornton, we called in a new doctor, John Petro. He told Ian to take two blue pills a day as a tonic, which he did. After a few weeks I noticed an extraordinary change in him. He was losing a great deal of weight, was eating almost nothing, and had become strangely garrulous. He would talk ceaselessly, sometimes far into the night, in a rambling way, and kept referring to his early childhood.

Ian's behaviour worried and puzzled me until I discovered that the blue pills were in fact drinamyl (purple hearts), an amphetamine drug that can be dangerous and should be taken very sparingly—if at all. Ian had been taking, on a doctor's prescription, two a day for weeks.

One morning in January, 1957, he suddenly announced that he was leaving me, and for no apparent reason. He seemed quite sober, but his eyes had a strange, staring look. I was stunned, because nothing had happened that morning to cause such a crisis. Pleading was useless, and he left me after a few minutes, saying, 'By the time you get home this afternoon I shall be gone.'

I immediately telephoned Petro and told him about Ian's behaviour, how he had looked and what had just happened. I also insisted that he stop giving Ian the drinamyl tablets. Petro said, 'I shall continue the dose of two a day for as long as I think fit. They are quite harmless.'

When I returned home in the afternoon I found that Ian had gone as he had threatened, leaving no address. I telephoned Inveraray and White's, but no one knew where he was. I finally discovered that he was staying, under another name, at Claridge's.

As I came back to the house one evening, I found a reporter waiting on the doorstep. He said, 'We hear that the Duke has left you.' I told him, 'The Duke is staying at Claridge's for a few days because the painters are in the house and he hates the smell of paint.'

The reporter looked puzzled, and said, 'This is very odd. I was told that the story came from a former secretary of the Duke. I'm sorry to have bothered you about it.'

I then telephoned Claridge's and got through to Ian—with great difficulty, because of his incognito. I said, 'The Press have discovered that you have left this house, and they seem to think that the story came from a former secretary of yours. I know that you are seeing quite a lot of Yvonne at the moment. Do you think she has mentioned it to anybody?'

Ian denied the suggestion irritably and said that she would never do such a thing. Ten minutes later he called me back, saying, 'Margaret, will you just repeat what you said about Yvonne?' There was a faint click, as though a telephone extension was being picked up, and I suddenly felt apprehensive.

'There is no need for me to repeat anything,' I replied. 'You heard quite well what I said.'

Ian continued to stay at Claridge's, but each morning he came to Upper Grosvenor Street to open his letters and work in the library. It was the most bizarre situation, but I kept very quiet and left him alone.

On January 24th, three days after he left the house, I gave a dinner party planned long beforehand, but I now had no idea whether Ian would appear. To my surprise he did.

After one glass of sherry he made no sense at all, talking everybody down in a very loud voice throughout dinner. He told Duncan Sandys, who was then Minister of Defence, and Sir Humphrey Trevelyan, now Lord Trevelyan, how to run their affairs. Everyone was horribly embarrassed, and my guests had all left by 10.30. As he said goodbye, David Kilmuir, the Lord Chancellor, whispered to me, 'Ian is obviously ill. He must have a doctor.'

'He *has* a doctor', I said. 'That's the trouble.'

After the dinner Ian once again left the house to spend the night at Claridge's. The following morning he returned and said, 'I am going to Paris. I don't know how long I shall be there, but I want to be left quite alone. Please don't try to follow me or telephone me.' I said nothing except to beg him to stop taking the drinamyl. He promised to do this.

Four days later, to my great relief, a telegram arrived from him asking me to come over. I prepared to leave immediately, and told my family doctor, who knew the whole story, about Ian's telegram. He warned me that if Ian had really stopped taking the pills he would be quite ill and in a state of deep depression for a long time. He advised me to humour him like a child and to agree with everything he said, however unreasonable or ridiculous.

What I was facing was made plain when I arrived at the Ritz in Paris. I found a note from Ian saying that he had booked a room for me, and had paid for it, but that he was staying at the Travellers' Club.

Within half an hour he telephoned me and asked me to dine with him, to which I immediately agreed. He arrived with his luggage, and moved in with me. I asked for no explanation.

As soon as I saw him I realised that he was very ill, and was obviously suffering from the terrible let-down predicted by my doctor. My only thought was to get him home—quickly.

The following day we returned to London, and as soon as possible I arranged that we should go to Inveraray. When we were alone there Ian was gentle and loving, and I hoped that at last he was recovering. One night he woke up, turned to me and asked, almost pathetically, 'Maggie, why did I ever go to Claridge's?' I said, 'Because you were very ill, Ian.' I began to realise then how insidious were the effects of those pills.

'Doctor' John Petro had a lot to answer for, and when finally he was sent to prison I could not be sorry that the law had caught up with him.

Back in London several weeks later I received a call from a friend of mine, Magda Buchel, a cousin of the Duke of Norfolk. Magda was always 'dropping in', so I was not surprised when she asked if she could come round at five o'clock that afternoon. She had only been in the drawing-room for a few minutes when Ian walked in unexpectedly. He did not like Magda and usually tried to avoid her.

To my astonishment, he was followed into the room by Yvonne MacPherson. He then said, 'I have brought Yvonne here for you to apologise to her for the allegations you made about her giving information to the press.' I then got up from my chair and walked out of the drawing-room and upstairs to my bedroom, closing the door behind me.

Ian yelled up to me, 'Come downstairs and stop acting like a coward. You're a yellow-belly.'

If only I had ignored the scene and stayed in my bedroom, years of unhappiness and litigation would have been avoided. But with my children and the servants in the house I could hardly allow Ian to go on yelling at me for all to hear. I also thought he was having some sort of a brainstorm and that I had better go down and try to calm him.

So I made the great mistake of returning to the drawing-room. I advised Magda to leave, saying that I did not want to involve her in the ugly scene that was obviously pending. 'It's all right, Margaret,' she replied, looking very uncomfortable.

Ian immediately said, 'You accused Yvonne of telling the newspapers that I had left you.' I replied that I had merely repeated what the reporter had told me, and asked whether he thought Yvonne might have mentioned it to anyone.

Yvonne was very busy taking notes in shorthand, and demanding an apology, which I refused to give. I had told the truth, and spoken only to my husband.

I then said to Yvonne that if she ever appeared in my house again she would be shown the door. She and Magda then left.

All this seemed to me very trivial and petty, but it was to become the foundation upon which many lawsuits and years of calumny were based.

Two years afterwards my husband told me that he had deliberately invited Magda Buchel that afternoon to try to trap me into making a statement in her presence. He even admitted it by letter to my solicitor:

Argyll House
Upper Grosvenor Street
London, W.1.
26.4.59

Dear Jobson,

Yesterday my wife told me that she did not know that Mrs. Buchel had been invited by me to be present at an interview between my wife and Mrs. MacPherson.

I twice telephoned to Mrs. Buchel to ask her to come to this house at 5 o'clock on the day in question to be a witness to Mrs. MacPherson's demand for an apology after a repetition of my wife's original statement.

Yours sincerely,
Argyll.

Not then realising I had walked blindly into a trap laid for me by my husband, I dined alone with him that evening. To my surprise he made no reference to the episode. I became anxious that he and I should take a holiday together. So in March we left for Florence, and planned to motor around Tuscany. It should have been a pleasant and happy trip, but throughout it I felt uneasy, and I had a premonition that something unpleasant was brewing.

I also knew that Ian was writing to Yvonne, which did not make me feel any happier.

On our return to London my premonition was certainly justified, for there was a letter awaiting me from Yvonne's lawyer, claiming damages. Mrs MacPherson's modest income seemed to have stretched, for she wrote to her new friend, Magda Buchel:

> There is no violent hurry for me. I am taking advice and I may say that my further decisions will not be governed by lack of finance.

She also added that she had told her employers, Maureen and John Maude, all about it, and that they were most understanding.

I could not believe that Maureen would continue to employ any woman she had known for only a year who was attacking a friend of long standing, but she and John did continue to employ Mrs MacPherson. As the summer wore on I was left in no doubt about where their support lay.

Ian continued to insist that I apologise to Yvonne, which I refused to do. He told my solicitor, Cecil Jobson, that he was determined I should 'eat humble pie'. He repeated this in a most unpleasant letter to my father, who answered him on June 25th as follows:

> Dear Ian,
>
> After our talk at the club I received your letter of May 28th and I wish first of all to say that I deeply resent my daughter being accused of lying and also of having been responsible for the 'mess' and your suggestion that she should 'eat humble pie' and apologise. I was completely disgusted at the tone and gist of your letter, so much so that I did not reply to it until now as I was determined to get to the bottom of things. I have made many enquiries and sounded out various people, some of them our mutual friends, and in my opinion you and *not* Margaret are responsible for this 'mess' by your going behind her

back and repeating confidential conversations she had with you as man and wife. I consider that your behaviour, especially recently, has been despicable and cowardly and that you have been completely disloyal to Margaret. I may add that Margaret has been a very popular and respected member of London society for over twenty-five years. I do not expect you to reply to this letter.

Yours,
G. H. Whigham.

In his letter to my father, Ian had used one significant sentence: 'Mrs MacPherson has no legitimate claim for damages in my opinion.'

Indeed she had not; how could she have been damaged, since she was still in the job which I had managed to get for her?

Yet Yvonne was demanding damages. The figure had started at £600 and quickly risen to £5,000. Ian was shaken when he heard this, and he went round to see her and reason with her, but she had now got the bit between her teeth—at last Ian realised just what he had started.

Outwardly our lives went on as if nothing was wrong. We went to the State Opening of Parliament. I appeared in the 'Pageant of Fabulous Beauties down the Ages' held at Sir Alfred Bossom's house as Marie Antoinette, wearing the necklace that had belonged to her. This had been lent to me by the Duchess of Sutherland.

On November 1st, 1957, Yvonne MacPherson issued a writ against me for libel and slander. The libel pertained to a mysterious telegram, which was the subject of the case when it finally came to court.

The battle was on!

Chapter 18

Ivor Griffiths, a renowned Harley Street throat specialist, telephoned me one day and asked me to call and see him. He said, 'I think you should know that a man called Petro, who is apparently Ian's doctor, has been trying to get me to sign a paper certifying you as being insane. He went on to say that Ian believed your fall down the lift shaft in 1943 had caused brain damage, and that this was the reason for your refusal to apologise to Yvonne MacPherson.'

Ivor, my physician and a personal friend for twenty-five years, also told me that as he listened to Petro he had burst out laughing, and said, 'Brain damage—fourteen years after the accident? If you believe that, Petro, then I am afraid it's you who need certifying. Margaret Argyll is one of the sanest people I know.'

Petro was sent away with his tail between his legs. He, too, was to appear as a witness against me in court. But like several of the people involved in that sinister series of lawsuits, he did not prosper long afterwards.

Ian and I returned to Inveraray, and I tried to ignore the evil influences that were building up against our marriage. I now know that I should have left him then, in 1957, but there were many reasons why I decided to remain with him. Although I am a renegade Catholic convert, having married twice, I still believe that marriage should be an unbreakable partnership, and the idea of a second divorce was abhorrent to me. Also, it must not be discounted that Ian Campbell, the 11th Duke of Argyll, had great personal charm and plausibility which he had used to influence people all his life. He played with me just as a cat toys with a mouse. Many times during our marriage I had been on the verge of leaving him for good, but always at that very moment he sensed it without my saying a word. He would then choose to become his most amiable, amusing self, ready to do anything to please me. Each time this happened I would try to forget the past unhappiness and pray that Ian had at last decided to become a more tolerable person to live with. I argued with myself that, after all, no marriage is perfect and perhaps mine was not so very bad.

I loved Ian deeply, and in his strange, perverse way, I think he loved and needed me. The idea of leaving him and Inveraray was unbearable.

Last, but not least, I was convinced that the drinamyl tablets had temporarily unhinged Ian's mind, and that if I was patient he might return to his senses. I also hoped that I could finally persuade him to cut down on his drinking, which had been one of the main problems of our marriage from the very outset.

Ian would have been perfectly happy to remain alone with me in the castle all the time. Inveraray was very isolated, and but for my insistence on asking them over we would never have seen even our nearest neighbours, Michael and Anne Noble, now Lord and Lady Glenkinglas, at Strone, or Sir Fitzroy and Veronica Maclean at Strachur.

When people did visit Inveraray, Ian's attitude to me would be curiously double-edged. Two of my oldest friends, Sir Henry and Lady d'Avigdor Goldsmid, came to stay one Whitsun. Rosie wrote the following account of their visit:

For the Whitsun weekend of 1957 my husband and I were invited to Inveraray Castle, and we went. There was staying in the Castle the Duke of Argyll, whom I have known for many years, and his wife, Margaret, her daughter Frances, and Mr David Tennant.

Some time on the Saturday, the Duke was showing me over the Castle, and I believe the Duchess was or had been with us.

I think we were standing by the entrance to the big Gallery, when the Duke said, indicating the pictures and armoury, 'All these belong to Margaret. I made them over to her because if anything happened to me she would be turned out tomorrow. If I could have done, I would have given her the lot.' He also said that his wife had done a marvellous job in arranging the Castle so that it could be open to the public.

The Duke was a perfectly charming host to us, and this stuck in my mind particularly because curiously enough it was rather in contradiction to his general attitude towards his wife. During the weekend we were there, he was constantly needling her, in, I thought, a rather disagreeable way, which she took very well, changing the subject or laughing it off.

Yet, during the same visit, while Ian was showing Rosie and Harry over the castle, he pointed out with pride the initials which he had had painted on the ceiling of the Great Hall: I.—M. and the year, 1952. Our initials are still there.

Ian's remark to Rosie was quite true. In return for the help and support my father and I had given him, he had indeed made over all the contents of the 8th Duke of Argyll's Trust to me, for my lifetime only, in a Deed of Gift.

My father and I had been surprised by this gesture because the Trust comprised the most valuable contents of the castle—the tapestries, the armoury, the French furniture and the pictures. The Deed, which was signed and witnessed in 1953, looked most impressive with many seals and ribbons attached to it, but it proved to be the strangest quirk of all in my husband's character —I was later to discover that the Deed was not worth the paper it was written on.

Brian, in the meantime, had distinguished himself at Ampleforth by winning a scholarship to Oxford at the age of seventeen with an outstanding PPE paper (politics, philosophy and economics). We were all delighted, and I felt tremendously proud of him. Frances, at twenty, was surrounded by good-looking, eligible young men. One, however, seemed to be the most persistent of them all—Charles, Duke of Rutland.

Charles, who had divorced his first wife two years previously, was eighteen years older than Frances, and obviously deeply in love with her. He was a handsome, distinguished-looking man with a very pleasant manner.

Ian had always wanted to re-visit the Middle East where he had been many years before, and in the winter of 1958 he suggested that we take a trip there. I was delighted, and asked him if he would mind if Frances came with us, as she loved travelling as much as I did.

Ian had no objection to this, and we began planning a detailed itinerary for our visit to the Lebanon, Jordan, Iraq, Iran and Israel. He was most enthusiastic. I then thought of inviting a younger man to accompany us and to make the trip more amusing for Frances. I suggested this to the lovesick Charles Rutland, who jumped at the idea.

I need hardly say that ten days before we were due to leave, Ian announced that he was not going. His decision lacked the element of surprise, as well as the charm of novelty!

This time, however, it was not only a disappointment but an inconvenience, since four is company, three is none. However, I simply cancelled his tickets and set off for Beirut with Frances and Charles on January 29th.

The press were at Heathrow, and they immediately noted Ian's absence. A party of four would have looked quite natural, but a mother, plus a pretty daughter and an unattached Duke, was quite enough to start rumours of a romance before the plane had even left the ground.

As a result, we arrived in Beirut to be met by more press, all demanding an explanation of the trip. 'If you don't give us a statement we'll hound you all the way round the Middle East,' said one London newspaper reporter. I refused to make any statement, and the press did hound us. There were flash bulbs in the hotel lobbies, and telephoto lenses trained on our windows; even the hotel hall porters were in their pay. At one point we sent a cable reserving rooms in Russia in an effort to confuse them.

After Beirut we flew to Amman, the capital of Jordan, and there our Ambassador, Mr Charles Johnstone, and his wife, Natasha, arranged that we should fly to Petra, the 'rose-red city, half as old as Time', in a private plane lent by King Hussein. The plane landed at Ma'an, where we were met by a detachment of soldiers and escorted on horseback to the Caves.

Here we did expect to be free from the press, but suddenly from behind a boulder a little Arab appeared with a camera. Frances said, 'Mummy, look. The press.' The officer riding next to me gave orders for him to be caught, and he was brought back to us, obviously terrified, by a soldier holding the poor man by his collar. The officer asked me, 'Shall we kill him now?' I assured him that this was the last thing I wanted, and asked for him to be released. Before he was allowed to go, however, he was made to confess that he was on the payroll of the same London newspaper whose representative had threatened me in Beirut.

In Ma'an we stayed the night at Army headquarters. It was so cold that we gathered all the paraffin stoves we could find and put them into one room which Frances, Charles and I shared.

We escaped the press temporarily and continued to have a fascinating trip lasting five weeks. I doubt, however, if Charles Rutland remembers anything he saw or anybody we met. His only thought was to be with Frances, holding her hand, preferably on a beach or in a cosy restaurant—without me!

It was in Tel Aviv, at the Accadia Hotel, that the romance between Charles and Frances really blossomed. One evening Frances came to me and asked for my advice about marrying him. We talked for hours and I tried to help her weigh the advantages against the disadvantages. Frances said little, listened carefully, and thanked me. I knew that the one thing worrying her as a Catholic was the fact that Charles's first wife was still living. I had not tried to influence her in any way, for I knew from my own experience that it was essential she make up her own mind. The following morning she came to me looking radiant, and told me that she had decided to marry Charles. I was so happy for them both. Charles was beaming, and the three of us had a celebration lunch—all very emotional.

The press had caught up with us again in Israel, and, rather than trust the concierge at the Accadia, we went to the post office where I cabled Ian the good news, and Charles cabled his mother.

Our precautions were in vain. Before our cables had even reached their destination, news of Frances' and Charles's engagement was on the front page of the London editions of the *Daily Mirror*.

We then deliberately chose an all-night flight home, convinced that no reporter would bother to be at an airport at dawn.

We were wrong. We landed at Heathrow at five in the morning to be met by a bevy of our old friends, the press, and—to my astonishment—Ian. As usual, he had not communicated with me during the entire trip. On our return to London poor Frances suddenly found herself under a barrage of criticism by various Catholic Bishops who disapproved of her intended marriage to a divorced man. This worried Frances so much that she even considered breaking off the engagement, but as Charles had agreed that any children of their marriage should be brought up in the Catholic faith until they became of age, she decided to go ahead with the marriage.

The press had been encamped outside 48, Upper Grosvenor Street twenty-four hours a day since our return, and Charles had to go in and out of the house by the back door. Their patience was rewarded finally when the engagement between Charles and Frances was announced in *The Times*.

The wedding had originally been planned for June, but because of the religious controversy Frances asked me to bring the date forward. This I did, and it was on May 15th, 1958, that the marriage took place at Caxton Hall.

My daughter looked a vision in a dress designed by Hartnell of pale pink organza, its skirt lined entirely with pink ostrich feathers which showed below the hem. The skirt dipped at the back, almost like a train. On her head she wore a minute cap of pink ostrich feathers.

Both she and I wished that it could have been a church wedding, but I tried to make up for this by having a large reception afterwards at Claridge's, with a dance orchestra playing, and our piper, Ronnie McCallum, who piped the bridal couple into the ballroom.

My ex-husband, Charles Sweeny, and I received the guests, along with Kathleen, Duchess of Rutland. It felt strange to stand there at Charlie's side at our daughter's wedding, and I was a little sad. It was also hard for Ian to be there merely as an on-looker, but the situation was inevitable.

I hoped that I would never be the traditional tearful mother-of-the-bride, and I was absolutely stoical until the time came when they were actually leaving Claridge's for their honeymoon. It was a very final moment, and I found myself fighting back the tears. Ian put his arm round me and said, 'Maggie, Maggie, you're breaking the rules. No tears,' and that pulled me together.

1958 was a year of great activity at Inveraray. I revived the Inveraray Games, which used to be held annually in the castle grounds but had lapsed during the 10th Duke's lifetime. Although it rained all day, the whole town turned out and it was a great success.

I had discovered that two of the neighbouring towns—Loch-Gilphead and Campbelltown—both had famous Gaelic choirs. After hearing them and falling in love with their singing, I had the idea of inviting them to the castle for *ceilidhs*. I also asked the townspeople to come and join in. The word *ceilidh* began as meaning 'visiting', when neighbours would call on each other and sing together. Now it really means a concert. Soon the *ceilidhs* at Inveraray Castle became quite a tradition, and we discovered that the lofty hall had exceptionally good acoustics. We had some marvellous evenings in front of two open log fires, listening to those very beautiful Highland voices singing their island songs. These songs were never written down but were passed on from parents to children, and I did think of trying to have them professionally recorded.

Later that summer I was approached by the Chairman of the King George V Fund for Sailors and asked to help raise money for their Navy Week, during which three destroyers were to be anchored on Loch Fyne. To entertain the Royal Navy and raise money for the fund, a series of fetes and similar functions at Inveraray and the other towns and villages bordering Loch Fyne were planned. I suggested to Ian that we give a ball at the castle, which would be the first one held there for a hundred years. The idea seemed to capture Ian's imagination, and he was very enthusiastic. With the help of Provost John Campbell and his town committee, the Navy Week proved to be a great success, and the climax was on July 21st, when six hundred people came to Inveraray for the ball. We had two bands—one playing only Scottish music—and people were still dancing as dawn broke.

At five o'clock that morning Ian and I slipped away and drove up to the top of Duniquaich, which overlooks the town.

The floodlit castle and the ships on the loch, all of which were lit up from stem to stern, were beneath us, and it was a breathtaking sight. As we stood there for several minutes, there was a real happiness between us. I forgot the wretched past and once again hoped that we might make a fresh start.

The ball and the entire Navy Week had been such a success that I suggested to Provost Campbell that we might have the same thing the following summer. I had no idea that by then Inveraray would no longer be my home.

That August Ian and I left for a holiday in Greece, and ended up in Cyprus. Ian had been asked to go by the Colonel of the Argyll and Sutherland Highlanders stationed there. The morale of the Regiment was very low at that time, and it was felt that a visit from Ian would give them a boost.

He was advised that it would be unsafe for me to accompany him, but I dared him to leave me behind! We were the guests in Nicosia of the Governor and his wife, Sir Hugh and Lady Foot— now Lord and Lady Caradon. Cyprus was a grim, troubled island at that time, and Hugh Foot, an idealist, talked to me at length about his anxiety to avoid bloodshed.

While we dined in the garden of Government House I noticed soldiers patrolling the grounds and prodding the bushes with their bayonets. When I asked what they were doing, Hugh Foot answered grimly, 'Searching for terrorists'.

The next day we drove to the Regimental Headquarters at Limni, with two soldiers in the car to guard us. These two Jocks never left our side throughout our stay in Cyprus. They followed us on to the beach when we bathed, and one of them slept outside our room at night.

On the way to Limni I developed an agonising, almost unbearable toothache. I was unable even to eat lunch, and I asked an officer's wife if there was any dentist nearby. She told me the only one was an Army dentist miles away in Kyrenia.

At this point Ian sauntered off to bathe, so it was a kindly young officer who drove me over the mountains to Kyrenia, where the dentist was awaiting me. His surgery was an Army truck. After an examination he told me that I had an abscessed tooth and that it must come out immediately. 'There is only one problem,' he added. 'My anaesthetist is away, and I am not qualified to give you an anaesthetic.' I replied 'You are, today.' Reluctantly he did, and extracted the tooth as perfectly as any Harley Street dentist.

With a rapidly swelling face I was driven back by my escort to Limni. There I found that the ceremony of Beating the Retreat, which usually takes place at sunset, had been delayed for my return, so Ian and I watched it under the light of the moon.

The Regiment was in full dress—feather bonnets, white spat and all—marching to the pipes and drums, and accompanied by their mascot, a Shetland pony called Cruachan.

It was a stirring sight, and I little dreamed that ten years later I would be called upon to help save that historic Regiment from disbandment.

The following October we left again on another tour, this time to Canada to visit the Canadian Argyll and Sutherland Highlanders in Toronto, and also to meet the Canadian members of the Clan Campbell. Ronnie McCallum, our piper, accompanied us.

We sailed to Montreal on the SS 'Homeric', and in Canada Ian was his most urbane and pleasant self. In Toronto the Canadian Argylls gave a dinner in our honour. They were again in full regimental dress, and I was flattered to be invited, for women are rarely present on these occasions.

As good tourists we visited Niagara Falls and then went to on New York. On December 1st Elsa Maxwell gave a birthday party for me at El Morocco. It was a happy occasion, and no premonitions disturbed my pleasure. I would perhaps have done well to remember another birthday party of mine long ago at the Embassy Club, at which the fortune teller had warned me against treachery by those around me.

We returned to London, and Frances and Charles invited us to spend our first Christmas at Belvoir with them. We motored up on Christmas Eve, and I could tell from Ian's mood at the beginning of the journey that it would be far from pleasant; indeed he did nothing but complain about the fog. I decided to take a nap as the most diplomatic way of avoiding a row, and I awoke to hear Ian telling the chauffeur to stop the car at Grantham, and saying he would take a train back to London. Without an explanation he got out of the car, and I later heard that he spent Christmas at St James's Club!

I made the usual excuses to my daughter and son-in-law. I had never discussed my marriage problems with Frances, but after living with Ian and me for seven years she can have had few illusions. That first Christmas at Belvoir was not the happy one it should have been for me, but there was one moment of real joy. While I was there Frances told me she was expecting a child in the early summer.

Chapter 19

Sometimes, to my surprise and delight, I meet people—foreigners perhaps, or the younger generation—who have never heard of the Argyll legal cases. These are things I rarely discuss. I believe in the saying, 'Never explain, never complain, never apologise.'

I also know that even to outline the tangled web of these lawsuits to 'Learned Counsel' takes countless hours.

The macabre year of 1959 began with my organising the packing of many dresses into many suitcases. Ian told me we had been invited to make a semi-official visit to Australia and New Zealand for the purpose of meeting all the Campbells living 'down under'. The itinerary was to be tough and crowded. For more than two months we were to be continually 'on parade' at public functions and staying at Government Houses. As I never travel with a lady's maid, the packing was a problem. A week before we were due to leave, Ian reversed his usual strategy. As the Campbells were expecting to see their clan chief, this was one trip he could hardly back out of. So, instead, he told me that he would prefer it if I did not accompany him—with no reasonable explanation. I simply said that as most of my suitcases were already in Sydney, and as people were expecting me, it was too late to change my plans.

So on January 13th—nine years to the day that Ian had first

entered my house—I set off with him on what was to be our last trip together. It was an exhausting journey; after all, we were going halfway round the world, and there were no long-run jets in those days.

Our last fuelling stop was at Biak, New Guinea, and from there we flew across Australia all that day. I only then realised what a vast, uninhabited continent it was.

We arrived in Sydney to face a damp, grey heat with the temperature at over 100. I do not think I have ever been so tired. After staying one night with Sir William Woodward, the Governor of New South Wales, and Lady Woodward, we moved into the Australia Hotel. My old friend, Sir Frank Packer, the Australian Press tycoon, had a suite in this hotel which he put at our disposal, and we used it as a base during our seven weeks' visit.

When I was alone with Frank and his enchanting wife, Gretel, he quizzed me as to the real reason for our coming to Australia. 'To visit the Campbells,' I answered in all innocence. It was only later that I discovered Ian's main reason for accepting the invitation, which was to raise still more money for Inveraray—this time from Australian Campbells.

When I learned this I was both angry and embarrassed that we were accepting such lavish hospitality from people who were *my* friends—not Ian's—in order to raise funds for his castle. Ian had purposely misled me before we even left Britain, and I now understood why he had not wanted me to go with him.

From the beginning it was almost like a royal tour. At every city we visited we would be met at the airport by the Governor's aide-de-camp and a Scots band piping us off the plane to the tune of 'The Campbells are Coming'. We would then be driven to Government House, where I usually had barely an hour to get my evening dress unpacked and pressed in time for a dinner given in our honour. The following day there would probably be a Lord Mayor's reception, followed in the evening either by a Campbell gathering or by a full-dress Highland ball for as many as two thousand guests.

Each of these balls would end with the band playing 'Will Ye No' Come Back Again', which was always heart-rending.

In public Ian's behaviour was impeccable, and the Australians loved him. I purposely remained in the background and watched with pride how well he conducted himself on various television programmes and in 'Meet the Press' television interviews.

It was during this tour that I realised how accomplished and relaxed a public speaker Ian was. He seemed to be gaining self-confidence, the lack of which I was sure had been the cause of some of the trouble between us. I began to have hopes that when we returned to London, Ian might at last make his maiden speech in the House of Lords and take his rightful place in Scottish public life.

After Sydney we stayed at Government House, Canberra, as guests of the Governor-General of Australia, Field-Marshal Sir William Slim, and his delightful wife, Aileen. Here, more than anywhere, one was conscious of military precision and efficiency in the running of the household. Protocol was exacting. At dinner all the guests had to be assembled (the women wearing long white gloves) before the Slims entered the room. After dinner the women left the room in pairs. At the door each couple turned and curtsied to the Governor-General, while the men stood and raised their glasses to us. It was an old-world custom, and a charming one.

No one sat in Sir William's presence while he himself stood. One evening he remained standing for so long after dinner that I was forced to protest. 'Dear Sir William, my back is breaking. Will you *please* sit down.' He burst out laughing and promptly seated himself.

In Canberra we were also invited to stay with the British High Commissioner, Lord Carrington, and his wife.

As 'Meet the Campbells' was the purpose of our trip we concentrated on visiting the big cities, but I longed to see the Outback. Every time I suggested going to the Great Barrier Reef or Alice Springs I was told it was at least three thousand miles away and it would be impossible for us to go in our limited time.

Perhaps the most memorable event of the whole tour, however, was the rodeo staged specially for us in Wellington, New South Wales. The cowboys who took part rode three hundred miles just to meet us for five minutes, and a group of aboriginals came across the continent to present me with a pair of boomerangs which they threw in a demonstration for my benefit. I still have those boomerangs.

In Queensland we were the guests of the Governor, Sir Henry Abel-Smith, and his wife, Lady May, the daughter of Princess Alice, Countess of Athlone. Princess Alice was due to arrive for her annual visit just after our departure.

In Melbourne our hosts were the Governor, Sir Dallas Brooks, and Lady Brooks, and they arranged for us to visit Geelong School which became famous in Britain when Prince Charles went there on an exchange education system.

Our longest stay was in Adelaide, as Sir Robert (Bobbie) George, the Governor, and Lady George were old friends of Ian's. As we were staying there ten days we offered to take our host and hostess out to dinner and a cinema one night to relieve the staff. Bobbie insisted on our dining in Government House, and we then drove to the cinema in a large official Rolls with the flag flying. On our arrival, and as we left, the whole audience rose and sang 'God save the Queen', and during the interval the manager had a reception for us in his private sitting-room. So much for our idea of a casual night at the movies!

I was most touched by the interest in, and loyalty to, Britain that I found throughout Australia, ten thousand miles away from the Mother Country. I have never felt that we in Britain fully appreciate this loyalty.

After Australia we flew to New Zealand and stayed with the Governor-General and his wife, Viscount and Viscountess Cobham, before making an informal motoring tour of the South Island. On our route south I noticed that the names of many of the towns had a Lowland Scots look about them. We flew to Dunedin, and the solitary piper who met us was in RAF uniform. 'The Scots here seem to be mostly Lowlanders,' I said to Ian. 'If I were you I wouldn't wear Highland dress at the reception tonight'. He ignored my advice, and when we entered the Town Hall a few hours later Ian found that he was the only man in the room wearing a kilt. In full Highland evening dress, lace jabot and all, he suddenly looked overdressed and rather foolish. As I had expected, all the Scots there were Lowland farmers who had emigrated from Dumfries, Ayrshire and Renfrewshire.

Although we were now even farther away from Britain, I found the same loyalty to the mother country that I had in Australia, and I felt very much at home with these people from my part of Scotland.

On leaving New Zealand we began our homeward journey, stopping for a week in Honolulu where we were entertained by Mr Walter Dillingham, who owned most of the island of Oahu. He took us on a tour of Pearl Harbour, and we stood on the wreck of the 'Arizona' in which 1,177 men were entombed. This may now be a hackneyed tourist 'attraction', but I found it an eerie and emotional experience. We also went to the island of Maui, and to me these were Paradise Islands.

Still en route home we visited San Francisco for a few days. Until now our trip had been a wonderful one and a great success, especially for Ian, but now that he was no longer the centre of attention he began drinking heavily again and became correspondingly unpleasant.

One day he suddenly said to me, 'The trouble is, Maggie, I can't divorce you, can I? I've got no evidence.'

As he refused to elaborate on this bewildering remark I could only conclude that he was under the influence of drink. He then changed the subject and announced that he was going to Los Angeles to see an old friend of his called Jack Morgan. I assumed that I was going with him, and looked forward to meeting Mr Morgan, but Ian was adamant in insisting he should go alone. I was hurt and unhappy about this, but I had no choice, so I told him that I would go on to New York, meet my father there, and wait for Ian to join me.

In New York, on meeting my father (who was then in his eightieth year), I learned that his second marriage had turned out unhappily. He confided to me that he had been miserable with Jane since the day he married her. I was most disturbed to hear this, and tried to concentrate on his worries instead of my own.

I had no idea if and when Ian might decide to join me, but three days after my arrival he suddenly appeared in my room at my hotel and moved in as if nothing had happened. I told him that I was lunching with four close friends, the Carman Messmores and the Angus Walkers, and he seemed happy to join us. We all lunched in the Sheraton East Hotel, where I was staying, and afterwards Ian said, 'Come upstairs. I've got something amusing to show you all.'

I had no idea what he meant, but we all went upstairs to our sitting-room where Ian produced a packet of extremely porno-graphic photographs and showed them around to my friends, proudly announcing that Jack Morgan had given them to him in Los Angeles. The man and woman who figured in these photo-graphs were unrecognisable, as the photographer had cut off their heads. Ian was notorious for showing 'feelthy pictures' around White's Club, but to exhibit them in mixed company and to people he hardly knew was a very different matter and quite unpardonable. I was horrified, Lee Messmore and Amber Walker were obviously embarrassed, and their husbands were 'not amused'. In deathly silence they all put their coats on and left.

Once we were alone I lost my temper with Ian, and I barely spoke to him for the next few days. He then decided to fly back to London ahead of me. I shall never forget the afternoon of April 13th, 1959, when I watched Ian walking down the corridor and out of the hotel. I had the feeling that he was walking out of my life. But on April 21st I received a terse cable from him: 'Absolutely imperative you return immediately to Scotland not repeat not to London.'

It was unlike Ian to send cables, and I wondered why on earth he was sending this peremptory message. I tried to telephone him, but he would tell me nothing, merely repeating that I had to come straight to Prestwick.

In consternation I took an overnight plane to Scotland and landed at Prestwick in the afternoon of April 23rd. I was met by Peach, Ian's valet, and during the journey he said, 'His Grace is in a very strange mood. He keeps talking about divorce, but he isn't making much sense.'

On arriving at the castle, tired though I was I went straight to Ian in the library and asked him what it was all about. 'This is what it's about,' he said, pointing to his desk on which was a pile of letters. I stared at them in amazement, realising that they were all letters that had been written to me. I demanded from Ian an explanation of how they had got there.

It appeared that on arriving back in London he had gone straight to 48, Upper Grosvenor Street, and, finding a cupboard locked in my drawing-room, he had called a locksmith to open it. In the cupboard he had found letters I had kept since the age of seventeen. Every one I had ever received from my children was there, as well as love letters and also some important letters and cables from my parents. (Several of these letters have been included in this book.) Ian had also, for some inexplicable reason, extracted all his own letters to me and destroyed them.

When I recovered from the shock of this I challenged Ian, saying that there was nothing secret about that cupboard and if he had ever wanted to see its contents he could have done so at any time. I only locked it because I was going away on a long trip. I finally proved to Ian that none of these letters had anything to do with our marriage, and he seemed much happier.

The next day he said, 'From now on things are going to be very different between us. I would like you to spend less time in London without me. Your place is here at Inveraray.'

I agreed immediately as it seemed a reasonable request, and I was pleased that at last Ian seemed to be showing some concern for our marriage.

Chapter 20

On May 8th, 1959, Frances gave birth to my first grandchild—a wonderful little boy, David, who is now the Marquis of Granby, and heir to the Dukedom of Rutland.

On the day following his birth, I met Ian in South Audley Street as he was coming back to the house for lunch. He was carrying a briefcase. 'It may interest you to know,' he said, 'that I have got all the evidence I need against you inside this,' indicating the briefcase. He refused to tell me anything more.

By now I was not surprised by anything that Ian said, and honestly believed that he was in a very confused state of mind. I knew that nothing in his briefcase could be of any danger to me, but I was certainly curious to see what was inside it. After lunch I managed to get the briefcase and hide it, intending to look at it later. When he discovered it was gone Ian went absolutely berserk and attacked me violently. My maid, Carpenter, mercifully came into the drawing-room and stopped him. He then said to me, 'I refuse to stay in this house until you return that briefcase.' With that he left for Inveraray, and I brought the briefcase downstairs, to find it locked. I could very easily have forced the lock open with a pair of scissors, but I thought that, if I did, it would put Ian into an even blacker rage than he already was, and, as I was going to Inveraray with my father and Jane the next day to spend Whitsun at the Castle, I was most anxious to avoid any more ghastly scenes.

So, innocent that I was, I took the case up to Inveraray with me the next day and handed it back to Ian—still locked. I have always wondered what use the contents were to him, but my returning it seemed to mollify him, which was what I had hoped for.

My father was clearly very worried about the threatening atmosphere around me, and discussed the situation with me during his stay. I noticed that Jane seemed quite unconcerned, and spent most of the holiday taking long walks alone with Ian.

When my father, Jane and I were leaving for London, and Peach, our chauffeur/valet, was driving us to the airport, Jane suddenly said, 'Remember, Peach, you take your orders from the Duke now, not from the Duchess.' My father and I then realised without any doubt that my stepmother was no friend of mine.

A few days later, on May 22nd, Ian and I lunched together in London at Pruniers. Suddenly he produced a long list of men's names which he had compiled from my dinner-guest book, and said, 'The only hope we have for our future married life is if you will admit that all these men were your lovers.'

Beyond observing that if this were the case I deserved to be in the *Guinness Book of Records*, there seemed to be nothing I could say, except to refuse absolutely to resume our life on the basis of a lie. I also refused to admit to something that was quite untrue.

The following day I returned to the house after lunch and saw Ian's suitcases piled in the hall. He was obviously preparing to leave. I went upstairs and saw that he had done a very thorough job; not a handkerchief, not a collar stud had been left behind.

The only thing he had not packed was a small china rabbit that always stood on his desk. It was a silly-looking rabbit, with a crocus in its mouth, and I had given it to him, saying, 'Here's a picture of me.' It was christened 'Dumb Bunny'.

I was quite aware of Ian's reasons for packing up so completely and for leaving only Dumb Bunny behind. It was all done to hurt me, and it succeeded.

Noise, heat and heartbreak are my only memories of the summer of 1959. It was one of the hottest summers on record, and I had the American Embassy building going up opposite me and an old building being demolished next to me. Through all this I was sitting for an oil portrait which was being done by Rene Bouché, the American artist. Poor Rene could not have chosen a worse time to paint me, and because of my unhappiness it is a haunting picture.

At the end of May Ian asked me to meet him in Paris, and we stayed at the Ritz. (His lawyers later had a hard time explaining why he should have stayed with me after the enormities I was supposed to have committed.) He was pleasant and reasonable at this time, and on leaving Paris he said, 'I am going back to Inveraray, and hope you will come up in a few days.'

Although I hoped and prayed that Ian's erratic behaviour towards me would cease, in my heart of hearts I already knew that the moment had come when the tears had to stop, that my marriage was over and that a long, ugly battle probably lay ahead of me. When I returned to London and told my father, he said, 'Margaret, you certainly must fight all the way, but be prepared for a great deal of very unpleasant publicity.'

In London, on September 2nd, I suddenly woke up in the middle of the night. A thought had struck me, and I immediately went downstairs and began looking through all my papers. Finally I found what I was looking for, tucked away amongst the dog licences. It was Ian's Deed of Gift, signed in 1953:

I, the Most Noble Ian Douglas Campbell, Eleventh Duke of Argyll . . . . hereby give, make over, donate and gift to my said wife, Margaret, Duchess of Argyll, the whole family portraits and other effects acquired by me under the foresaid Codicil dated Ninth September Eighteen hundred and ninety six and registered in the Books of Council and Session on Twentieth June Nineteen hundred to the said General Disposition and Settlement executed by my great grandfather, George Douglas Glassell Campbell, Eighth Duke of Argyll.

I had no wish to rob Inveraray Castle or the Argyll family of its treasures, and I would willingly have returned the Deed to Ian if he would agree to be quietly divorced for desertion and desist from attacking me publicly. If not, here, surely, was a weapon to fight with.

Later I paid a farewell visit to Inveraray. I was alone, and my two days at the castle were sad ones. Realising that they were the last I would ever spend there, I wandered round the house and through the grounds, trying to memorise every detail. It seemed cruel that, when Inveraray was beginning to look just as I had always dreamed it might, I was leaving it.

Throughout all this period of trouble and anxiety, the person who consistently stood by me was Anthony Marreco, a brilliant young barrister, and my friend since our days together in Berlin in 1948. Had I been able to follow his advice, my enemies would never have achieved the success they did. On September 7th Anthony told me that I must change the lock on my front door immediately, as he was sure that Ian would try to enter the house. He was convinced that Ian was now so determined to divorce me that he would stop at nothing to get evidence. I planned to have the lock changed, therefore, but most unwisely told my then secretary, Diana Crossland, of my intention. She, too, had previously worked for Ian, and according to his own later admission she telephoned him and told him of my plan. At five o'clock in the morning on September 9th I awoke with a strong feeling that Ian was very near me. He was, in fact, in my drawing-room, with his daughter, Lady Jeanne Campbell, removing all my four-year diaries. But the current one was lying on my bedside table.

Upstairs in my bedroom, after reading a little, I put out the light, but not long afterwards I saw the silhouettes of two figures entering my room from my bathroom, which was lit. I switched on the light and, to my amazement, saw my estranged husband and his daughter. She was wearing trousers and a head-scarf.

I immediately began dialling 999, but Ian pinioned my arms to prevent this, while Jeanne snatched up my diary. After this they made a rapid exit. It was a horrible experience, and the next day I suffered from delayed shock.

Lord Wheatley, the divorce judge, later said that what Ian had done that night made him a thief at common law. I sued Jeanne for trespass and theft and she settled out of court by paying me damages.

Stealing my diaries availed Ian very little in the end, and he was reduced to circulating lurid rumours about their contents. These rumours became so insistent that when I made a trip to New

York that autumn I took with me photostat copies of the diaries, which my lawyer had demanded and obtained. Bill Hearst, the newspaper owner, and a friend of mine, suggested that since I had received such bad publicity as a result of the vicious rumours —which I had had no chance to deny—he should send a feature writer to my apartment to see the copies of the diaries and write a feature article about them. This he did, and the heading of the article published was: 'The Duchess' "hot diaries" are only dull'. It went on: 'Friends of the couple who have seen the diaries are hooting down this allegation. The only thing scarlet about the diaries, they said, is their calfskin binding. . . . The diaries' pages are spaced and dated so that the diarist can only write a short three-line entry for a given day.'

Lord Wheatley later echoed this. The diaries, he said, were 'of limited evidential significance.' They were 'not the repository of the defendant's innermost thoughts, but a written-up record of her movements and engagements on each particular day.'

This was certainly an ugly period of my life and I seemed to be surrounded by ugly people. Poor Frances and Brian were constantly receiving poison-pen letters reviling their mother. Brian, recognising the handwriting as Ian's, signed a statement for my lawyers to this effect. More despicable still were Ian's efforts to drag a number of eminent and innocent friends of mine into the scandal surrounding the threatened divorce.

One person who suffered was a Cabinet Minister, one of my oldest friends, who had stayed at Inveraray with Ian and me. Shortly before the October election of 1959 he called on me in London, looking worried. He told me that rumours were rife in London that he would be cited in my divorce, and he thought he should go to Macmillan and offer his resignation. There was no truth whatsoever in the allegations, let alone any evidence, so I said that I was amazed that the Conservative Government could be so fragile as to be shaken by mere unsubstantiated rumour; that no divorce between Ian and myself had even begun yet, and if it finally did, there was no possible evidence that could be used involving him. I strongly advised him to 'stay put'.

He remained in the Cabinet and again became a Minister when the Conservatives were re-elected to office.

On September 18th—nine days after Ian and Jeanne had raided

my house—a press reporter handed a piece of paper to my butler at the front door asking if I had any comment to make. The piece of paper informed me that my husband had applied for an interdict banning me from Inveraray Castle from that day forward. I was told that this application, which made a savage attack on my morals, had been pinned to the walls of the Edinburgh Law Courts for all the world to read—a barbaric custom which has now been discontinued. This method of denigrating me was inexcusable, as no divorce action had begun and I had no chance of refuting Ian's allegations.

The result was that Judge Wheatley gallantly allowed me exactly one day—'from dawn until dusk'—at the castle in order to pack my belongings.

Ian's behaviour in banning me from the home which I loved and which my father and I had done so much to restore created a general revulsion in Scotland. Immediately after the interdict the Countess of Erroll—the hereditary Lord High Constable of Scotland, who walks directly behind the Queen on State occasions —invited me to stay at her home, Easter Moncreiffe, in Perthshire. 'Puffin' Erroll and her husband, Sir Iain Moncreiffe of that Ilk, took me to the Perth Ball, the Perth Races, and deliberately posed for photographs with me. They were certainly loyal friends in a time of stress, and I shall never forget this.

I chose Thursday, October 22nd, as the day of my last visit to Inveraray Castle. I told nobody of my plans, and yet when I arrived in Inveraray the town was full of reporters.

I was accompanied by my London and Scottish lawyers, for I had not come just to pack my few personal possessions remaining there—I could have sent my maid up to do that. I had come up to identify the various heirlooms of the 8th Duke's estate, given to me in Ian's Deed of Gift. I was the one who had put green labels on them in 1950 and I remembered them well.

My lawyers, my maid and I arrived at Arrochar at eight in the morning and had breakfast at the George Hotel, Inveraray. It had been made quite clear to us that we were to be shown no hospitality by the Duke of Argyll during that day. But I was heartened and touched when Ronnie McCallum and many of the townspeople came to visit me in the hotel during breakfast, obviously most upset by what was happening.

I had made a vow when the onslaught had begun, never to take a tranquilliser or sleeping pill of any kind. That day, however, I had been persuaded to take one benzedrine tablet which I was told would bolster me up and prevent me from crying—which I was determined not to do.

It certainly worked.

When we arrived at the castle, Ian appeared (fifteen minutes late) and his greeting was curt and cold. I gave him a great big happy grin in return. Then, followed by my lawyers and a disgruntled Ian, I systematically toured the State Rooms pointing to every object that I recognised as belonging to the 8th Duke's Trust. In each room I said, 'That, that, and that is mine,' pointing to the tapestries, armour and portraits.

By now the benzedrine was working beautifully, and I was as gay as could be. In the end, Ian burst out laughing and said to my solicitor, Cecil Jobson, 'For God's sake stop her.' Poor Cecil said, 'I can't.'

At lunchtime Ian was ready to say goodbye, supposing that I had finished my tour.

'Finished? Not at all, Ian. I've hardly begun. I've got until dusk, remember? We're going down to the George for a very quick lunch and we'll be back at two o'clock on the dot.'

After lunch we returned, and there we stayed until the light faded over Loch Fyne. By this time my lawyers had succeeded in identifying everything that I could lay claim to.

Ian and his elder son, the Marquis of Lorne, stood in the Great Hall to watch me leave. It was a bitter moment, for I knew I should never again enter the castle that I shall always love. I wondered if Ian also had memories of our work together to save his home.

As we drove away from the castle my day at Inveraray was over and a chapter in my life had ended. We passed the watch-tower at Duniquaich, and we went over the beautiful Rest and Be Thankful pass.

Cecil and my Scottish solicitor were with me in the car, and these poor gentlemen had to suffer the embarrassment of my silent weeping all the way down Loch Lomond and back to Glasgow. The benzedrine was no longer working!

We then applied to the Scottish courts for leave to claim the

Argyll heirlooms. This was refused, for the Deed of Gift, with all its official seals, proved to be a complete fraud on Ian's part. The heirlooms were not his to give away, for he had already mortgaged them, and it was this mortgage that had provided him with the £1,000 a year he was living on when I first met him.

Air-Marshal 'Bill' Thornton, the wise and loyal friend of both Ian and myself, now intervened in an attempt to have the threatened divorce settled peacefully. He arranged that Ian should come to my house to discuss this.

When Ian arrived with Bill he was at his most arrogant, and dictated his terms to me: if I would admit to adultery with one man and give him money to cover his 'legal expenses', he would give me a quiet divorce. The sum he mentioned was a large one, far exceeding any possible legal expenses.

Trying to keep my temper, I said that I would not admit to something I had not done, and that I had always believed *gentlemen* offered to let their wives divorce them. Ian replied, 'I have been divorced twice already. This time *I* am going to do the divorcing. Since you refuse my offer, I shall destroy you and make it impossible for you to live in this country.'

One result of this most unpleasant meeting, which lasted barely twenty minutes, was that Ian broke his friendship with Bill Thornton, who, however, remained loyal to me until his death.

By now my father had left Jane for good, and had come to live with me in Upper Grosvenor Street. He, Brian and I spent Christmas together at home, and so the worst year of my life— up to then—at least and at last ended on a happy note.

Chapter 21

It was the first Monday in May, the traditional start of the London season. But in 1960 the circumstances were very different from my coming-out ball thirty years earlier. Then I had danced till dawn; now I sat in the Royal Courts of Justice listening to Counsel for the Plaintiff trying to tear my reputation to shreds.

He was an old man, with stooping shoulders, sharp eyes, and a hawk-like nose in his gaunt face. His name was Gilbert Beyfus. He was known as one of London's most bombastic advocates, and he was already a dying man. This was his last case and he was clearly determined to make the very most of it.

The words he had chosen to apply to me, the defendant in the case, were certainly histrionic and melodramatic. I was, he said, 'a dazzling figure, high in rank, the possessor of great wealth and famous beauty.'

As prosecuting counsel it was his job to discredit me, and I waited for the inevitable sting in the tail. Sure enough it came.

'As one contemplates her,' he continued, 'one thinks back to the fairy stories of one's youth when all the good fairies assembled for a christening and showered their gifts upon the infant. In some of the fairy stories there is a bad fairy who is not invited to the christening. One can imagine that the bad fairy said, "I can't withdraw the gifts showered upon you, but I will give you my own gift. You shall grow up to be a poisonous liar!"'

Yet, cruel as they were, his words had little effect on me. The events of the year before had anaesthetised me against shock and attack.

For three years, since my refusal either to apologise to Yvonne MacPherson or to pay her damages, her case against me had hung suspended like the Sword of Damocles. Now it was being heard in the High Court. Ian, true to his threat made three years earlier at the Ritz in Paris, had taken her side against his own wife.

On September 10th, 1959, eight months before the case came to court, he had written as follows to my solicitor: 'I have already supplied Mrs MacPherson with all the documents in my possession which may be helpful to her in her action against my wife.'

In spite of that incredible admission, I still could not believe that Ian would actually give evidence against me.

Dumb Bunny! How right his name for me had been. For he had arrived at the court with Mrs MacPherson, posed with her for photographs, and escorted her inside. And the usher now called for the 'Most Noble' Duke of Argyll to enter the witness box and testify against his own wife!

I watched him. I heard what he said. The last scales remaining on my eyes fell away on that May afternoon. I realised at last that I had been married for nine years to a man who had the devil in him.

As he stood there in the box, wearing a red carnation, vindictive, giving a performance of supreme arrogance, I stared at him, hoping that he would meet my eyes and realise what I thought of him at that moment. But he avoided looking in my direction.

Asked by my counsel, Gerald Gardiner, about the theft of my diaries, Ian replied pompously, 'That is not a matter for this court.' One would have thought he was the judge!

Gerald Gardiner gave Ian full rein. 'I want to give you every opportunity of saying everything you want against your wife,' he said.

And Ian did. ' "S" for Satan—my wife,' said the Duke.

But the denigration did not dismay me. I had expected it. At the end of the first day my lawyers were confident, as the other side had not presented a convincing case. My father and I went home in a mood of optimism. I felt fairly certain that justice would be done and that I would win.

On the second day there was evidence from several GPO telephone officials about a mysterious telegram that now formed part of Mrs MacPherson's libel claim. Their evidence proved nothing for either side.

The telegram had been sent to Ian at Inveraray Castle just before Easter, 1957, at 9.30 a.m. 'Rushing off for ten days leave,' it said, 'but all is ready as we planned to tear strips off Margaret financially and otherwise. A million thanks for your love, support and invaluable information without which I would be helpless. Happy Easter and then into battle side by side. Yvonne.'

The telegram had Mrs MacPherson's telephone number on it, but she denied sending it. My husband had accused me of doing so, but, unfortunately for him, my maid, Kathleen Carpenter, made the following statement and gave it to my solicitors:

On this particular occasion Her Grace was in her bedroom with me there all the time between 9 a.m. and 11 a.m.

During that period she made only one telephone call which was to Mr Lumley-Savile between 9 and 10 a.m. and she was speaking to him for about 30 minutes. At no time did she send or dictate a telegram. . . . I certainly was not asked to despatch a telegram and did not do so.

But Carpenter never got a chance to tell this to the judge. Evidence was given in support of my husband's accusation—notably by Diana Napier, the actress and widow of my son's godfather, Richard Tauber. During the forty-five-minute adjournment at lunchtime my father said to me, 'If she's lucky MacPherson will get a farthing's damages.' Afterwards my Counsel, Gerald Gardiner, who was to become Lord Chancellor, and Colin Duncan, with Cecil Jobson, met us in a private room all looking very gloomy. Gardiner then said I could not go into the box to give evidence for reasons that neither my father nor I could understand.

I had not said a word yet, and they did not even know what I was going to say.

I argued with them that it was imperative that I should go into the box, but both Counsel were adamant. I then asked for an adjournment to have time for further discussion, but the other side would not agree to this. So reluctantly I gave in to my advisers.

As a result, the evidence called by Yvonne MacPherson went unchallenged; indeed, Gardiner said to the jury, 'My advice, given after careful consideration, is that the defendant is not calling evidence. As there is no evidence by the defence, you will accept the evidence called by the plaintiff.'

This meant that the jury was not given the chance of weighing the evidence of Yvonne MacPherson and her witnesses, including Diana Napier, Magda Buchel and Ian Argyll, against that of myself and my witnesses, the most important of all being my maid Carpenter.

This was the first law case in which I had ever been involved and I imagined that one's Counsel was omniscient. It was not made clear to me or to my father that I could have insisted on giving evidence and that if I instructed my lawyers to defend me they would have had to do so. I was never given a choice, and so my father and I naturally assumed that if I rejected Gerald Gardiner's advice I would be left without Counsel to represent me.

It is my belief that the course which was taken was quite wrong. In fact the jury awarded damages of £7,000—more than ten times the amount Mrs MacPherson had first demanded. I am firmly convinced that I should have been encouraged to defend this case.

Ian, Yvonne and Maureen Maude—Yvonne's employer and my friend—posed together jubilantly for photographs outside the court, and Maureen paid Ian for a bet they had had over how long the case would last. The newspapers also reported that Ian had made a bet of four shillings with Yvonne that I would lose the case. It was not a pretty scene.

It has always been one of my greatest regrets that my father was present to hear his daughter vilified and undefended in public.

For two months I had suspected that he had cancer. His voice was growing increasingly husky. One day, after seeing our mutual throat specialist, Ivor Griffiths, my father quietly told me that he had cancer of the throat.

Instead of my comforting him, he had to comfort me. It was such a shock because, although he was eighty, he was upright, very fit and seemed blessed with the cast-iron Whigham constitution. He played golf almost every day, his hearing and eyesight were near-perfect.

'He's got about a thirty per cent chance,' Ivor Griffiths told me frankly. The odds were low, but knowing my father's iron will and love of life I thought that thirty per cent might be enough.

All through that summer he underwent cobalt ray treatment. After it he would come back to the house drained and exhausted. He now had difficulty in eating, so I would have a tray waiting for him in the library and would leave him alone to be quiet and to rest.

That August we spent a happy month together in Folkestone, and while he was there he signed a Deed of Separation from Jane Whigham, upon which he paid her £20,000 in settlement.

'All I want at my time of life is peace and quiet,' he wrote to his solicitor, Sir Charles Russell, 'and I can well afford £20,000 to achieve this. Even if I were to take divorce proceedings which were successful, I would make financial provision for Jane on an approximately similar scale. As it is I do not wish to subject myself to the bother, strain and publicity of doing so.'

In spite of my father's reasoning, I had grave misgivings. Jane had been cut out of both my father's wills—one for his English estate and the other for his property in the Bahamas—and I doubted that the Deed of Separation would be the last we heard of my stepmother. Although my father had given her nearly £100,000 in three years, I felt quite sure it would not satisfy her, and I told Charles Russell so.

All too soon I was proved right. We returned to London, and about a month later a man came to the door with a letter in his hand, asking to see my father personally. I showed him in, only to find that the 'letter' was a writ. Jane was suing my father for divorce on the grounds of 'cruelty'—a kinder man had never lived. Her petition was headlined in the newspapers.

My father loathed publicity—even to the extent of refusing to be included in *Who's Who*—and these headlines caused him great distress. His condition deteriorated rapidly, and he finally had to enter the London Clinic. I was most careful to tell no one that he was either ill or in hospital.

When Jane did hear of his illness she made an offer (again much publicised) to withdraw the divorce petition, but my father refused and entered his defence, strenuously denying the charge of cruelty.

In the meantime Brian had taken his Oxford finals and gained second-class honours. There had been a nasty moment when it looked as if he would not pass at all. But, when at last he recognised approaching doom, Brian managed to cram three years' work into six weeks!

Brian's father, Charlie, had now arranged for him to go to America and take a course at the Harvard Business School. He was due to leave at the end of October, so I planned a dance for him as an advance celebration for his twenty-first birthday, which was not until the following April.

I was so anxious that my father should be well enough to come to the dance, but by now he could barely talk above a whisper, so he spent that evening quietly at the Clinic.

The day of Brian's dance, October 11th, was marked by a most extraordinary occurrence. A 'lady' tried hard to ruin the occasion. She telephoned every one she thought I might have invited. 'Surely you're not thinking of going?' she said to each of them. 'Don't you realise it's going to be the fiasco of all time? If you *do* go, you'll be the only one there.'

Her efforts did not meet with much success. I had a dinner of about seventy guests at Claridge's, and five hundred more came to the dance afterwards.

'Rarely have blue blood, money and sheer merit been mingled in such heady proportions,' said next morning's *Daily Mail*. 'The rest of the season's hostesses will have to work hard to match this assembly.'

I was most anxious to have a really good cabaret for the party and suggested asking Jean Sablon if he would fly from Paris and sing for us, whereupon Brian pulled a very long face and said, 'Oh, Mummy, he's so old hat. All my friends will be bored stiff by him.'

Nothing daunted, I approached Monsieur Sablon and was delighted when he agreed to sing.

Needless to say, he was charm itself, and sang the right songs for all ages. Much to Brian's amazement his young girl friends were all ecstatic about Jean Sablon, begged him for several encores, and then besieged him for his autograph.

My father sat up in bed that day reading all the newspaper accounts of the dance. He was very thrilled at its success and, thankfully, the last headlines he read about me were happy and triumphant ones.

Brian flew off to America soon afterwards, and I felt lonely as I watched him go, for I knew that I would be losing my father very soon. He was obviously sinking, slowly and reluctantly. 'One day,' Ivor Griffiths had warned me, 'he will just decide to give up.'

My father complained several times, 'They're giving me so much morphia that I can't even read to see what the stock market's doing.'

One afternoon he suddenly put down the newspaper and said, 'To hell with it.' I knew that the moment Ivor had warned me of had come. For the next forty-eight hours he was almost in a coma, and I sat with him most of the time in case he should wake up and want me. The doctors thought that he would survive a few more days. On the evening of Sunday, November 6th, I came home for a bath and a quick meal before returning to the Clinic. A woman friend came in to see me who was known to be quite psychic. During dinner she suddenly said, 'Listen to the bells.' I said that I could hear nothing, and she insisted, 'Don't you hear them? All the bells in a church on the Clyde are ringing for your father, and all his family are waiting for him, especially your mother.' (My parents had married in a church on the Clyde.)

I immediately called the Clinic, and the sister said, 'I was just about to telephone you. Your father has had a sudden change for the worse.'

I hurried back to the Clinic to find Jane Whigham sitting outside my father's room. He had given strict instructions that in no circumstances was she to be allowed into his room.

The night sister and I asked her to leave, as my father did not wish to see her.

I went into his room and sat holding his hand until he died, an hour later. But for my psychic friend I might have been too late.

My father had been the only person upon whom I could always depend. Without him to turn to, the world seemed a lonely place. He had once written in my first autograph book that I was given as a child, 'This above all—to thine own self be true, and it must follow as the night the day thou canst not then be false to any man.' It was his favourite quotation, and he certainly lived up to it throughout his life.

Jane gave press interviews about our confrontation at the Clinic, and she gave so many interviews about the funeral that my father's solicitors had to issue a public statement saying that it was his express wish that Jane did not attend his funeral. But she came and sat at the back of the church unnoticed by me or by any of my family.

On December 15th Jane entered a caveat contesting my father's English will, in which she was left nothing.

On July 12th, 1961, the case was heard. She lost and had to pay the costs. James Comyn, QC, who appeared for the three administrators of the estate (Sir Charles Russell, Mr Gerald Russell and Mr Robert King Graham), called her action 'A defence that never was.'

Jane also contested my father's Bahamas will. The property consists of three pieces of land and a house on Cable Beach. Although my father had also cut her out of this will, under an old Nassau law Jane claimed a Dower right as his widow entitling her, for her lifetime only, to one-third of the estate. So far she has not succeeded in the action, despite fifteen years of trying.

In 1965 Jane married again—a man called Clive Beadon—and went to live in Portugal.

Chapter 22

I have always believed that travel is the best tonic when one is worried or upset. It inevitably takes your mind off your problems, puts them into perspective, and is bound to focus your attention on seeing new things and meeting new people.

Also, I have always loved travel for its own sake (although I hate all resorts and resort life), and in the winter of 1961, while the divorce case and the endless other litigation I was enmeshed in were continuing on their weary ways, I decided to take a trip around South America, which I had never visited before although I had many friends there.

I went to New York first for several weeks to see my son Brian, who was then working there, and in that time I received a telephone call from a man offering me the services of a hired car and driver at a temptingly low rate. He said that he was anxious to have my name, for prestige purposes, on his list of clients. I accepted but only used the car three times—I was rather surprised at the old, dirty car that turned up.

Once I took Sir Charles Russell, one of my trustees, on a tour of New York, which he had never visited before. Charles noticed at the back of the car what he thought was an air-conditioner.

The second time I used the car to take Brian and myself to a matinee and back.

The third time was to take me to the airport when I was

leaving for Buenos Aires. There was a blizzard that night, and the only plane daring to take off was mine, of Varig Air Lines. It was in the evening, and Brian, who was accompanying me to see me off, fell asleep in the car and snored away the tedious journey out to Idlewild.

In Buenos Aires I was met by the entire Uriburu family, who are one of the most prestigious in the Argentine. Their father had been Ambassador to Britain for many years and was the doyen of the Diplomatic Corps.

They gave me the most wonderful time, and we even spent a few days in Uruguay at Punta del Este, the favourite resort of the Brazilians and the Argentines. The hours nearly killed me: lunch at 5 o'clock, cocktail parties at 11 o'clock at night, and dinner parties beginning at 1 o'clock in the morning.

I then went on to Brazil for the Carnival in Rio. This I frankly found disappointing, except for the last night when the natives, who live in the favelas (villages) in the hills around Rio, have their big night, which is the finale of the Carnival. It is fantastic to see these very poor people, who have barely enough to eat, coming down the mountains in groups, with each group wearing the locally designed costumes, all matching. To my amazement the women of some of these groups were dressed in pink satin crinolines carrying ostrich feather fans, and the men were in top hats and tail coats to match.

I was told afterwards that they spend every penny they have on making their costumes, and their greatest pride is to get the prize for being the most spectacular group of the year.

They danced down the hills and through the towns, all to their hypnotic samba music, and I stayed up till six in the morning watching them.

I then took a night flight to Caracas, Venezuela, and I was told afterwards that this is the most dangerous flight in the world because it is over jungle all the way with no possible place to land.

After returning to New York, on March 13th I received a letter from the District Attorney asking to see me. With my hair standing on end I telephoned Brian and learned that he had received a similar letter, and we wondered what on earth we *both* could have done to merit this.

I made arrangements for us to see the District Attorney the next day, accompanied by my American lawyer.

We discovered that the car I had been so generously offered was actually owned by a mortician (undertaker). It had been bugged—this was the instrument that Charles Russell had noticed.

As bugging is illegal in America there was a criminal charge against the firm who owned the car, and Brian and I were merely being asked to be witnesses. We duly appeared before the Grand Jury and gave evidence.

The sad part of the story is that the 'evidence' obtained was practically unintelligible—and useless to the other side. It had cost $3,000 to obtain it.

The end of this weird incident came when I received the following letter from the International Security Bureau, 75 Maiden Lane, New York:

Dear Madam,

This Corporation, its officers and directors, wish to present to you their sincere apologies for any steps taken to record conversations occurring in the automobile you used during December, 1960 and January, 1961.

We greatly regret this incident and any inconvenience it may have caused you.

You may be assured that there can and will be no recurrence.

In August 1961 I was invited to visit Antenor and Beatrice Patino in their beautiful quinta above Estoril, Portugal. They had just finished building it—in fact I believe that I was their first visitor.

I had stopped in Biarritz on the way to go to a ball given by Mr and Mrs Rodnam de Heeren (she was Aimee Lopez, the Brazilian beauty), but I was worried and depressed and in no mood for anything but a quiet holiday with my very dear friends, the Patinos.

After my arrival in Portugal on August 24th, we were all invited to dinner at a friend's house in Lisbon.

In my anti-social mood I wished that I could refuse, but I realised that I had to go, out of politeness.

When we arrived, an attractive man with very blue eyes and a

190

wonderfully infectious smile came up to me saying, 'You don't know who I am, but I know who you are.'

'Along had come Bill,' and so began a friendship with the most important, and only, man in my life for the next six years.

But, unlike the words in the song from *Show Boat*, Bill was no 'ordinary guy', and that entire evening we sat talking together, ignoring everyone else.

The following day he took me to dine in a restaurant outside Lisbon called the Choupana, overlooking the sea.

Who can explain mutual attraction? One thing I do know; it was not only physical, although Bill was one of the most attractive men I have ever met. He also had the gift of being an interested, intelligent listener, and I found myself telling him of many problems that I had not discussed even with close friends. He listened intently, and from the encouraging observations he made afterwards I felt confidence returning for the first time in many years.

He was a business man with an important position in a large firm in London. It was only when we were both back in London that he told me he was married—unhappily married, but married.

But he told me this too late. By now he was deeply in love with me and I with him.

Chapter 23

After three and a half years of delays and postponements, while Ian tried in vain to obtain evidence against me, the Argyll divorce case finally came to court on Friday, March 1st, 1963. It was already the longest and costliest divorce in Scottish legal history.

It was heard before the Court of Session in Edinburgh, the same court in which, two centuries earlier, my Dundas of Arniston ancestors had presided as judges. Now I had come here to be judged myself.

The public gallery was full, but it held only about thirty people. Most of them were women. The press box was packed. The American and European correspondents were scribbling hardest. They were allowed to report the actual evidence; the British reporters were not.

In the event, only three men were named in Ian's petition.

The first was Baron Sigismund von Braun, a high-ranking diplomat, who became German Ambassador to France. He and his wife were both friends of Ian's and mine, and they had stayed with us at Inveraray.

The second was an American, John Cohane, whom I had known for only three days during my visit to New York with Frances in 1955. John Cohane was not dragged into the case until 1960, and to defend myself against the charge concerning him I was told that it would be necessary to take the Edinburgh Court over to America to obtain evidence on commission. In September 1961 I did so. The court consisted of two Counsel on each side and a lawyer deputed to take evidence on commission. Evidence was given on oath in a private room in New York.

During this phase of the case, there were two people to whom I shall be eternally grateful. One is Mrs Carman Messmore, wife of the head of Knoedlers Gallery, who, at my request, interrupted a well-deserved holiday to give evidence on my behalf. She refuted a specific allegation made by Ian against me. The second is Helen Smith, who had been my personal maid, and who, according to my lawyers, proved to be a most intelligent and staunch witness. Afterwards she wrote to me from New York saying:

Dear Lady Duchess,

I only hope I helped—was glad to do so. The Duke's Lawyer called me a liar in a nice way—for a while I was a little scared of him but Mr Stein (my American solicitor) seemed to think I was O.K. . . . I hope and pray everything goes well with you.

Sincerely,
Helen Smith.

Nice as Jack Cohane was, and obviously anxious to see me before I left for England in 1955, I had already made all my engagements for lunches and dinners, and the only times I could see him were for a six o'clock drink in my hotel suite (which I was sharing with Frances) and during the drive when he kindly took me out to the airport—not exactly a heavy romance!

Five years later, several friends of mine, including Ted Rousseau, were able to prove this by giving evidence to show that it was they who had occupied my time during those three days—not Jack Cohane.

The third man Ian named was a dear friend of mine called Peter Combe, the son of Lady Moira Combe, one of the great beauties of her day.

The addition of Peter Combe in July, 1961, two years after Ian had left me, was almost laughable. Peter is a Scot, and I had known him and his family for many years. He was the staunchest of friends, and when I was on my own after 1959 he had given me a wonderful time by taking me out to restaurants and theatres.

The divorce had presented me with a great dilemma: to defend or not. My morals and integrity were under attack, and my natural inclination was to fight all the way. Some of my friends advised me not to defend, for the sake of peace and dignity and the avoidance of further scandal. But instinct told me that, if I did *not* defend this case, the malicious, lying rumours that had been spread about me would follow me all my life, and I knew that my enemies would never allow them to die.

So I decided to fight. But there was still the need to avoid involving either my friends or my children, even at the risk of losing valuable witnesses. That was the most important consideration of all, but, at the same time, a tremendous handicap.

Throughout this period strange happenings were constantly taking place. Not only were my children and friends bombarded with poison-pen letters, but abusive telegrams arrived under bogus names. Anonymous telephone calls were made to my house, one of them suggesting that I had just had my face lifted—which reassured me that I must be looking well!

Once, when I was about to give a big dinner party, a woman posing as my secretary telephoned each of the guests. She informed them all that the dinner was to be at 9.30 p.m. instead of 8 p.m., and that each guest would be welcome to bring a friend. If this ingenious plan had worked, the evening would have been well and truly wrecked, but fortunately my guests were suspicious and checked back with me first.

At breakfast the next morning a parcel arrived containing a boot-polish tin. When I opened it I found it filled not with boot polish but with a mass of live worms!

It was quite obvious to me, and to my friends, that the 'joker' was an erstwhile acquaintance obsessed by jealousy, and I quickly became quite accustomed to these little pranks.

During the hearing, Ian's behaviour in the box was a repetition of what it had been in the MacPherson case. This time he also pleaded frailty, having just recovered from influenza. The judge immediately offered him a chair. (When it came to my turn in the box, I stood for thirteen hours in four days without being asked if I would care to sit. I actually preferred standing but it would have been nice to be offered the courtesy of a chair.)

I was impressed that Ian's elder son, the Marquis of Lorne, should have flown over from Canada specially to be at his father's side on every day of the hearing.

I would not have cared for my own children to have been in the court room while this very unpleasant case was going on, but the question did not arise. Brian was in New York working, although he cabled me several 'Good luck' messages. Frances was now preoccupied with her young family and her life at Belvoir Castle. She had given birth to a second son, Lord Robert Manners, on June 18th, 1961, and, on November 11th, 1962, my first granddaughter, Lady Teresa Manners, had arrived.

Frances telephoned me once in Edinburgh during the action. 'How's it going, Mummy?' she asked briskly. I nearly told her the ghastly ordeal that it was, but I simply said, 'It's unpleasant but it will soon be over.' My daughter had her own life and her own problems.

My mainstay through all this was Bill. In the several lawsuits that had preceded the divorce he had been an invaluable counsel, often much wiser and more astute than my own solicitors. He was the son of a lawyer and he was the one person who understood the legal maelstrom in which I found myself. In spite of the fact that he had an unhappy marriage to contend with, and also held one of the most high-powered jobs in London, Bill somehow found the time to get away in the middle of the week and come to Edinburgh to support me (sometimes even against my own lawyers) throughout the case.

Bill was one of those friends who were anxious that I should defend. He said, 'I want the world to know that this whole thing is a pack of lies.' In spite of the outcome, he still believes that his advice was right—and so do I.

The first three days of the case were the hardest. I thought that those who had heard Ian's evidence might be openly hostile to me, but I soon realised that the crowd waiting daily outside the law courts and the Caledonian Hotel, where I was staying, were friendly, and that I had the sympathy of many people. I was greeted by cries of 'Good luck' and 'Go for him', and had many bunches of heather pressed into my hand.

I later heard that Ian and his solicitors did not expect me to go into the box. After my non-appearance in the MacPherson case, they anticipated another failure to face the music. But I was three years older and had more knowledge than on that day in May 1960 when Gerald Gardiner had advised me against speaking in my own defence.

Ian Fraser (now Lord Fraser), Dean of the Faculty of Advocates, opened the case for me, and normally, as Defender, I should have been first in the box.

But Peach, the Duke's valet, who was one of my witnesses, was called before me in order to catch a train. I saw Ian and his advisers gloating, thinking that I had given in again.

After Peach, I was called to give evidence, and as I rose to go into the box Ian's jaw literally dropped and his face went very, very red.

From the box I also looked once more into the eyes of Yvonne MacPherson, who had already given evidence for Ian. She was looking as shaken as Ian.

The moment came for George Emslie, QC, to cross-examine me. Emslie was a plump little man, and certainly did not look terrifying to me. He began by swishing his gown in a theatrical manner and shouting his questions at me.

I turned to the Judge, Lord Wheatley, and told him I was not accustomed to being shouted at in that way, as I was not deaf. I asked if it was really necessary. The Judge told Emslie to moderate his voice when addressing me. Mr Emslie altogether became increasingly more moderate as the minutes passed.

What I remember best about those days in court is the total exhaustion that followed. I would return to the Caledonian so drained that I barely had the strength to get to my suite. Once in my room I would collapse on to the bed and lie there like a limp rag for an hour, without even taking off my coat. It was a tiredness unlike any I had known in my life.

The court reporters told me at the end of the case that they had been convinced throughout that, although Ian had slung endless mud at me, he had not won a single legal point, nor had he been able to disprove anything that I had said on oath.

As I was leaving the court room after my last day in the box, I was handed the following letter:

To Her Grace, The Duchess of Argyll.

We, the women in the public gallery, at the hearing of the Duke's divorce petition, wish to express our admiration for your courage in standing in the witness box and speaking so eloquently and bravely in your own defence.

You touched our hearts. We have watched and listened with sincere sympathy for you.

Whether you are guilty of the charge of adultery does not matter to us one bit, but if your character should be unnecessarily smeared, that would matter a lot—and we would deplore any attempt to do this.

We would like to wish you great happiness in the future, and give you our sincere affection. We shall miss seeing your enchanting beauty.

The letter bore seven signatures, and reading it in my room I was reduced to tears. I was not fighting a lone battle after all, it seemed. My spirits lifted, and I left Edinburgh to wait for Lord Wheatley's judgement. It was given two months later, on May 8th, while Bill and I were in Paris, where I heard the news that I had suffered a crushing defeat.

Lord Wheatley had sat in the Court of Session at Edinburgh and delivered his gargantuan judgement—40,000 words.

He granted Ian a divorce mainly on the basis of one occasion—the evening of July 13th, 1960—when Peter Combe took me home from a nightclub and remained in my house for ninety minutes.

When calling for me earlier that evening Peter had left three large dogs in my house, and when we returned my maid, Kathleen Carpenter, was waiting up to tell me that Peter's dogs—'not ours'—had wreaked havoc in the house. The three of us spent some time putting the house in order again.

Peter then came to the library and stayed half an hour for a drink. Carpenter was still up and about on the floor above us. She had already warned us that there were two men parked in a car opposite the house who looked like private detectives. While we were having our drinks, Peter suggested asking them to join us!

Yet Lord Wheatley considered that 'the circumstances of that night are sufficient to infer that adultery took place on that occasion.'

His findings brought a sarcastic reaction from that shrewd observer, the Earl of Arran, who wrote:

> I cannot help raising an eyebrow at the learned judge's decision on one point. If it were ever to be generally assumed that because a man stays for 90 minutes in a woman's house after taking her to a nightclub that the worst has happened, then I am a monumental sinner. On that basis or argument, I have been to bed with at least 30 women, some of them a great many times.

That was the view generally taken. It was felt that Lord Wheatley must have led an extremely sheltered life. It was also felt that he had far exceeded his function as a divorce judge, and his cruel and devastating condemnation of my character seemed to cause revulsion and criticism almost everywhere. Bernard Levin, who is certainly no admirer of the aristocracy, felt that Lord Wheatley's 'unnecessarily prolonged judgement in the Argyll case only maintained the reputation for impertinence—in both senses of the word—that the Bench in this country has unhappily acquired.' He went on to say that the judge's remarks 'threw some light on his own psychology, but most of the "moderns" I know would agree that a Divorce Court judge's function is to decide the case before him, and that he might with advantage leave sexual psychology and social *mores* to those better equipped to discuss them.'

It was *The Observer*, however, in an editorial article, which took Lord Wheatley most severely to task. The writer expressed surprise that Lord Wheatley should have thought fit to repeat so much of the evidence he had heard in court. He must have known that his judgement would be published at length in nearly every newspaper and quoted by the BBC both because of the prominence of the individuals concerned and the salacious nature of the evidence. It went on:

> One cannot escape the conclusion that he did so because he also wished to publicise his moral strictures—some of them

rather brutal—on the case. As a man and a Roman Catholic, Lord Wheatley is entitled to his own opinions on sexual morals, marriage and divorce. But as a judge he need only find which of the parties before him is 'guilty' in the eyes of the law. . . .

But cruelty to individuals, including the wholly innocent children and grandchildren of individuals thus publicly pilloried, is not justified by moral indignation at the offence. We believe that divorce judges should give in their judgement only those facts which are strictly necessary to explain their findings.

Bill and I hurried back from Paris in the hope that I could lodge an appeal against the judgement. But my solicitors had found no point of law we could attack. It was all Lord Wheatley's opinion, and judges are entitled to their opinions, however savagely they express them.

Not only was I unhappy and angry, but I was also bewildered by the inconsistencies of Scottish law. Although my Edinburgh advisers were never optimistic about my case, they had repeatedly told me that in Scottish law a divorce is much more difficult to obtain than in England. It demands that there be 'two eye-witnesses of a couple crossing the threshold of a bedroom and staying there for the night.' In my case I asked myself, 'Where were those four eyes, and where was that bedroom threshold?'

Shortly afterwards, Lord Wheatley gave another judgement—again in Ian's favour. He ordered me to pay seven-eighths of the divorce costs, including Ian's. The fact that Ian's costs came to £8,000 rather than the inflated amount speculated upon by the press did not make the injustice of it any easier to bear.

Once again I was bewildered, because I had always been told by my Edinburgh 'advisers' that in Scotland, 'Any woman has the right to defend her fair name at her husband's expense.'

In spite of the outcome, the one thing I have never regretted is defending that divorce. I did my best.

From New York my son sent me a sweet cable when he heard the news: 'Desperately sorry verdict and humiliation. Disbelieve evidence completely. All possible moral support. Love.—Brian.'

When Wheatley's judgement was published, scores of letters

and telegrams arrived for me. I opened them with considerable apprehension, but I was touched beyond words by the kindness of the people who had written to me. Amongst them were letters from old friends like Lady Daphne Straight, Eric (Earl of) Dudley, Barbara Cartland, (Prince) Charles d'Arenberg, who all sent their love and encouragement.

The letters were not only from friends. They also came from members of the public, people I had never even met. One came from a young couple to whom I had once given a lift on the Rest and Be Thankful Pass in Argyll. Another was from an ex-ARP warden with a wartime memory:

> Were you one of the 'Brave Ones' staying at the Dorchester in January 1941 when two bombs missed it by a hundred yards?
>
> I was on duty on the roof and did I pray when they whistled down behind the chimney stack!
>
> Having survived the onslaught I tore down to the lounge to see all of you assembled in your negligees, the men, I recall, in uniforms. Quite a large crowd. The explosions had been deafening.
>
> Now I am sure I recognised the beautiful lady in pink who asked me, 'Is Albemarle Street O.K.?'
>
> Was it you, brave one?

During the golden years when I entertained a great deal, I occasionally wondered how many of my guests would remain loyal to me if my fortunes changed. My guess was—about twenty per cent. People often say that they can count their real friends on the fingers of one hand. After my divorce I discovered that I was much luckier. I found myself protected by a group of intelligent, angry and intensely loyal people, all the ones I would have expected. First to arrive on my doorstep the morning after my divorce was the best friend anyone could hope to have— Lady d'Avigdor Goldsmid. Susan Ward, wife of Colonel John Ward, the former Silver Stick in Waiting, telephoned and offered me all her support—and so they rallied round.

But a very few—four to be exact—intimate friends of many years' standing, and whom I had entertained in my house count-less times, suddenly became invisible. These consisted of one married couple and two well known single women (one of them a Peeress) whom I certainly had thought I could rely upon, and I was amazed at their behaviour.

For a week after the judgement I stayed in the house and moped. Then Bill insisted on my going out, and he took me shopping at Aspreys. Everybody I met that day seemed to be exceptionally warm and friendly.

A month later Sir Charles Clore invited me to his annual dance. It was the first public occasion I had attended since the divorce, and I wondered how I would be received. I need not have worried. People in their unique British way greeted me as though nothing had happened—so much so that I began to wonder if what I had been going through was merely a bad dream.

The summer was pleasant and peaceful, which made a welcome change. Then, just as the divorce was beginning to fade from public memory, the Denning Report on the Profumo case revived it all over again.

As the Report concerned itself with Government Security, the publicity leakages surrounding Lord Denning's enquiries seemed very strange to me. A story—quite untrue—that 'the Argyll divorce papers were sent down to Lord Denning from Scotland' became front page headlines, and there was a surprising number of press photographs of various witnesses entering and leaving Lord Denning's chambers. Consequently, when Cecil Jobson told me that Lord Denning wished to see me in connection with one aspect of the case I agreed on condition that Lord Denning came to my house.

Lord Denning did visit me, and I explained what I knew about the minor incident he was investigating.

Three weeks after our divorce became final Ian Argyll was married again, for the fourth time, to a Mrs Matilda Heller. She had been in Ian's life for some years before our divorce.

One happy memory of my work at Inveraray is enshrined in a touching message of condolence that I received from the Inveraray Town Council when my father died, and in the many loyal letters from the Royal Burgh after the divorce judgement. I had continued booking films for the Argyll Cinema from London for three years after I left Inveraray Castle, and ten months after Ian's remarriage, the former Provost, Mr John

Campbell, wrote to me when the Argyll Cinema was closed—
TV had come into its own. He said:

> Your good work has not been forgotten. Speaking on my
> own behalf and also on behalf of the members of the Trust,
> may I thank Your Grace for those wonderful meetings we
> had at the Castle, for the work which you put into the running
> of the cinema, and above all for your unselfish interest in all
> the affairs of the Burgh. Believe me, Your Grace, when I say
> we do miss you very much.

To this day I receive Christmas cards from Provost Campbell
and from other of my Inveraray friends. I am also always delighted
when they visit me in London.

In November 1964 I heard that Ian was publishing a series of
articles for a 'popular' Sunday newspaper. I had heard rumours
of these articles during the past three years but I could not believe,
even now, that Ian could stoop so low. The articles purported
to tell his life story, but he disposed of his five years as a prisoner
of war, and his two former marriages, in a few paragraphs.
Clearly the sole purpose of these articles was to attack me, and
to revive details of the divorce action.

There was also a 'report' by Petro on my physical and psycho-
logical health during the marriage. Petro was *never* my doctor.

This time I had Counsel who urged me to fight: Sir Andrew
Clark, QC, and Paul Sieghart.

On Friday, November 13th—two days before the first article
was to appear—I applied to the High Court for an ex-parte
injunction to restrain Ian from publishing details of my 'private
life, personal affairs or private conduct,' communicated to him
in confidence during our marriage and 'not hitherto made public
property.'

This is known in America as the 'Invasion of Privacy' law,
brought over from this country by Judge Brandeis. It was a law
that had seemingly died out here, but Sir Andrew Clark and
Mr Paul Sieghart revived it with a vengeance.

This writ took *The People*, in which the articles were to appear,
by surprise. They begged us to allow them to publish the first
article which was comparatively harmless, describing the first
years of our married life. We consented to this. They then offered

to submit the other five articles to Sir Andrew the following week for him to read.

I shall never forget the scene in Sir Andrew Clark's chambers on the day that he received the five articles. As he read them with Sieghart he said repeatedly, 'These are the most terrible things I have ever read.' He could not believe that any gentleman, let alone a Duke, could write them. He said they *must* be stopped.

The application was heard on November 17th, 1964, and Sir Andrew Clark described Ian's articles as 'a scurrilous and vindictive attack.' Referring to the 'medical report' on me, Sir Andrew commented, 'How any man with any decent feelings could seek to publish such a thing to the world for his own pecuniary gain passes comprehension.'

The Judge, Mr Justice Ungoed-Thomas, agreed: 'A relationship more intimate can hardly be conceived of than the relationship based upon mutual trust and confidences between husband and wife,' he said in his judgement.

He granted my application and restrained *The People* and Ian from publishing any of the private matters to which I had objected. Only four of the six articles were allowed to be published.

This judgement became popularly known as the Argyll Law, and it greatly disturbed publishers and newspaper editors. For the first time in British courts, the doctrine of the binding validity of a confidence based purely on trust was proclaimed.

Ian's attempt to write about me in this way had antagonised many of his friends. As a result of the unpleasant publicity over his articles in *The People*, many members of White's complained to the Club's committee. The committee debated the matter, and the chairman, Mr David Stacey, wrote to Ian suggesting that he might care to resign. Faced with the alternative of a committee vote to expel him, Ian resigned from White's in January, 1965. It must have been a bitter moment for him. I can still remember the day in 1950 when he nervously paced up and down the library at Inveraray waiting to hear if he had been elected as a member.

'Though the mills of God grind slowly, yet they grind exceeding small.'

Chapter 24

In September, 1963, Frances seemed sad and preoccupied, and I soon learned the reason. Robert, my second grandson, had developed an unknown illness.

He was taken to a specialist at the Great Ormond Street Hospital in London, and after various tests it was found that he needed a blood transfusion—the first of several.

My son-in-law, Charles Rutland, broke the news to me, but I had already guessed. Robert had leukaemia. He was not kept in hospital at that time but was allowed to return home. We all spent Christmas at Belvoir together, and even then we thought that Robert had a good chance of recovery.

I was again at Belvoir on a weekend in February when there came a crisis in Robert's condition. He had to be taken down to London by Frances in the car, and I came with them. Robert was only two and a half years old, but he must have had strange intuitive powers far in advance of his age. As the car left the castle he looked up at his mother and said 'Shall I ever see Belvoir again?' Frances reassured Robert, but she and I both knew that he would never return.

We took him straight to the hospital, and the doctors told us that there was now little hope for Robert—he remained in hospital from then on. Frances and I dined together at my house that evening, and she telephoned the news to Charles at Belvoir.

He motored down immediately to join us, and when we were all together I suggested calling the Medical Centre in Texas as they were reputed to have made a breakthrough in leukaemia research. We did call and were told by one of the most famous specialists there that they were on the verge of finding a cure—in five years' time.

For eighteen terrible days Robert clung to life, then he developed pneumonia, perhaps mercifully. In the late afternoon of February 28th, 1964, my former husband, Charlie Sweeny, telephoned for me to go at once to the hospital, and about an hour later Robert died.

He was buried in the family mausoleum in the grounds of Belvoir, with only the family and tenants present at the funeral. The sight of that very small coffin being carried over the hill towards us was heartbreaking.

Frances was dry-eyed and calm, for all her tears had been shed. She was still as self-controlled and reserved as she had always been, even as a child. I am afraid that Charles Rutland and I were far less stoical.

Robert was a very special child in every way, and his death was a sad illustration of the saying, 'Whom the Gods love die young.'

In the spring of 1965 I was spending a few days in Paris, and on April 23rd I was lunching with my oldest and dearest friends there, Baron and Baronne de Cabrol, in their apartment in the Avenue Foch. This time I was staying at the Plaza-Athenée, and the concierge happened to know where I was lunching. While I was with the de Cabrols I received a call from Charles Sweeny in London.

He told me that he had just heard that our son Brian had been in a bad car accident in New York at 2 o'clock that morning. He said that the only information he had was that Brian was suffering from multiple head injuries. This, of course, made my blood run cold. I said to Charlie that I would catch the next plane to London, and suggested that we meet at Heathrow Airport and fly to New York together.

Charlie made many helpful suggestions about the planes I could catch and where I could stay in New York, but said that he was involved in a business deal and could not come with me. He told the *Evening News* that Brian had had a lucky escape, and that he did not intend flying out. He added, 'His mother will let me know how Brian is when she gets to New York.'

Because of the difficulty in getting plane accommodation I finally left London early the next morning, and on arrival in New York went straight to the Lennox Hill Hospital where Brian had been taken and put into the Intensive Care Unit.

I had imagined every possible horror for twenty-four hours, and once in the hospital I dreaded what was awaiting me. I saw him immediately, as the doors are never closed and the lights are permanently on in each bedroom. Brian was lying very still, very white, with his eyes closed. I got hold of a male nurse who told me that he was not unconscious but under sedation. He also told me that he had been badly smashed all down his right side from shoulder to foot. His pelvis was out of its socket and he had broken his shoulder, arm and leg. Luckily, contrary to what we had been told, neither his head nor his spine had been injured.

I suggested leaving him undisturbed while I went to find the doctor, but the nurse said that Brian had been asking for me and would like to know that I was there. When I touched him he woke up with a start, shouting, obviously having some kind of nightmare. He seemed very relieved when he realised that I was there, and dozed off again.

When I found the doctor he told me just how bad his injuries were. He said that Brian would have to have several operations and would be in hospital at least three or four months, but he assured me that finally he should be perfectly whole and well.

He also explained to me how the accident had happened. Brian apparently had been driving his little Porsche car across 84th Street. A lorry, towing an enormous pantechnicon, had jumped the red light in Park Avenue and turned into 84th Street, hitting Brian's car, with the pantechnicon falling on top of the Porsche. If his car had not had a hard top Brian would have been killed. The girl he was with escaped with slight injuries, but Brian got the full brunt of the impact and the car was pulverised. In fact, although I avoided seeing it, I was told that the police deliberately left it out in the street for at least ten days as a warning to motorists.

It was naturally an enormous relief to me to hear that Brian would finally recover, and I immediately telephoned Charlie and woke him up, which annoyed him considerably—I had forgotten about the time change and that it was the early hours in London.

Then began the difficult business of getting a lawyer to represent Brian, an insurance company to enable him to make a claim against the owners of the lorry, and all the other technicalities of such an affair. I stayed in New York to arrange all this and to see Brian through the worst, until May 29th. By then I knew that there was no more I could do for the moment, and since any number of his friends were visiting him in hospital, I decided to return to London. I hoped to be there in time for the birth of Frances' fourth child, but Lord Edward Manners beat me to it and was born on 29th May. He was the most beautiful baby boy, and grew up to look uncannily like poor little Robert. With his looks, his voice, his mannerisms, he could have been Robert's identical twin, and Charles Rutland and I said one day, almost in unison, 'Robert's come back.'

During the summer I was constantly in touch with Brian's doctors in New York and learned that the bones which had been broken in his leg would not knit together, even after a month and more in plaster. I was then told that a piece of bone would have to be taken out of his hip and inserted in his leg to enable the broken ends to join.

This was obviously worrying news, and I flew to New York on September 8th to try to cheer Brian up before the operation on the 10th. Although very painful, the operation seemed successful, but during the next three days Brian was frighteningly pale and I asked the doctors about his needing a blood transfusion. They said it would be highly necessary, but there was no risk as he had already had one transfusion immediately after the operation. So they arranged for him to have another one on September 13th.

I went to the hospital early that morning and insisted that for once he had the telephone unplugged, otherwise I knew he would spend the day talking to his broker and girl friends. The transfusion was expected to last several hours, so, instead of pacing the floor in the waiting room, I decided to go to Bloomingdale's store

—a visit to Bloomingdale's is usually a sure cure for all worries. When I arrived at the store I had a strong hunch that I ought to return to the hospital quickly, and, without even getting out of the taxi, I did so.

On entering Brian's room I found it filled with nurses and doctors, all scurrying round and looking very worried. Poor Brian's face was horribly swollen, and his eyes were so puffy that he could hardly open them. Apparently he had had a violent allergic reaction to the blood he had been given, and if the nurse in the room at the time had not been alert, and inserted a tube into his throat, he would have died from asphyxiation because his throat was closing.

Antihistamine injections helped to reduce the swelling, but at the end of the day Brain was an exhausted wreck. It had all happened within a matter of minutes, and none of the doctors could give me an explanation. Charlie visited Brian in October, and Frances, meanwhile, was very busy preparing to give a ball at Belvoir Castle for her stepdaughter, Lady Charlotte Manners. It was a magnificent affair and Frances deserved a lot of credit for the hard work that she put into it. Most of the guests came from some distance, and Frances not only reserved accommodation in the nearby hotels but also arranged that other neighbouring houses would put up her guests for the night. Charlotte, who had the famous Manners good looks, was a vision of beauty that night.

On October 17th Brian was allowed out of the hospital, and he flew straight back to London. He stayed in my house for many months, having daily treatment on his leg, but I am afraid the accident has left him with a steel rod in his hip, and a limp. However, he is lucky to be alive.

Poor Brian's troubles were not yet over. After a year of convalescence he went back to work in New York in the brokerage house of Haydon Stone International. In 1969 the international branch of this firm went into liquidation and Brian moved to another well-known firm of stockbrokers, Blair & Co. 1969 and 1970 were bad years for businessmen, and at the end of July, 1970, Brian telephoned me to say that Blair & Co. had also gone into liquidation. So he was once again out of a job, through no fault of his own.

I had been invited to spend that August in Santa Fe, New Mexico, as the guest of George Frelinghuysen, brother of the Congressman, and when I heard how depressed Brian sounded I immediately telephoned George in Los Angeles and asked if he would mind Brian joining us. George, generous and hospitable as always, was delighted, and Brian met me at the airport at Albuquerque on August 3rd. George was a wonderful host and guide to us on this visit. We motored to Taos and saw the 'Adobe Skyscrapers'. We also went to the surrounding villages and watched the Harvest Corn Dances, when the Indians pray for rain.

At Los Alamos, carrying special security passes, we saw the underground research centre where the first atomic bomb was developed.

This trip ended in Gallup where we watched the unforgettable Ceremonial dances. Here, all the Indian tribes—including Cherokees, Sioux, Iroquois, Navajos, Apaches—gather once a year to perform their ritual tribal dances. It was a fascinating spectacle which we were lucky to see, as I was told that this was the last time it would take place.

Brian had now decided—I think rightly—to give up being a stockbroker and to form and manage a company of his own in London. This was more easily said than done, so in the meantime he returned to live with me in my house. While he was unmarried and not working, it seemed a good time for us to explore the world together. He had inherited the travel bug from me, and we decided to take some exciting trips to far-off places. Brian is a perfect companion, as he is not only enthusiastic but drinks in knowledge everywhere he goes—and retains it.

In 1969, our first trip, to Pakistan, Afghanistan and Iran, lasted a month. In 1971 we made a five-week tour of Russia with the Smithsonian Institution, travelling by train, bus and plane as far north as Novgorod, and as far south as Tashkent and Samarkand. We loved Russia and the Russians, but the only chance we had to communicate with the local people anywhere was in Kiev. I remember one occasion when Brian and I were having a drink in the hotel bar while waiting to board our next plane which was, as usual, leaving at 2 a.m. The bar tender and his wife offered us 'drinks on the house', and we tried to ask why.

They said, 'This is to drink to peace between our countries and no more rat-tat-tat'—meaning war.

In the winter of 1973 Brian and I went to East Africa, South Africa and Ethiopia. In Cape Town we were invited to lunch in the House of Parliament by the famous Mrs Helen Suzman, who is one of the most vital and attractive women I have ever met. At that time she was the head, and only parliamentary member, of the Progressive Party—extremely advanced in her ideas.

From South Africa we went to Ethiopia, and the highlight of our trip there was provided by our hostess, Princess Ruth Desta (granddaughter of Emperor Haile Selassie), and Johannes, son of another granddaughter, Princess Aida. We stayed with them at Government House in the Province of Makelle. From there they flew us in their private plane to the Danekil Depression. Armed guards travelled with us, not only to protect the Royal family but because the area was full of brigands.

The Danekil Depression is the lowest place on earth and was once a sea bed. It is full of bubbling cauldrons of potash and sulphur—bright orange and lime green. You have to be guided every inch of the way, as one false step could mean being sucked down to a scalding death.

In February 1966 I had been invited to go to Mexico, which I had always longed to see, and I decided to extend the trip and go to some of the places I had missed in South America in 1961.

I flew direct to Los Angeles, where I met a charming couple from Houston called Baron and Baroness Portanova. They were both unusually handsome. Riccy Portanova, whose father was Neapolitan, was half Texan on his mother's side, and his grandfather had been the richest man in Houston. Luba Portanova was Yugoslavian and had a beauty resembling Sophia Loren's. When they heard that I was going to visit South America, Riccy said to me, 'Why don't you end your trip in Houston? If you do, let us know and we will look after you.'

I loved the idea but dismissed it as one of those casual invitations that are not meant to be taken seriously.

George Getty, whom I had met through his father, Paul, gave me a wonderful time in Los Angeles and also made the arrangements and provided introductions for a trip I planned to the

Yucatan in Mexico. Without his help I should never have managed this, as all the planes and hotels tend to be full in the winter season.

From Los Angeles I flew to Mexico City, and visited Merle Oberon in Cuernavaca, and from there to Merida, capital of the Yucatan, where I spent two or three days being shown around the fabulous ruins by Mr and Mrs Barbachanos, the leaders of Yucatan society.

I had intended to go straight to the Argentine, but decided to break my journey in Guatemala. For some reason the plane could not land at Guatemala, so we had to go to El Salvador, where we all spent the night at the Intercontinental Hotel. On being shown into my room I noticed a large rift, four inches wide, running down the wall. I asked what it was and was told there had been an earthquake the day before!

We reached Guatemala the following day, and I discovered that there was both a minor revolution and an election going on. Everybody was warned to stay indoors, but I was determined not to waste my visit. The next morning I hired a car, an English-speaking driver, and I motored up to Chichicastenango, one of the most fascinating towns in all of Central America. The drive itself was full of interest, and I lunched at the beautiful Lake Atitlan on the way.

Luckily I have no fear of travelling alone—in fact I would much prefer to be on my own than with an irritating companion. But here I did rather wonder what was going to happen next, as the country was practically in a state of war and I did not speak a word of the language.

I did a great deal of sight-seeing in Chichicastenango, and next day found myself, by mistake, in a line of people who were queueing up to cast their votes in the election.

I was almost the only tourist there at the time, and not a very popular one, I'm afraid, as I was always trying surreptitiously to take photographs of the people, which they do not like. Anyway, I did get some wonderful pictures.

I had great difficulty in getting out of the country, thanks to the political situation, but I finally flew down to Buenos Aires, crossing the fabulous Andes on the way.

I was met at the airport by my Argentine friends, the Uriburus.

Their maternal grandfather was General Rojas, who liberated Patagonia from the Indians, making it part of the Argentine. Consequently everywhere we went doors were opened to us. Patagonia is a beautiful country, not unlike Switzerland but on a grander scale and with marvellous fishing—so good, in fact, that anglers often come direct from Scotland specially for that. The wild life, too, is extraordinary, and, mercifully, many of the animals and birds, such as the vicunas, llamas and condors, are now being preserved.

I was strongly tempted to continue my journey down to Tierra del Fuego at the southernmost tip of South America, but it was another two thousand miles on, and when I was told that I would meet nothing but penguins and face a permanent eighty-mile-an-hour gale, I decided to go to Chile instead. This meant taking a succession of buses and boats for two days crossing the lakes, and as I never travel light—I had ten pieces of luggage with me—and I do not speak a word of Spanish, my Argentine friends firmly believed that I would never reach Chile.

They would probably have been right had I not met 'Happy' Hatton, a young American working in the Peace Corps, who was making the same trip with his girl friend. I was feeling, and must have looked, rather forlorn sitting on the boat deck surrounded by a pile of luggage. It was also raining. Dear 'Happy' came up to me and said, 'Ma'am, you look as though you are in trouble. Can I help?' I accepted his offer with the greatest alacrity, and if it had not been for 'Happy' I think I might still be sitting at the Argentine/Chilean frontier, as nobody there even understood my passport.

Finally, arriving in Porto Varas on a bone-shaking bus with no springs, I took the night train up to Santiago, spent a night there, and then flew to Peru.

Lima is a most interesting city, but the main object of my visit to Peru was to see Cuzco and Macchu Piccu. When I got to the airport I discovered that my aeroplane was not pressurised, and Cuzco is 14,000 feet above sea level. Once I boarded the plane, however, I forgot all about this until I found myself trying to suck an oxygen tube, eat a sandwich, and take photographs out of the window all at the same time.

We were warned on the plane that it was necessary to lie down for an hour on arrival in Cuzco because of the height. This I obediently did. I also took coramine tablets, as advised. After my hour's rest I felt perfectly well, and rushed out to see all that I possibly could, which meant scrambling over many ruins. Everything was fine until two o'clock the next morning when I woke up unable to breathe. The effect of the altitude had hit me sixteen hours after my arrival. Later that morning I crawled on to the auto-rail that takes one to Macchu Piccu, and as we were descending all the time I began to feel more normal.

Everybody told me that I must stay the night to see Macchu Piccu at sunrise. So next morning I was up at dawn and I realised how very worthwhile the effort had been. I stood, quite alone, watching the sun rise, and clambering over these ancient ruins. It was a memorable experience.

I had cabled the Portanovas from Lima giving them the date I was arriving in Houston, but quite expected that they had forgotten my existence.

It was raining when I arived there—dead-tired and very travel weary. In fact during the drive into the city I wondered why I had ever come. There were no messages awaiting me at my hotel, so I decided to leave for New York the following day.

That afternoon I was lying on my bed feeling rather sorry for myself, when the telephone rang. It was Luba Portanova, who welcomed me to Houston and then said, 'We're taking you out to dinner tonight with a very attractive beau, and we are giving a dinner dance tomorrow night in your honour in the restaurant on the roof of the Warwick Hotel.' I began to realise what the famous Texan hospitality was like.

The 'beau' who dined with us on the first night was William Dugger, an oil millionaire, and a most generous, wonderful person, who became a great friend of mine. At the dinner dance the following night I met what seemed to be all of Houston, and I then spent ten of the gayest days, all organised by Riccy and Luba.

On March 28th I was presented with a document giving me the freedom of the City of Houston. The Mayor described me as 'The most stupendous stir to hit Houston since the Beatles.' I was taken on a special visit to NASA, headquarters of the American space programme. Officials explained their plans for a moon landing, and I tried very hard to follow them. In 1968, while watching Neil Armstrong (whom I had met in Houston) make his first step on the moon, I realised they were following in every detail the programme they had described to me two years earlier.

At the end of my visit to Houston I sent Luba dozens of roses from the hotel florist as a small 'Thank you' for the wonderful time that she and Riccy had given me. On asking for my bill at the hotel I was told by the manager that it had already been taken care of by Baron Portanova. I realised with horror that the Portanovas had paid not only for my laundry, cables etc., but for their own roses!

I shall never forget Riccy's reply to my protests the next day. He said, 'In Texas a lady travelling alone is never allowed to open her purse.'

In the meantime Bill Dugger had arranged for me to visit San Antonio, his home town, as his guest, so I was duly flown there in his private plane. I arrived at the Saint Anthony Hotel to find myself installed in a suite so grand and so full of flowers that I took photographs of it, for I knew that otherwise nobody would believe my description of it.

Bill also arranged a dinner dance for a hundred people. This time it was held in the Argyll Club. The name of this club did not surprise me, for I knew that thousands of Campbells had emigrated from Scotland to Texas.

I was then invited to a traditional dinner given on the river boat which sailed down the San Antonio, accompanied by the Mariachi Orchestra playing Mexican music. What with all this excitement, and with going every night to the Poco Loco night-club, I realised that I was seeing nothing of the city itself. It was difficult to get anybody to show me around, as the hours were very Spanish—lunch often began at 2.30 and ended at 5 p.m. Finally I literally dragged a friend of mine, Jeanette Jaffee, out of bed at ten in the morning and implored her to take me on a tour of the wonderful old Spanish Mission Churches. Above all I wanted to see the Alamo Museum. There I read, with a lump in my throat, of the soldiers from Virginia, Kentucky, Tennessee and even Scotland, who had enlisted to fight for a cause that was not their own.

From San Antonio I was flown to Dallas—again in a private

plane. By this time I was getting used to it. I was the guest of Mr and Mrs Joe Lambert and was lucky enough to find myself staying in one of the most beautiful penthouses in America.

Joe Lambert was known as the finest landscape gardener in the United States, and Evelyn, his wife, is one of the most amusing women I have ever met. She and I are still great friends, but Joe is now dead. With them I enjoyed the same scale of hospitality and fun in Dallas that I had enjoyed all over Texas.

Not surprisingly, I was very sad indeed to leave Texas, and have been back many times since.

In January 1967 I was invited to stay in Colombo, Ceylon, with Sir Oliver Goonetilleke and his daughter, Sheila.

Sir Oliver was the first Singhalese to become Governor of the island. After their independence he was appointed High Commissioner to London, and Sheila (now married to Mr Sathanathan, a Tamil Indian) was his hostess.

During my flight to Colombo I discovered that 'Dickie' Mountbatten was on the same plane. He, of course, was travelling first class; I, of course, was in the economy section. On arrival in Colombo Dickie was met by a group of VIPs, among them Oliver Goonetilleke. As he had come to meet me, I, too, enjoyed a very gay, prestigious arrival.

Dickie was on his way to India to make part of the television series on his life. For the first five days there were endless festivities in his honour, to which I was invited, and because of this I met the Prime Minister (Dudley Senanayake) and many of the Government officials.

As usual, I was longing to see as much as possible of the country and begged Oliver to take me on a tour. This he did, and I could not have had a better escort. Everywhere we went the people gathered around him with obvious affection. We visited Kandy and were allowed a private viewing of the Sacred Tooth. This happens only once a year, and the people were patiently queueing the whole day for a glimpse of it. We watched the Kandy elephants being taken down to the river for their daily bathe, and we visited all the impressive ruined cities. In fact, I don't think Oliver had ever before seen so much of his country in such a short time.

Oliver persuaded me, without much difficulty, to extend my trip and visit India—another place I had always longed to see—so, armed with introductions to everybody everywhere, I started off for Madras.

While staying there I saw an enormous American ship arriving, filled with wheat and all kinds of grain, as a gift from America to India. The ship was so large that it could not get into the harbour, and its cargo had to be unloaded into lighters. Once again I marvelled at the generosity of America, for which they get little thanks, as I am only too well aware.

I was told that there was an astrologer, famous throughout India, who happened to be visiting Madras at this time. I have always loved going to fortune tellers, and immediately made an appointment to see him on February 16th. Amongst other things, he told me that on March 12th I would be in Dallas, Texas, and that there I would receive either a letter or a telegram which would affect my life considerably. I thought the poor man was out of his mind because I had made definite plans to be in Calcutta on March 11th, and Calcutta is a long way from Dallas.

Some time earlier I had applied to the English Court to be allowed to break twenty trusts, inherited from my father, in favour of my children, to save them paying death duties and to enable them to enjoy the money while they were young. My lawyers were not at all sure that the judge would sanction this. One year after the astrologer's prediction I *was* in Dallas, Texas, and on March 12th I received a cable from London telling me that the judge had agreed to my breaking these trusts. The sum of money involved was considerable, and I immediately sent cables, changing many of my instructions regarding property in Nassau and on other matters. So, in a most uncanny way, the astrologer proved right about the place, the date, what I would receive, and the effects it would have on my future. He was only wrong by exactly one year to the day.

This money, plus other bequests my father had made to my children, has benefited them greatly throughout their lives. I only hope that they will learn to appreciate their remarkable grandfather and their Scottish heritage.

After Madras I made an extensive tour of India, sometimes with others and sometimes alone. I visited Mysore as guest of the Maharajah, Bangalore and Bombay. I saw the Caves of Ellora and Ajanta, which were restored thanks entirely to Lord Curzon. I went to Udaipur and Jaipur, I spent a week in Delhi and, of course, I went to Agra to see the Taj Mahal. Banal as it may be to say it, the Taj Mahal is the most beautiful thing I have ever seen in my life, anywhere. I saw it first at midday and marvelled at its perfection—no neon lights, no telegraph poles, no traffic signs anywhere near. I went again at sunset, and again at midnight under a full moon, which is the obvious tourist thing to do. Determined to see it at sunrise, I got up at five o'clock the next morning, woke up a cross, sleepy taxi driver, and sat in his taxi in the bitter cold waiting for the sun to rise. The driver by this time had given me up as mad and gone to sleep again. When the sun began to appear, the Taj Mahal turned a bright rose pink, which grew paler as the light grew stronger.

All this time I was completely alone there, and I took picture after picture as the colour changed.

I then proceeded to Benares for two nights before taking a plane to Nepal. Besides seeing as much as I could of Katmandu, the capital, I also toured the ancient towns of Badgaon and Pathan.

On March 10th I flew to Calcutta to meet friends, and the week I spent there was a welcome rest from the strenuous travelling I had been doing. From there I flew to Cambodia via Bangkok and went to Angkor to visit the temples there. They certainly lived up to their reputation as one of the wonders of the world. In moments of euphoria I had sometimes considered making a round-the-world trip. But I am never very good at consulting maps. Now, in Cambodia, I sat down and looked at a map for the first time, and realised that I was only a quarter of the way round the world. I was also very tired and suffering from mental indigestion from all that I had seen. And suddenly I decided to take the first plane home from Bangkok, which I did.

I had missed Bill very much during my long trip, but our separation had been a necessary one. In spite of the fact that his marriage was unhappy, I knew that I could not contemplate a future in which the ghost of his wife came between us, so I had left him to think things out by himself. Bill met me at London Airport, the same Bill I had loved so deeply for six years. I would have married him within five minutes if he had been free.

But he was not, and his wife had become almost suicidal at the idea of losing him. So, together, we decided that we would have to part. I try not to think about the misery that surrounded this decision. The following letter of farewell, which I received from Bill in March, explains better than I can all that I was losing:

My dearest Margaret,

Until about ten months ago I could never have believed this day would ever come. Since early this year I've been dreading it.

If this is really goodbye—my mind says it is but everything else about me denies it—let me give you these lasting impressions I have of you.

You are surely the most beautiful woman who ever lived. You are also one of the bravest, most charming and most generous.

You are capable of providing the greatest excitement, warmth and happiness.

Thank you for all of that,

love,

Bill.

Chapter 25

Being brought up in a city I never owned a pet, though I had always adored all animals.

I had one very clear-cut childhood dream. It was that I should own a country house surrounded by lots of lovely fields, with lots of shiny new stables and lots of shiny new kennels. I would be living in the house, surrounded by strong young men and strong young girls all in shiny white overalls who would look after any lost, hurt, neglected, old or unhappy animal of any kind for the rest of its life.

Early in January, 1968, I received an appeal from Bleakholt Animal Sanctuary in Lancashire. Nobody to this day has ever discovered how this came to me as the organisation never sent appeals to London. It was a most appealing appeal, and a heart-breaking one. It had photographs of horses, dogs, cats and donkeys all round the page, and it said that five hundred animals were in danger of being put down for lack of money.

The appeal made an extraordinary impact on me. I paced the floor for an hour, was about to write a cheque for far more than I could afford, and then pulled myself together sufficiently to telephone the RSPCA, to check that Bleakholt Animal Sanctuary was even genuine. They assured me that it was not only genuine but desperately in need of help.

I immediately made up my mind to go and see this sanctuary,

and the RSPCA offered to have their Northern Regional Inspector (Mr Goodenough) accompany me. On January 20th I stayed the night with a great friend of mine, Lady Barber, widow of General Sir Colin Barber, who has a house in Ripon. The next day Mr Goodenough called for me and we set off for Bleakholt, which proved to be a very difficult place to get to, deep in the Lancashire moors. Once there we were met by Mrs Olive Lomas, the remarkable woman who had begun the sanctuary by adopting one horse, and who had run it for eleven years. She greeted me by saying. 'Duchess, your coming is a miracle. I am not even going to try to apologise for Bleakholt—we are past apologies.' I said, 'I am not here for apologies. I have come to try to help.'

On touring the sanctuary I could see that it was hopelessly overcrowded and broken down. There was a cat or dog in every corner of every building. The horses and donkeys were housed n old railway carriages. But no living creature had been abandoned by Bleakholt. There was even a sheep which had broken its two front legs on a road, and various birds which had been found with broken wings.

Chaos though it was, at least the animals were safe, under a roof, well fed and happy, and I made up my mind on the spot to do my utmost to save Bleakholt. The first thing I did was to arrange for it to become a Registered Charity. Both for tax reasons and for its reputation this was vital. Next I arranged a meeting in London with the Charity Commissioners' lawyer and Mr Rowlands, Bleakholt's lawyer, plus myself. Mr Rowlands and I had to admit that there would be no accounts available for at least a year because Mrs Lomas had kept no bills. However, the Commissioners' lawyer was most understanding, and saw to it that Bleakholt was registered in record time.

The next thing I had to do was to pay off Bleakholt's numerous debts and try to eradicate the bad reputation which it had acquired because of these debts (which totalled over £9,000).

Mrs Lomas was a dedicated animal lover and a fantastic fundraiser, but her heart ruled her head, and every penny that she raised had gone to buying food for more and more animals. Bills and debts just did not interest her. I became Patron and President and formed an impressive Appeals Committee which included the Duchess of Norfolk, the Marchioness of Zetland, Lady

(Colin) Barber and the Earl of Derby, Lord Lieutenant of Lancashire. I paid monthly visits to Bleakholt, and the meetings we held during my visits I shall never forget. They took place in a little wooden house (now a very attractive tea-room), with a paraffin stove, and the whole room swarming with dogs and cats.

At these meetings it was becoming clear that the money I had given to build new kennels was all going on day-to-day expenses. It was all extremely worrying. After almost a year of struggling along in this haphazard way I decided that we must employ an accountant. This was done, and we held a most upsetting meeting on December 19th, 1968, with him there. His report was even worse than I had expected, and it shocked everybody present. As well as our disastrous financial position, there were other problems. We were breaking the law by leaving marrow bones in the fields; we were not attached to the main water supply, and the well water was unfit for the animals to drink. Last but not least, the risk of fire was very great.

However, this meeting proved to be a turning point for the sanctuary. Mrs Lomas decided to resign, and we immediately engaged a manager and formed a devoted and efficient working committee, thereby spreading the load of responsibility.

The next time I went to Bleakholt I arranged to meet the local Health and Sanitation Officer, and the head of the Fire Brigade. The Committee and I discovered that, far from being enemies of the sanctuary, these men were all very worried about Bleakholt and most anxious to advise and help us. I found the same attitude from the local RSPCA officials, who are now our best friends. Though much heartened by all this, we still had to face many desperately anxious moments struggling to get the charity on a firm footing. It became sadly necessary to put down seventy-eight dogs that were old and unwell. This was done on the advice of Mr Nutt, the vet, who I think suffered more than any of us on that day.

One of our triumphs was producing the sanctuary's first Annual Report in 1971.

Now Bleakholt has seventy new kennels which can house two dogs each, twenty-four new concrete stables which can house either two horses or four donkeys each, and a new cattery for forty-five cats, with ledges for them to lie on and dangling toys for them to play with. We also have an isolation building for six dogs and four cats. As each of these was built, we joyfully made a bonfire of all the old, dilapidated kennels and stables.

Bleakholt and I can never thank Mr and Mrs John Adamson adequately for their loyal support and hard work for sixteen years on behalf of the sanctuary. Mr Adamson was chairman, but because of overworking to help Bleakholt he had to resign, and is now vice-chairman. Mrs Adamson is the honorary York-shire representative for Bleakholt, and she raises over £4,000 a year by her own efforts for the sanctuary. Miss E. J. Searle, another wonderful friend to Bleakholt for sixteen years, became our chairman.

I would also like to say how helpful the press have been during this seven years' struggle. Every letter of appeal of mine that they have kindly published has always brought wonderful results. One editor, however, rapped me rather firmly over the knuckles in a letter by saying, 'I will publish this letter in aid of your Sanctuary, but not another one for at least a year.'

The struggle to keep Bleakholt going now is harder than ever in these very difficult times, but working for it is almost my childhood dream come true, and is one of the most satisfactory and satisfying things I have ever done.

While coping with Bleakholt's problems in the summer of 1968 I went on a cruise to the North Cape. When I returned on July 15th I read with dismay that the Regiment of the Argyll and Sutherland Highlanders was about to be disbanded by the Labour govern-ment.

There was a storm of protest against the disbandment, and much talk of collecting a million signatures in a petition against 'axing' them. Apart from the fact that I was still bearing the name of Argyll, several relatives of mine have served in this Regiment. A cousin, Brigadier Ronald Tod, parachuted into Yugoslavia with a group of them led by Sir Fitzroy Mclean. Therefore I, too, was concerned and immediately sent a telegram to Lieutenant-Colonel Colin Mitchell, the swashbuckling hero of Aden:

Have returned today from abroad and wish to say how dis-tressed I am as a Scot to hear the news of the impending disbandment of the Argyll and Sutherland Highlanders. The heroism of the Argylls in Aden and elsewhere will live forever and if there is anything at all which I can do to help you have this decision reversed please let me know.

I was delighted to receive his reply:

Thank you very much for your kind telegram. How very thoughtful of you. Will certainly tell you if there is anything you can do to help us.

I had assumed that my former husband, who had been a captain in the Regiment and was taken prisoner with them at St Valery in 1940, would be one of the leaders of this cause. A reporter telephoned asking me if I was going to take part in this campaign. I replied, 'Of course I would like to, but I feel that it is for the Duke to help his Regiment officially.' The reporter replied, 'I have just spoken to the Duke at Inveraray, and he has said, "Don't bother me with this, and tell people not to write to me about it." '

Once again I was amazed, and thought how empty Ian's life must have become. Now I began to wonder if I might be of some help in the campaign.

I nervously telephoned General Sir Gordon MacMillan, who was leading the campaign from Scotland. It had to be organised by retired officers of the regiment, as serving officers are not allowed to take part in any political controversy. I asked permission to form a base in London to collect signatures outside of Scotland. The General agreed. I began by putting an advertisement in *The Times* and *The Daily Telegraph*, saying that if anybody was interested I would be present at Scotch House, a shop in Knightsbridge, all through the day of August 1st to inaugurate the campaign and receive signatures.

It became quite a ceremony, with the Queen Mother's piper, Pipe Major Leslie de Laspee, piping me in to the tune of 'The Campbells are Coming'.

A surprising number of people came along to sign, among them Iona, the young Marchioness of Lorne, my step daughter-in-law.

During the day I sent a telegram to Lieutenant-Colonel Colin Mitchell reporting our progress:

Five hundred signatures collected by one p.m. and they are still signing. Will continue to campaign indefinitely.

His reply was:

Many thanks your message over success. We will win eventually. Colin Mitchell and all ranks the Argylls.

Now I felt we were really getting somewhere. A month later I received the following letter from Sir Gordon MacMillan:

Dear Duchess

I hope that you will not have written me off as being incredibly rude and ungrateful in not having written to you before to thank you for all that you are doing to Save the Argylls.

I keep hearing from all sides of your tremendous efforts and am very grateful indeed.

The response up to date has been terrific, but of course we have quite a task before us to collect a million signatures which is my aim. . . .

By September I was told that we had collected only 500,000 signatures. This was disheartening as I knew that we had squeezed the British Isles dry and that Scotland had signed to a man.

I assumed that the officials of this campaign had already approached the Commonwealth for signatures, and was dumbfounded to be told they had not. I enquired of Sir Gordon if I had his permission to tackle the Commonwealth on my own, and he, by now slightly dazed, agreed.

I immediately telephoned Associated Press and United Press Association to ask them how I could get a message to the editor of every newspaper, however small, in Canada, Australia, New Zealand and South Africa. They rose nobly to the occasion and said it could be done by telex within a matter of minutes.

The message I sent was: 'Would anybody interested in "Saving the Argylls" please get in touch with me, Margaret, Duchess of Argyll, 48, Upper Grosvenor Street, London, W.1, and I will send them official petition forms.'

The next morning a flood of cables arrived pleading for petition forms. From then on a mountain of letters came by every post. It became clear that many people had not known to whom or where to apply.

My library became a headquarters, with my invaluable secretary, Miss Winifred Medus, and myself working eighteen hours a day to answer the post. It was our proud boast that my desk was cleared by the end of every day.

Many of the letters were heart-rending, and many were very angry. They came from men who had fought side by side with the Argylls in both world wars. One letter I shall never forget came from an 84-year-old New Zealander offering his VC for the regiment to sell if they needed money.

Colin Mitchell was the 'star' of this campaign. He is a dynamic speaker, and whenever he went on TV the demand for petition forms increased noticeably. He used to tease me by saying that one day I would put the Argylls into the kennels at Bleakholt. Colin and I came in for much criticism, and questions were even asked in Parliament as to whether the 'Save the Argylls' campaign was being run by us from the drawing-rooms of Mayfair. There was also some confusion among tourists as to whether it was a campaign to save the Duke and Duchess of Argyll!

The Commonwealth and their press were magnificent. Without their help the final figure of 1,086,590 signatures would never have been reached. One of the most stirring articles was from the *Evening Star*, Dunedin, New Zealand. It ended by saying:

Now a million people want to save it (the regiment) regardless of the state of Britain's finances, regardless of changes in the nature of warfare, regardless of what role there might be for it to play. In short . . . regardless. But no matter what happens, no matter what sort of reception the Duchess of Argyll's petition receives from the Englishmen who head the Government, one thing remains certain. Even if the substance of the Argyll and Sutherland Highlanders is allowed to die, their name and their glory will live on in the hearts of Scotsmen, who will always accord them the right to march through the Royal burgh of Stirling with bayonets fixed, flags flying and drums beating.

Without asking permission, I brought America into this campaign, as I was convinced that there were thousands of Scottish Americans (some still holding British passports) who would be overjoyed to sign. They were and they did! I also wanted to make it a world-wide protest—which it became. By December 4th the target of a million signatures had been reached, and the petition closed soon afterwards.

On December 10th General Sir Gordon MacMillan and Lady MacMillan were gracious enough to give a luncheon in my honour at Stirling Castle, the headquarters of the Regiment. Major-General Frederick Graham, the Acting Colonel of the Argylls, and many of the officers were present.

Although the campaign had officially ended, petition forms were still pouring in, and I took up twelve thousand more signatures with me that day.

I received another charming letter, dated the day of the lunch, from Sir Gordon, saying:

Dear Duchess,

Thank you so much for making such an early start and taking all the trouble to come to Stirling with that splendid bag of signatures.

We are all so grateful to you for the wonderful part you have played in this campaign and for your never-failing enthusiasm and initiative.

I found more completed forms awaiting me when I got home and I expect that Upper Grosvenor Street will be flooded out with them again tomorrow.

Yours sincerely,
Gordon MacMillan.

The petition forms were finally packed in twenty-two cardboard cartons, which had once contained bottles of whisky. These cartons were brought to London by train on December 12th, formally escorted by General Sir Gordon MacMillan and his staff. Awaiting their arrival at Euston was an official reception party consisting of the four Scottish Conservative MPs who initiated the campaign—Mr Michael Noble (Argyll), Mr Gordon Campbell (Moray and Nairn), Mr Hector Monro (Dumfries) and Mr George Younger (Ayr and Bute)—Colin Mitchell and myself.

The train had broken down on the way and was an hour late. (By the time it arrived, the members of the reception party were feeling very merry, having fortified themseves with drinks while waiting!) But at last the cartons were unloaded to the accompaniment of 'Glendaruel Highlanders', piped by Pipe Major Robert Hill, and they were handed over to George Younger.

On December 17th Colin Mitchell and I watched the petition being formally presented to Parliament. The twenty-two cartons were solemnly brought in by liveried staff and placed in front of the Speaker two by two, accompanied by cheers from the Tories and jeers from the Labour benches.

George Younger read out the Petition, which said:

> I support the petition to Parliament which showeth that the Scottish regiments in general and the Argyll and Sutherland Highlanders in particular have an outstanding record in recruiting and military skill and have rendered notable service to this nation over many generations. Wherefore your petitioners pray that your House should resolve that none of the regiments should be disbanded at this time when the army is in urgent need for more recruits!

Much criticism was voiced by the Labour MPs, and in fact there were allegations that some people had signed more than once. (Perish the thought!) But what emerged loud and clear was the spirit behind the campaign. The Scottish *Daily Express* of December 18th published a leading article headlined 'NO JOKE' and reading:

> Some Members of Parliament appear to view lightly the Save-the-Argylls petition, with more than a million signatures, as it is presented to the House of Commons.
>
> They are greatly mistaken. It is possible that some signatures have been duplicated by well meaning people with more enthusiasm than responsibility. It is possible that the petition has been signed by some people with no right to sign.
>
> But these are trivial objections. There can be no serious doubt that this petition represents a large section of public opinion and hundreds of thousands of voters.
>
> Members of Parliament scoff at their peril.

The result of this campaign (one of the largest in history) and the world-wide storm of protest, was that the Argyll and Sutherland Regiment was saved. They are now back to full battalion strength, with their illustrious name unchanged.

After my children had grown up and left home I began to feel aimless and rather useless. I had done as much as I could for Frances and Brian, who now had their own lives. My grand-children, whom I adore, could not be termed 'under-privileged'. They had all the love and material things that life could give them. I seriously considered taking into my care a refugee child from Biafra, Bangladesh or Vietnam, but I realised the difficulties and possible unkindness that this might result in for such a child. The thought also occurred to me that charity does begin at home.

In the autumn of 1970 I asked two friends of mine—one was the Reverend John Andrew (formerly Chaplain to the Arch-bishop of Canterbury), who was then Vicar of Preston and is now the Rector of St Thomas Church in New York; the other was Mr Philip Rutter, headmaster of a school in Alcester, War-wickshire—if they knew of any child who was intelligent but under-privileged whom I could take under my wing.

Some weeks later Mr Rutter telephoned me. 'I think I have found the boy you are looking for,' he said, 'but I am afraid he has a brother.'

'Well then,' I replied, 'I may have to have two little boys instead of one.'

Richard and Jamie Gardner, then nine and seven respectively, came from a family which had fallen on difficult times. Their father was a retired sales manager, then sixty-seven, who had only a small pension. His second wife, mother of the two boys and younger than her husband, was working as a kindergarten teacher at Mr Rutter's private preparatory school, Kinwarton House, and was struggling to make ends meet.

The boys were at a grammar school, making little progress although obviously intelligent.

When I met them at Alcester I was impressed by their good manners and smart appearance. They were beguiling little toughies. I immediately decided that they were 'the ones', and told Mr Rutter so.

Their parents came to see me in London, and it was agreed that I should be financially responsible for the boys' health and education until they came of age.

I also discussed the question of their going to Kinwarton House, and afterwards to a public school. We all reached agreement on these matters.

I was advised by my family solicitor that the word 'sponsor' was an American term. 'Adopt' was the only correct word to use since I was taking over all responsibility for Richard and Jamie. A formal adoption was not possible because I was over the age limit of forty and no longer married. He advised what is known as a 'private adoption', which was perfectly legal but more elastic. The terms would be decided between the Gardners and myself, and I should have to sign adoptive papers that would be completely binding for me but not for the parents.

It seemed clear-cut and reasonable, and all was well—until the news broke in the press.

Largely through the boys' father's lack of experience in dealing with reporters, and the indiscretion of one of the trustees of Kinwarton House School, who afterwards resigned, an essentially private matter became magnified to front-page proportions.

People were led to believe that I was taking Richard and Jamie away from their parents. Nothing could have been further from the truth. The boys' mother, at the height of the controversy, said: 'The boys are staying with us and the Duchess is paying for their schooling, their future and all the things we couldn't give them. I don't know what all the fuss is about.'

Nor did I. Nevertheless, reporters besieged my London house day and night, and Mr Leo Abse, the Labour Member of Parliament, tabled a House of Commons question to Mrs Margaret Thatcher, then Minister of Education, asking if she was aware that 'the school's headmaster acted as an "intermediary" in the adoption', and if she was, 'now considering withdrawing Ministry recognition of the school.'

Suddenly my well-intentioned plan for Richard and Jamie was being described as 'a matter of national concern', and even Worcestershire County Council ordered an official enquiry into the circumstances. I was utterly bewildered.

I had been deliberately sparing in the comments I had made

to the press. 'I don't expect to love them immediately,' I had said of Richard and Jamie. 'You don't love people just like that. You grow to love them. I'm sure I'll grow to love these boys, and they may return my affection.'

Godfrey Winn commented on this: 'The duchess is very honest about it all,' he wrote in the *Daily Mail*, 'and I admire her honesty.'

But Jean Rook, in one of the unkindest and most unpleasant articles I have ever seen, wrote: 'What really gets me is the casual way Her Grace takes this fancy to two children, aged nine and seven, and simply Rolls-Royces off with them.

It's all too glossy. It's all too like popping into Harrods and choosing a couple of ornaments that'll look good either side of your Adam fireplace.'

It was not like that at all, Miss Rook, but you never bothered to find out. Neither did the press think it worth while to publish what my son said to every one of the newspapers. Brian was dining with me one evening and he answered all the press calls that were coming in every ten minutes, saying: 'My sister and I are perfectly happy about this. The parents seem to be quite content with the arrangement, and none of us can understand what all this fuss is about.'

Eventually the truth began to emerge, and it was left to that great columnist, the late John Gordon, to put the 'cause celebre' into its true perspective in the *Sunday Express*, dated November 22nd:

Although she takes over financial responsibility for the education and upbringing of two fine boys, with the full consent of their parents, a howl goes up from the people who sincerely believe that God appointed them to control the lives of the rest of us—especially duchesses.

I hope the duchess continues to cock a snook at them. There are many less admirable ways in which she could spend her money.

Richard and Jamie have now left Kinwarton and are both at a public school in Shropshire. They visit me every holiday and I take them to either a theatre of their choice or something such as the Tutankhamun Exhibition.

Not long ago I took them for their first flight in a jumbo jet. We flew from London to Ireland and back again the same day. They were very excited about the whole trip and about seeing Ireland also for the first time, but the highlight of their day was being allowed to go into the captain's cabin on the jumbo. They are growing fast, and show every sign of developing into intelligent, good-looking young men.

I am looking forward to the time when they will be old enough to accompany me on trips to far-away places.

Chapter 26

My most memorable visit to Washington came in January 1971 when I stayed for ten days with Perle Mesta—a great woman and a great friend.

The itinerary she had planned for me was so crowded and so glamorous that I kept a copy of the schedule for unbelievers to see. I met Senators Birch Bayh (Indiana), Lloyd Bentsen (Texas), Harry Byrd (Virginia), Charles Percy (Illinois), Wiley Buchanan (former Chef de Protocol); and as Perle's apartment was in the same building as that of Mr and Mrs Spiro Agnew, I was constantly meeting the then Vice-President in the elevator.

The climax of this visit came when we went to the Senate with Perle to hear President Nixon deliver his State of the Union Message at the opening of the 92nd Congress. I sat next to Mrs Agnew whom I found charming and very pretty.

After the ceremony I was given a luncheon party in the Senators' dining room by Mrs McClelland, wife of the Senator from Arkansas, and there I watched Edward Kennedy and his family lunching, with their faces shades paler and their buoyancy gone since Kennedy had failed in his bid to become Speaker of the House.

During this visit I was privileged to be taken to have tea with Mrs Alice Roosevelt Longworth by her niece by marriage, Mrs Archibald ('Lucky') Roosevelt. The two hours I spent with

Alice Longworth were the most amusing I had known for a long time. She is one of the most famous women, not only in Washington but in the world today. She is also something of an iconoclast, and when I noticed many photographs of Maharajas and Eastern Potentates in her drawing-room I was puzzled. Her explanation was, 'I only have photographs of Oriental Heads of State now—the Western ones are passé!'

Her regime is also unorthodox. She never lunches, but spends the hours from 2 to 4 o'clock in the afternoon talking to her friends on the telephone. She then 'receives' visitors every day at teatime. I was fortunate enough to be the only visitor she had that day and, therefore, could enjoy her wit and, more important, her sense of the ridiculous, to the full.

My equally famous hostess, Perle Mesta, has had so much written and said about her throughout her life that comment is almost superfluous. However, having twice been her guest for ten days at a time, I perhaps knew her a little better than some.

In her apartment at the Sheraton-Park Hotel there was an impressive array of signed photographs of the United States Presidents from, and including, President Eisenhower. There was one exception—John Kennedy, whom Perle did not care for. One of her closest friends was Mrs Mamie Eisenhower, whom she spoke to on the telephone every day. I once asked Perle if she was a Democrat or a Republican, and she answered, with a very knowing twinkle in her eye, 'I'm known as two-party Perle.'

She had the rare quality of absolute loyalty, and would not tolerate the usual cowardly attitude of 'I would rather not be involved.' If she liked a person it was through thick and thin, and the thinner it got the more staunch she became. On the other hand, anyone she did not like would be well advised to run for cover.

When I read, early in 1974, that she had moved to Oklahoma to be near her brother, Mr D. W. Skirvin, I felt very sad. I wrote to her saying that I would willingly go and visit her in Oklahoma City any time she needed company. I was sadder still at the news of her death on March 16th, 1975. However, I have a permanent reminder of her in my library. It is a large edition of the *American Heritage Dictionary of the English Language*, given to me by Congressman James Fulton on January 26th, 1971, at a dinner that Perle gave for me with a dance afterwards. All her forty dinner guests signed the dictionary, and the list includes many interesting names. I am ashamed to say that because of my poor spelling, I have to refer to this dictionary very frequently!

Perle will never be forgotten and always be missed by those who knew her.

During 1971 there was recurrent newspaper speculation in Britain and America as to whether I was going to marry J. Paul Getty. First of all it was amusing to us both, but it ended up by becoming a great nuisance.

Paul had been my very dear and staunch friend for many years, and there was a time in the late 1940s when we might have married, if it had not been for the intervention of a certain mutual woman 'friend' who deliberately convinced Paul that I was interested in an American colonel. This was quite untrue.

Paul has been a wonderful ally to me ever since, and unwavering in his loyalty. Through his kindness and wisdom I have received invaluable guidance over many problems, for which I shall be eternally grateful.

J. Paul Getty is so famous, and has been so much written about, that I hesitate to add my comments, but there are aspects to his character which are little known. He may purposely create an image of being 'canny' over money, but there are many people and many charities who have cause to be very grateful to him. Yet the world does not know about these.

He is essentially gentle and shy, not at his best in a large gathering of people. In a conversation alone with him, however, he is one of the most fascinating and entertaining men I have ever listened to, with great knowledge of many subjects, and an incredibly accurate memory spanning his entire life. In spite of his inscrutable mien he has a sharp, dry and very perceptive wit.

Although I say that sometimes he apparently 'turns off' in a conversation which bores him, I am not fooled by this, nor should anybody else be. Paul hears, sees and absorbs everything.

On December 15th, 1972, J. Paul Getty was going to be eighty years old, and I felt that he deserved the best possible party I could give to usher his birthday in on the night of December 14th. At first he was terrified of the idea, being fundamentally a modest man, but when the night of the party came he was thrilled and very touched. All that he asked of me was that he did not have to receive the guests or make a speech. To this I naturally agreed.

I was anxious to try to revive some of the pre-war party elegance, and I was determined to have pre-war dance music played by Joe Loss and his orchestra.

As they had never played for me before I insisted upon having a rehearsal at 10.30 one morning in the Dorchester ballroom where the party was to be held. The members of the orchestra were sleepy and disgruntled, and at one point Joe Loss, exasperated, suggested that I lead the orchestra instead of him on the great night! However, after two hours of my pleading for the real dance music such as we used to have at the Four Hundred Club in London and El Morocco in New York, Mr Loss and his orchestra all became enthusiastic and on my side.

At seven o'clock on the night of the party I was putting on my silver organza dress designed by Harald of Curzon Street (who now makes most of my clothes) when the telephone rang and an American voice said, 'The White House is on the line'. I hung up, thinking it was one of the many 'phoney' calls I receive. But the American voice rang again, saying this time, 'President Nixon would like to speak to Mr Paul Getty'. I said that Mr Getty had not arrived here yet, but perhaps the President could telephone later. The American operator pointed out that this just possibly might not be convenient for the President—he was a busy man!

Much chastened by now, I promised to have Mr Getty at the Dorchester by eight o'clock, and the call came through exactly then. Paul was overjoyed.

I had the blue and white Orchid Suite at the Dorchester candlelit for the party, and decorated with coral-coloured flowers. Because Paul is who he is, there were a hundred illustrious dinner guests, headed by Umberto, former King of Italy. Two hundred people came to the dance afterwards.

An added compliment to Paul was the arrival of President Nixon's daughter, Tricia, with her husband Edward Cox. They came—after dining with the Prime Minister, Mr Heath—in time for the midnight celebration of Paul's birthday.

At midnight, as the giant birthday cake was being wheeled slowly around the ballroom, Joe Loss's vocalist sang a special version of 'You're the Top':

> You're the top, you are J. PAUL GETTY,
> You're the top, and your cash ain't petty,
> You're a Franklin Fellow with a Paris medal
>   as well,
> Got your own museum, let's sing a Te Deum
>   to such a swell.
>
> You're the top, you are like Jack Benny,
> You're the top, wouldn't waste a penny,
> I have an open cheque that I would like to
>   pop . . .
> and if you'd kindly sign the bottom—
>   YOU'RE THE TOP.
>
> You're the top, you're our very dear friend,
> You're the top, may it never end,
> You're just the fellow to whom we'd like
>   to say
> Don't forget your home is in England—
>   WON'T YOU STAY?

During this I glanced at Paul and saw that his eyes were noticeably moist.

After he had cut the cake the Duke of Bedford proposed a charming toast, saying that we all hoped to be present at Paul's hundredth birthday. It was a memorable occasion, and Paul was clearly moved by the affection that surrounded him throughout the evening. As an interesting corollary, nearly every one of the 'Thank you' letters I received afterwards said how much the writers—even the young—had enjoyed the 'old time' music.

The following summer brought great sadness into my long friendship with Paul Getty.

I was giving a dinner party at my house on June 6th to which he was invited. Just as Paul arrived, an urgent call came from Los Angeles which had been passed on from his home in Sutton Place. He took it privately in my library, and after about five minutes he beckoned to me and told me that George Getty, his oldest son and a great friend of mine, had had a bad fall and was unconscious in a Los Angeles hospital. I tried to reassure Paul by saying that it could only be concussion and that I was sure that the next call, which was due to come at 11 o'clock that evening, would bring better news.

With his usual courtesy he carried on throughout dinner as though nothing was wrong, but we were both inwardly waiting for that second call. At 11 o'clock it came, and again Paul took it in my library. Again he beckoned me in, but this time it was to say, 'George is dead.' I was almost as shocked as he was, and also very worried as to what effect this dreadful news would have on Paul. He refused a drink, but I made him sit down, and somehow my son managed to persuade my guests to leave the house, without their knowing the circumstances.

Paul also refused to have a doctor, but I called his devoted secretary, Mrs Barbara Wallace, and found that she was on her way, as was his close friend and neighbour, Mrs Penelope Kitson. Until they arrived I sat with Paul trying to help him through his ordeal. All he said repeatedly was 'George has gone. He is with God.' I was most relieved when Barbara and Penelope arrived, and as we talked to him I became aware of what had made Paul the man that he is. After about half an hour of great distress, I actually saw him tighten up, pull himself together and begin to speculate about the future problems of his empire now that George was gone.

We all sat up until about three a.m. and then, without taking any tranquilliser or sleeping pill, he spent the rest of the night in my guest room. After his great friendship to me over the years, I was thankful to be with him during his tragedy.

One day in 1971 while I was dining with Paul Getty in the Grill Room of the Ritz in Paris, Ian Argyll appeared and sat alone at a table right next to us. Only a glass screen divided us. It was the first time I had seen him since 1963, and it struck me how much older than his years he looked. The dejected man he now appeared to be was a sad contrast to the handsome charmer I first knew.

That was the last time I saw Ian.

Early in 1973 I heard that he had suffered a stroke in France, where he and his wife had chosen to live four years earlier, after emigrating from Scotland.

After a month in the American Hospital in Paris he was flown to the Western General Hospital in Edinburgh and put in a public ward. An old friend of us both, Brodrick Haldane, who lives in Edinburgh, kept me informed of Ian's progress.

The news was grim. Ian was undoubtedly dying, and, sadly, he was dying in the same aura of controversy that had surrounded him in his life.

The Scottish Labour Member of Parliament, Willie Hamilton, had demanded a House of Commons statement from the Secretary of State for Scotland on Ian's stay in the Edinburgh hospital.

Mr Hamilton felt that the Duke should not be allowed to leave Britain for tax reasons and then come back to use the National Health Service.

Shortly after that, Ian was transferred to the Royal Scottish (Nuffield) Nursing Home.

In the early hours of Saturday, April 7th, I suddenly awoke feeling a strong urge to telephone the nursing home immediately. I did so, and asked the night sister how the Duke of Argyll was. She replied, 'I am sorry to tell you that the Duke died at 5 o'clock this morning.' Apparently he died alone, so I may have been the first person to hear of his death.

As I put the telephone down, my mind went back over the years of my life with this strange man. I remembered the many picnics we had on the tiny island of Innishail in the middle of Loch Awe. It was the island on which his father, Douglas Campbell, was buried, and Ian always told me that this was where he wanted to be buried. I used to put in an occasional bleat asking if we could not both be buried at Inveraray, but he was quite adamant.

He always said that he wished to be cremated, and declared that he was an atheist, but I never believed him. I suspected that he was a latent Roman Catholic, due to the strong influence of his mother in his childhood.

Six days after his death I read of Ian's ashes being rowed over the waters of Loch Awe to their last resting place on Innishail, with Pipe Major Ronnie McCallum standing in the prow of the boat piping a Celtic lament.

I also read of there being no religious ceremony—just Sir Iain Moncrieffe of that Ilk proclaiming the style and titles of the Duke of Argyll. This was followed by a minute's silence for personal prayer.

I knew then that Ian had the funeral that he would have wished, even to the placing on the urn of his beloved shabby bonnet, this day adorned with the three eagle's feathers of a Clan Chieftain.

Why exactly did we fail, Ian and I? What poisoned our life together?

One comes back, finally, to the words of Somerset Maugham: 'Give a man five pounds and he will hate you for life.'

Perhaps it was my having money that began the trouble.

'I only marry rich women,' Ian had once said, cynically, in front of the servants.

Then I had not understood. I thought it was just one more cruel twist of the knife to wound me. Ian's first two wives had money of their own. He, who had none and was not prepared to work for it, needed to marry money—but he resented that need.

It undermined him as a man. That, I believe, is why he had begun to drink—many years before he ever met me.

Chapter 27

I visited Chicago in February 1974 as the guest of Mr and Mrs William Wood-Prince. I was feted there all the week—one head-line was, 'The Princes roll out the red carpet for the Duchess.'

However, I was very worried about the situation in Britain and the miners' strike. Mentioning this to oil tycoon John Swearington, he said: 'Duchess, don't you worry. If Britain is short of coal you may be sure that America will send you all you need.'

Remarks such as this, which I have heard all my life from Americans, convince me that there are more nice people to the square mile in America than anywhere in the world.

In the autumn of that year a major change took place in my household. My housekeeper, Mrs Elizabeth Duckworth, after a serious operation, decided that she could not do full-time work any longer.

She first came into the family at the age of twenty-two when she had just become engaged to my father's butler, Leslie Duck-worth, whom she married in 1932. They both continued in my employ after I moved into this house in 1945, although, sadly, Duckworth died on December 8th, 1956, still in my service.

Acknowledged as one of the finest cooks in London, Mrs Duckworth has been a loyal and devoted friend to me and to my family. Although she has never mentioned it, I know of the many difficult times she must have gone through on my behalf.

I am delighted to say that, although she is now officially retired, she still comes regularly to my house to take my poodles, Alphonse and Antoine, out for their walks, and to see that things are running as they should and as they always did during her forty-six-year reign over my household.

In the spring of 1975 my stepson Ian, the 12th Duke of Argyll, came to see me in my house—the first time for sixteen years.

I was delighted to see him. He had come to discuss with me certain complicated matters concerning the Argyll estate, and I willingly gave him all the help I could.

I hope he will come again and bring his pretty wife, Iona.

I call this book 'Forget Not', a translation of the Argyll family motto, *Ne Obliviscaris*. I choose it not only because I am a Scot who bears the title Margaret, Duchess of Argyll, but also because it is true of my whole life.

I do not forget. Neither the good years, in which I laughed and danced and lived upon a cloud of happiness; nor the bad years of near despair when I learned what life and people and friendship really were.

At this point it would be most gratifying to be able to relate how much wisdom I have acquired throughout these years, and how by now I know all the answers.

Unfortunately I am only too aware that I am still the same gullible, impulsive, over-optimistic 'Dumb Bunny', and I have given up hopes of any improvement.

Perhaps a change of scene is the answer, and in the near future I shall move to America to live, visiting Britain as often as possible.

I have made this decision not because of our political situation or our punitive taxes (reasons for emigrating with which I have no sympathy), but because I left a large chunk of my heart in the United States when I was a young girl, and I look forward with joy to living once more in that vital, exciting, warm-hearted country.

Index

Abel-Smith, Sir Henry & Lady Mary, 168

Aberconway, Lady (Christabel), 98, 99

Aberconway, Lord, 98

Abse, Leo, 229

Adamson, Mr & Mrs John, 222

Adler, Larry, 83

Agnew, Mr & Mrs Spiro, 232

Aitken, Hon Janet, 117, 125, 131

Aitken, Sir Max, 61, 62, 64-7, 75

Aitken, Hon Peter, 79

Alba, Duke & Duchess of, 131

Alfonso, ex-King of Spain, 41

Alwyne, The Farquharson of Invercauld, 146

Ambrose, 36, 42

Andrew, Rev John, 228

Anouilh, Jean, 120

Anything Goes, 78

Arden, Elizabeth, 114

Argyll, (Ian, Douglas Campbell) 11th Duke of, 2, 3, 4, 6, 19, 70, 117-203 *passim*, 223, 237-9

Argyll, (Ian Marquis of Lorne) 12th Duke of, 122, 132, 133, 178, 195, 241

Argyll, (Iona) Duchess of, 122, 223, 241

Argyll, (Niall) 10th Duke of, 117, 120, 124

Arlen, Michael, 48

Armstrong, Neil, 214

Armstrong-Jones, Anthony (Lord Snowdon), 114

Armstrong-Jones, Mrs Ronald (Countess of Rosse), 56, 59

Arran, Earl of, 198

Ashley, Lady (Sylvia), 95

Ashley, Mary, 32, 33

Astaire, Fred & Adele, 48, 101

Astor, (Nancy) Viscountess, 30, 31, 88

Baillie, Lady (Olive), 88, 89, 114, 127, 132

Baillie, Sir Adrian, 88

Bangs, Eleanor, 114

Barbachanos, Mr & Mrs, 211

Barber, Lady (Colin), 220, 221

Barnardo, Dr Thomas, 83

Barnato, Woolf ('Babe'), 50

Bayh, Birch, 232

Beadon, Clive, 187

Beaton, 'Baba', 28, 74

Beaton, Nancy, 28

Beaton, Sir Cecil, 28, 112

Beatrice, H.R.H. Princess, 81

Beaverbrook, Lord, 9, 61, 62

Bedford, (Ian) Duke of, 236

Beloved Enemy, 90

Bennett, Isabel, 5, 107

Benny, Jack, 101

Bentsen, Lloyd, 232

Berry, Lady Pamela (Lady Hartwell), 96

Berry, Hon Michael (Lord Hartwell), 75

Berry, Hon Sheila, 74

Beyfus, Gilbert, QC, 3, 14, 180

Biddle, Anthony J. Drexel, 101

Biddle, Mrs Anthony, 101, 102

Bingham, Mrs Robert, 82

Bingham, Rose, 46, 48

Birkenhead, Earl of, 75

Bossom, Bruce, 23

Bossom, Sir Alfred, 154

Bossom, Sir Clive, 23

Bouché, Rene, 174

Bourn, Dale, 58

Bowater, Sir Ian, 99

Boys from Syracuse, The, 94

Bracken, Brendan, 115

Brandeis, Judge, 202

Braun, Baron Sigismund von, 192

Brett, Angela, 74

Brinckman, Napoleon ('Naps'), 66

Brinckman, Sir Theodore, 66

Brooks, David ('Winkie'), 30

Brooks, Sir Dallas & Lady, 168

Buchanan, Jack, 48

Buchanan, Wiley, 232

Buchel, Magda, 127, 151-3, 183

Burke, Marie, 31

Burns, Robert, 104

Byng, Douglas, 47

Byrd, Harry, 232

Cabrol, Baron & Baronne, 205

Cadogan, Earl & Countess, 140

Campbell, Ellen Murray, 8

Campbell, Gordon, 226

Campbell, Lady Jeanne, 125, 131, 175, 176

Campbell, (Provost) John, 161, 202

Campbell-Walter, Fiona, 49, 112

Campbell-Walter, Rear-Adm Keith, 112

Caracciolo, Roberto (Duke of San Vito), 120

Carlow, Viscount, 32

Carpenter, Kathleen, 173, 182, 183, 197

Carrington, Lord & Lady, 167

Cartland, Barbara (Mrs Alexander McCorquodale), 48, 56, 200

Case of Human Bondage, A, 84

Castle, Irene & Vernon, 33

Castlerosse, (Valentine) Viscount, 33, 49

Cavalcade, 48

Cayzer, Sir Nicholas, 98

Channon, Sir Henry ('Chips'), 116

Chelsea, (Charles) Viscount, 140

Chevalier, Maurice, 48

Churchill, Baroness, 100

Churchill, Randolph, 75, 79

Churchill, Sir Winston, 100, 106

Clark, Sir Andrew, QC, 202, 203

Clore, Sir Charles, 201

Cobham, Viscount & Viscountess, 168

Cochran, C. B., 79, 83

Cohane, John, 192-3

Combe, Lady Moira, 193

Combe, Peter, 193-4, 197

Comyn, James, QC, 187

Cooper, (Dame) Gladys, 59

Cooper, Lady Diana, 47

Coward, Noël, 48, 116

Cowdray, Lady, 39

Cox, Edward, 235

Cox, Mrs Edward ('Tricia Nixon'), 235

Crabbe, 'Buster', 130

Crosby, Bing, 101

Crossland, Diana, 175

Cunningham-Reid, Bobby, 33

Curzon, Lady Georgiana, 31

Czernin, Count Hans, 91

d'Arenberg, Prince Charles, 200

d'Avigdor Goldsmid, (Rose) Lady, 139, 156-7, 200

d'Avigdor Goldsmid, Sir Henry, 156-7

Dawson, Lord, 80, 81

Day, Edith, 31

de Flores, Admiral Luis, 109

de Heeren, Mr & Mrs Rodnam, 190

de Laspee, Leslie, 223

Denning, Lord, 201

de Peña, Madame Florence, 47

Derby, Earl of, 221

d'Erlanger, Mrs (Edith Baker), 41

de Salis, Poppy, 115

Dickson, Dorothy, 48

Dietrich, Marlene, 101

Dillingham, Walter, 169

Donahue, Mrs Woolworth, 94

Donegal, Marquis of, 32, 36, 49

Dorsey, Tommy, 49

Douglas, Mr & Mrs Lewis, 115
Douglas, Mrs Barclay, 114
Douglas, Sharman, 47
Douglas-Hamilton, (Malcolm) Lord, 145
Dreyfus brothers (Henri & Camille), 25
Driberg, Tom, 49
Drogheda, (Joan) Countess of, 98
Drogheda, (Garrett) Earl of, 98
Duckworth, Elizabeth, 107, 115, 240-1
Duckworth, Leslie, 240
Dudley, Countess of (Gertie Millar), 73
Dudley, (Eric) Earl of, 200
Dudley-Ward, Mrs Freda, 41, 87
Dugger, William, 213, 214
du Maurier, Gerald, 48
Dumfries, Earl & Countess of, 73, 91
Duncan, Colin, 182
Dundee, (James) Earl of, 145

Eden, Sir Anthony, 63, 117
Eisenhower, Dwight D., President, 105, 106
Eisenhower, Mamie, 233
Elizabeth, H.M. the Queen Mother, 28, 56, 91, 146
Elizabeth II, H.M. the Queen, 72, 135, 140, 147
Elwes, Simon, 59
Emslie, George, QC, 196
Erroll, ('Puffin') Countess of, 177

Fairbanks, Mr & Mrs Douglas, Jnr., 79, 115
Fairbanks, Douglas, Snr., 95
Faucigny de Lucinge, Jean-Luis, 132
Ferry, Fefe, 94
Field, Sid, 101
Fitzwilliam, 7th Earl & Countess, 92
Flagstad, Kirsten, 131
Foot, Sir Hugh & Lady, 162
Fox, Roy, 49
Foy, Mr & Mrs Byron, 93
Fraser, Ian (Lord Fraser), 196
Frazier, Brenda, 47
Frederika, Queen of Greece, 141
Frelinghuysen, George, 209
Fulton, James, 234
Furness, (Thelma) Viscountess, 40, 87

Gardiner, Gerald, QC (Lord Gardiner), 181, 182, 183, 196
Gardner, Richard & Jamie, 228-31
George, Sir Robert & Lady, 168
'Georges' (Paris-Ritz concierge), 2, 5, 117
George V, H.M. King, 40, 82, 86
George VI, H.M. King, 82, 91, 105
Getty, George, 210, 236, 237
Getty, J. Paul, 116, 117, 122, 234-237
Gibbons, Carroll, 49
Gibson, Harvey, 101
Giltrap, Gertrude, 107
Glenkinglas, Lord & Lady, 155
Goalen, Barbara, 49
Gold, Dawn, 74
Goonetilleke, Sheila (Mrs Sathanathan), 215
Goonetilleke, Sir Oliver, 215
Gordon, John, 230
Gort, Colonel Viscount, 66
Graham, Robert King, 187
Granby, (David) Marquis of, 172
Griffiths, Ivor, 4, 155, 183, 184, 186
Griffiths, Stanton, 131
Guest, Mr & Mrs Winston, 94

Haldane, Brodrick, 238
Hamilton, Willie, 238
Hannay, Douglas Mann, 11, 13, 25
Hannay, Margaret, 36, 89
Harald (of Curzon Street), 235
Harmsworth, Mr & Mrs Esmond, 95
Harriman, Averell, 101
Harris, Jack, 42
Hartnell, Norman, 36, 40, 56, 59, 72, 93, 140, 160
Hatton, 'Happy', 212
Haxton, Gerald, 83, 84
Hearst, Mrs Randolph, 91
Hearst, William, 176
Heath, Edward, 235
Heller, Mrs Matilda, 201
Hellzapoppin, 94
Hewitt, Miss, 21, 22, 94
Hill, Robert, 227
Hohenloe, Prince Alex, 91
Hope, Bob, 101
Hore-Belisha, Leslie, 95
Horlick, Peter, 139
Hussein, King of Jordan, 158
Hutton, Barbara, 17, 91, 94, 96
Hutton, Edna Woolworth, 17

Innes-Ker, Alistair, 30
Innes-Ker, David, 30
Inverclyde, Lady (June), 50
Inverclyde, Lord, 73

Jaffee, Jeanette, 214
Jersey, Earl & Countess of, 79
Jobson, Cecil, 152, 153, 178, 182, 201
Johnstone, Mr & Mrs Charles, 158
Jones, Jennifer, 115

Kennedy, Edward, 232
Kennedy, Joseph P., 97
Kennedy, Rose, 97
Kern, Jerome, 22
Khan, Prince Aly, 41-5
Kidston, (George Pearson) Glen, 50-8, 59
Kilmuir, David, Viscount, 116, 150
Kirkwood, Sir Robert, 134
Kiss Before the Mirror, A, 77
Kittredge, Mr & Mrs Ben, 137
Kitson, Penelope, 237

Lambert, Mr & Mrs Joe, 215
Land of Smiles, 32
Latham, Lady Patricia, 98
Latham, Sir Paul, 98
Lawrence, Gertrude, 48, 79
Laye, Evelyn, 48
Leave It to Me, 94
Lenare (see Sources of Illustrations)
Levin, Bernard, 198
Lewis, Rosa, 49
Lillie, Beatrice, 42, 48
Livingstone-Learmonth, Margaret, 74
Lloyd, Geoffrey (Lord Geoffrey-Lloyd), 88, 95, 133
Logue, Lionel, 18
Lomas, Olive, 220, 221
Londonderry, (Robin) Marquis of, 50
Longworth, Alice Roosevelt, 232
Loss, Joe, 235, 236
Louise, Princess, 132, 134, 135, 145
Lowenstein, Alfred, 26
Lynn, Dame Vera, 101

MacArthur, Duncan, 6, 127
McCallum, Ronnie, 140, 160, 163, 177, 238
McClelland, Mrs, 232

McIntyre, Captain & Mrs Alexander, 146
Maclean, Sir Charles ('Chips'); Lord Maclean, 146
Maclean, Sir Fitzroy & Lady Veronica, 156, 222
MacMillan, General Sir Gordon, 223, 224, 226
Macmillan, Harold, 176
McNeil, Hector, 115
MacNeill, Jane, 79
MacPherson, Clunie, 148
MacPherson, Yvonne, 148, 149, 150, 151, 152, 153, 154, 155, 181, 182, 183, 196
Makins, Sir Roger, 112
Manners, Lady Charlotte, 208
Manners, Lady Teresa, 195
Manners, Lord Edward, 207
Manners, Lord Robert, 195, 204, 205
Margaret, H.R.H. Princess, 146
Margesson, (David) Viscount, 88, 95, 133
Marina, H.R.H. Princess, Duchess of Kent, 82, 83, 127, 135
Marreco, Anthony, 113, 175
Martin, Mary, 94
Martindale, Rev C. C., 80
Mary, H.M. Queen, 40, 77, 82, 83
Massigli, M. & Madame, 135
Matthews, Jessie, 48
Maude, Judge & Mrs John (Marchioness of Dufferin and Ava), 147-8, 153, 183
Maugham, Liza (Lady Glendevon), 83, 91
Maugham, Somerset, 48, 83, 84, 239
Maugham, Syrie, 83-5, 91
Maxwell, Elsa, 116, 117, 141, 163
Medus, Winifred, 225
Mendl, Lady (Elsie de Woolf), 91, 95
Messel, Oliver, 91
Messmore, Mr & Mrs Carman, 169, 193
Mesta, Perle, 139, 232-4
Milland, Mr & Mrs Ray, 112
Miller, Mr & Mrs Gilbert, 9, 91, 119, 138
Miller, Marilyn, 22
Milton, (Peter) Viscount, 92, 96
Milton, Viscountess (Olive Plunket), 92
Mitchell, Colin, 134, 222, 224, 225, 226, 227

Moncrieffe, Sir Iain of that Ilk, 177, 239

Monro, Hector, 226

Moore, Derry, 132

Morgan, Jack, 169, 170

Morrison, (Provost) Robert, 128

Mountbatten, Lord Louis (Earl Mountbatten of Burma), 41, 50, 215

Mylne, Robert, 145

Napier, Diana, 182, 183

Neagle, Dame Anna, 48

Negri, Pola, 51

Niarchos, Eugenie, 115, 141

Niarchos, Stavros, 115, 141

Nicholl, Pamela, 74

Nichols, Beverley, 84

Nicholson, Ruth, 34

Niven, David, 31, 32

Nixon, Richard, President, 232, 235

Noble, Michael, 226

Norfolk, (Lavinia) Duchess of, 220

Oberon, Merle, 90, 211

O'Connell, R. J., 113, 114

Olin, Mr & Mrs John, 117

Packer, Sir Frank & Lady, 166

Paley, Mr & Mrs William, 94

Parker, Bertram, 92

Parsons, Desmond, 30

Patino, Mr & Mrs Antenor, 190

Paul, King of Greece, 141

Peach (valet to Ian Argyll), 170, 173, 196

Pearson, Brenda, 39

Pearson, Joan, 39

Percy, Charles, 232

Petro, John, 4, 148, 149, 150, 155, 202

Philip, H.R.H. Prince, Duke of Edinburgh, 72, 140, 146

Phipps, Nora, 31

Pickford, Mary, 95

Pidgeon, Walter, 115

Plunket, Lord & Lady, 79

Plunkett, Aileen, 148

Portal, Viscountess, 101

Portal, Marshal of the R.A.F., Viscount, 115

Portanova, Baron & Baroness, 210, 213, 214

Porter, Cole, 78

Portland, Duchess of, 135

Poulett, Lady Bridget, 46, 47, 48, 74, 91, 111

Queensberry, (Cathleen) Marchioness of, 88, 89

Queensberry, 11th Marquis of, 88, 91

Raft George, 95

Randall, May, 20, 21, 23, 25, 38, 42, 68, 77, 79, 81, 92

Reading, Lord, 63

Reardon, Billy, 33

Rede, Baron Alexis, 118, 119

Richardson, Margaret, 13

Ring Round the Moon, 120

Road to Morocco, The, 105

Robeson, Paul, 31

Rockefeller, Winthrop, 24

Rook, Jean, 230

Roosevelt, Mrs Archibald ('Lucky'), 232

Roosevelt, Mrs Eleanor, 102

Roosevelt, Theodore, 9

Rose, David, 105, 137

Rousseau, Theodore, 113, 193

Rubinstein, Helena, 114

Russell, Gerald, 187

Russell, Sir Charles, 184, 187, 188, 190

Rutland, 10th Duke of, 135, 157, 158, 159, 160, 163, 164, 204, 207

Rutland, Duchess of, (Frances Sweeny), 3, 4, 20, 60, 91, 97, 98, 107, 109, 111, 117, 120, 125, 127, 131, 132, 139, 140, 141, 146, 148, 156, 157, 158, 159, 160, 163, 164, 172, 176, 193, 195, 204, 205, 207, 208, 216, 228

Rutland, (Kathleen) Duchess of, 160

Rutter, Philip, 228

Sablon, Jean, 185, 186

St Clair-Erskine, Hon Hamish, 30

Sally, 22

Sandys, Duncan (Lord Duncan-Sandys), 150

Sanford, Mr & Mrs Stephen, 93, 94

Searle, E. J., 222

Selby, Viscount, 39

Selfridge, Gordon, 73

Selznick, David O., 115

Senanayake, Dudley, 215

Shearer, Moira, 95

Show Boat, 31, 191
Sieghart, Paul, 202
Sinclair, Sir Archibald (Lord Thurso), 100
Skirvin, D. W., 233
Slim, Field-Marshal Sir William, 167
Smith, Helen, 193
Smith, Pamela (Lady Hartwell), 28
Spaatz, General Carl, 105
Stacey, David, 203
Stand Up and Sing, 48
Stark, Admiral Harold Raynsford, 105
Stars in Your Eyes, 94
Steel, Sir Christopher, 113
Stiebel, Victor, 36, 135
Stourton, Jeanne, 74
Straight, Lady Daphne, 200
Sutherland, (Clare) Duchess of, 117, 135, 138, 154
Sutherland, Duke of, 117, 138
Swearington, John, 240
Sweeny, Bobby, 67, 75, 79, 90, 98
Sweeny, Brian, 3, 4, 28, 32, 96, 97, 98, 100, 107, 109, 111, 112, 117, 125, 127, 131, 132, 141, 142, 157, 176, 179, 185, 186, 188, 189, 195, 199, 205–8, 209, 216, 228, 230
Sweeny, Charles, 67–112 *passim*, 126, 127, 142, 147, 160, 185, 205, 207, 208
Sweeny, Colonel Charles, 100
Sweeny, Mrs Robert, 87
Sweeny, Robert, 17

Tauber, Richard, 32, 96
Tennant, David, 156
Tennant, Ethel, 13
Tennyson, (Lionel) Lord, 50, 55, 64
Thatcher, Margaret, 229
Thomas, Joseph, 114
Thornton, Air Vice-Marshal, 126, 134, 148, 179
Throckmorton, Sir Robert, 83
Tiarks, Henrietta (Marchioness of Tavistock), 47
Tiarks, Mr & Mrs Henry, 127
Timpson, Louise, 117, 119, 120, 121, 124, 125, 127, 130
Tod, Ethel, 13, 16
Tod, Ronald, 222

Tomkins, Sir Edward, 115
Trevelyan, Sir Humphrey (Lord Trevelyan), 150
Tristan und Isolde, 131
Truman, Mrs Harry S., 112
Tunney, Gene, 32

Umberto, ex-King of Italy, 236
Ungoed-Thomas, Mr Justice, 203
Uriburu, Clara, 33

Vacani, Miss, 40
Van Horne, Sir William, 13, 14
Vaughan, Molly, 74
Von Cramm, Baron Gottfried, 17
von Herwath, John, 116

Walker, Mr & Mrs Angus, 169
Wallace, Barbara, 237
Warburg, Paul, 111
Ward, Colonel John, 200
Ward, Susan, 200
Wardel, Mike, 62
Warwick, (Frances) Dowager Countess of, 63
Warwick, (Fulke Greville), Earl of, 63–70, 73, 126
Warwick, Marjorie, Countess of, 65
Weir, Sir John, 19, 93
Wellcome, Sir Henry, 83
Welles, Mr & Mrs Benjamin, 115
Westminster, (Loelia) Duchess of, 90, 115
Wheatley, Lord, 2, 4, 175, 176, 177, 196, 197, 198, 199
Whigham, Charles, 9, 25
Whigham, David Dundas, 8
Whigham, Ellen Murray, 11, 53
Whigham, Ethel, 9
Whigham, General Sir Robert, 9, 25
Whigham, George Hay, 10, 11, 16, 17, 23, 24, 25, 26, 32, 35, 39, 48, 65, 68, 69, 71, 72, 73, 80, 83, 84, 96, 102, 107, 108, 109, 114, 120, 121, 125, 127, 133, 134, 139, 142, 146, 153, 154, 169, 173, 174, 179, 183, 184, 186, 216
Whigham, Mrs George Hay (Helen Hannay), 11, 16, 18, 19, 22, 23, 24, 25, 26, 33, 34, 35, 36, 37, 38, 50, 51, 62, 71, 72, 73, 80, 81, 102, 107, 114, 120, 127, 139, 186
Whigham, Gilbert, 9, 10, 11

Whigham, Henry James, 9
Whigham, James, 15
Whigham, Jane (Jane Brooks; Mrs Clive Beadon), 147, 173, 179, 184, 185, 186, 187
Whigham, Maud, 9
Whigham, Molly, 9
Whigham, Sybil, 9
Whigham, Walter, 9, 13, 15, 25
White, Sam, 2
Whiteman, Paul, 49, 94
Whitney, Jock, 116
Whitney, William C., 88
Widener, Joe, 94
Wilding, Dorothy, 102
Wilson, Woodrow, President, 15

Windsor, Duchess of (Wallis Simpson), 87, 88, 93, 112, 127
Windsor, Duke of (H.R.H. Edward, Prince of Wales), 41, 42, 47, 73, 83, 87, 88, 112
Winn, Godfrey, 230
Winston, Mrs Norman (Rosita), 117
Woodlock, Rev Francis, 71, 91
Wood-Prince, Mr & Mrs William, 240
Woodward, Sir William & Lady, 166

Younger, George, 226, 227

Zetland, Marchioness of, 220